Phyllis T. Stien, MSN
Joshua C. Kendall

Psychological Trauma and the Developing Brain
Neurologically Based Interventions for Troubled Children

Pre-publication
REVIEWS,
COMMENTARIES,
EVALUATIONS . . .

"The idea that the events occurring at the beginning of human life can, for better or worse, indelibly impact the development of the self over the entire life span has long been held as a major principle of the psychological and biological sciences. In this remarkable book, Stien and Kendall present in a clear and comprehensible form a compelling body of very recent research that forges deep connections between early relational trauma, disturbances of attachment in infancy, altered brain development, and the creation of a personality predisposed to significant enduring deficits in regulating emotion, processing cognition, and maintaining human relationships. Skillfully weaving together studies in developmental psychobiology and well-sketched portraits of children who have experienced abuse, the authors address head-on perhaps the most important and disturbing problem facing American culture today—the enduring negative impact of attachment trauma on the brain/mind/bodies of a disturbingly larger number of our children. The central question now is what we as a society will do with this extremely relevant information. Will we allot the resources that can transform this pragmatic knowledge into neurobiologically informed early prevention programs and thereby positively alter our collective future?"

Allan N. Schore
University of California at Los Angeles,
Author of *Affect Dysregulation and Disorders of the Self* and *Affect Regulation and the Repair of the Self*

More pre-publication
REVIEWS, COMMENTARIES, EVALUATIONS . . .

"**S**tien and Kendall provide a great service. In this clearly written and important book, they synthesize a wealth of crucial information that links childhood trauma to brain abnormalities and subsequent mental illness. Equally important, they show us how trauma also affects the child's social and intellectual development. I recommend this book to all clinicians and administrators. It should be required reading in all child psychiatry and psychology training programs."

Charles L. Whitfield, MD
Author of *The Truth about Depression* and *The Truth about Mental Illness*

HMTP

The Haworth Maltreatment and Trauma Press®
An Imprint of The Haworth Press, Inc.
New York • London • Oxford

Psychological Trauma and the Developing Brain

*Neurologically Based Interventions
for Troubled Children*

Psychological Trauma and the Developing Brain
Neurologically Based Interventions for Troubled Children

Phyllis T. Stien, MSN
Joshua C. Kendall

HMTP

The Haworth Maltreatment and Trauma Press®
An Imprint of The Haworth Press, Inc.
New York • London • Oxford

Published by

The Haworth Maltreatment and Trauma Press®, an imprint of The Haworth Press, Inc., 10 Alice Street, Binghamton, NY 13904-1580.

"Charting Your Baby's Emotional Milestones," from *First Feelings* by Stanley Greenspan and Nancy T. Greenspan, copyright ©1985 by Stanley Greenspan, MD and Nancy Thorndike Greenspan. Used by permission of Viking Penguin, a division of Penguin Putnam Inc.

S. Wieland, *Techniques and Issues in Abuse-Focused Therapy with Children and Adolescents: Addressing the Internal Trauma*, pp. 55-56, copyright ©1998 by Sage Publications, Inc. Reprinted by Permission of Sage Publications, Inc.

PUBLISHER'S NOTE
Identities and circumstances of individuals discussed in this book have been changed to protect confidentiality. Any resemblance to actual persons, living or dead, is entirely coincidental.

Cover design by Jennifer M. Gaska.

Library of Congress Cataloging-in-Publication Data

Stien, Phyllis T.
    Psychological trauma and the developing brain : neurologically based interventions for troubled children / Phyllis T. Stien, Joshua C. Kendall.
        p. cm.
    Includes bibliographical references and index.
    ISBN 0-7890-1787-3 (hardcover : alk. paper)—ISBN 0-7890-1788-1 (softcover : alk. paper)
    1. Post-traumatic stress disorder in children—Treatment. 2. Brain—Growth. 3. Pediatric neuropsychology. 4. Pediatric neuropsychiatry. I. Kendall, Joshua C., 1960- II.Title.
    RJ506.P55S856 2003
    618.92'8521—dc21

                                                                                        2002151041

For Karl, Erik, Pamela, and George

Shoyo and Hanna

And all the children of today and tomorrow

ABOUT THE AUTHORS

Phyllis T. Stien received her BS in nursing from the University of Wisconsin–Madison, and her MS in psychiatric nursing from the University of California–San Francisco. She has over thirty years of experience working as a child and family therapist, infant mental health specialist, educator, and consultant. Currently, she is working as a supervising therapist and as a mental health consultant for Head Start and Early Childhood Education programs. She presents workshops and training courses on the psychology and biology of child development, behavior problems in children, childhood disorders, and topics related to childhood maltreatment.

Joshua C. Kendall graduated summa cum laude from Yale, receiving his BA in comparative literature. He also did doctoral work in comparative literature at Johns Hopkins. He has been a freelance health care writer and editor for more than ten years. He has published dozens of scholarly articles and book chapters on childhood trauma, child development, and literary criticism. His journalism has appeared in various national magazines and newspapers. He won the 2001 National Magazine Award from the National Mental Health Association for a feature story in *BusinessWeek* on psychiatric disorders in the workplace.

CONTENTS

Foreword   ix
        Frank W. Putnam

Acknowledgments   xi

Introduction   1
  Overview of the New Neurobiology   7
  Organization of This Book   13

Chapter 1. Brain Growth and Organization   17
  How the Brain Grows   19
  How the Brain Organizes   25

Chapter 2. Birth to Five: Factoring in Biology   39
  Interaction, Brain Maturation, and the Stages
    of Development   40
  Conclusion   67
  Appendix: Charting Your Baby's Emotional Milestones   68

Chapter 3. PTSD: Biology Impinging on Behavior   73
  Identifying PTSD in Children   75
  The Two Types of PTSD   79
  The Psychobiology of PTSD   81
  Conclusion   96

Chapter 4. Complex PTSD in Children:
Brain and Behavior   97
  Child Maltreatment: The Scope of the Problem   98
  Complex PTSD: A Psychobiological Syndrome   100
  Brain Impairments Associated with Complex PTSD   101
  The Effects of Maltreatment on a Child's Psyche   112
  Conclusion   132

Chapter 5. Healing the Brain: An Interactive Approach to Treating PTSD and Complex PTSD in Children   **133**

Therapeutic Goals: An Overview   134
Demystifying the Therapy Process   139
Stage One: Safety and Stabilization   141
Stage Two: Symptom Reduction and Memory Work   147
Stage Three: Developmental Skills   168
Adjuncts to Therapy: Reconnecting to the Body   175
Conclusion   182

Chapter 6. Complex PTSD Compounded by Attachment Problems: Billy's Story   **183**

Children in the Child Welfare System   184
Introducing Billy   186
Analysis   187
Treatment   192
Conclusion   202

Chapter 7. Early Experience and Psychobiology: Translating Scientific Advances into Policy Prescriptions   **203**

The Two Approaches: White House Conferences I and II   205
The Underlying Sociological Ills   212
What's Been Working So Far: Interventions to Build On   221
Principles for the Future   223
Conclusion   228

Notes   **229**

References   **233**

Index   **253**

Foreword

I am always amazed by the ability of our society to overlook the consequences of child maltreatment. To be sure, everyone knows about the existence of child abuse. It is in the newspapers and on television almost daily, especially recently with the Catholic Church scandals. But many of these are only reports of individual cases, a few sparse details, with little, if any, follow-up. If the child died or was kidnapped, or if the perpetrator is convicted, then a more in-depth story with pictures may be published. What is missing from these reports is some account of the damage done to the child, and to society. Without such an account, we cannot really understand what it means for that child, or for us.

As I have long argued, child maltreatment is the single most costly public health problem in the United States today. It is a major contributor to scourges ranging from alcohol, tobacco, and drug abuse, to mental illness, AIDS, and violent crime. Of course, child abuse is not solely responsible for every case with these outcomes, but it is a critical risk factor that is preventable.

Why does child maltreatment have such powerful influences on mental and physical health, on one's behavior toward self and others? In the last decade, we have begun to learn just how deeply physical and sexual abuse and neglect can affect the minds and brains of children. This book brings together much of this new information. Even more significant, the authors also integrate these scientific findings with burgeoning knowledge of normal child development. As a result, we begin to appreciate how fundamentally damaging child abuse can be, and how it can shape a life forever. The book also emphasizes what we may be able to do to prevent or repair this damage.

As a scientific field, the surface has barely been scratched. It will probably be decades before we fully understand the mechanisms by which the many neurobiological systems affected by maltreatment lead to the negative outcomes associated with child abuse and neglect. Certainly, some of the content in this book will be revised as we learn more. Nonetheless, this comprehensive overview of the major scientific findings to date amply documents that child maltreatment often leads to dysfunction in basic brain systems associated with affect regulation, impulse control, and social behavior. We know less about the neurobiological effects of treatment. As noted by Stien and Kendall, animal research suggests that positive experiences may be able to reverse some of the biological havoc created by maltreatment. However, we need new studies because the scientific data do not yet exist for human beings. In any event, proper treatment can reverse some of the symptoms such as depression and post-traumatic stress disorder common in child maltreatment victims. Though we still need to deepen our understanding of what interventions work best, the course charted by this book sets forth the fundamental principles necessary to improve and individualize treatment.

If, as a society, we were to significantly reduce child maltreatment, we would see an enormous and almost immediate return on our investment. We would realize that return in terms of dramatic reductions in major psychiatric/psychological disorders, in reduced aggression and violence in our youth, and in improved school performance. The tools are available to begin this process and more are being developed. What is lacking is a widespread appreciation of why this is a critically vital task for our society. This book makes clear why we must do everything that we can do to prevent and treat child abuse and neglect.

Frank W. Putnam, MD
Professor of Pediatrics and Psychiatry
Mayerson Center for Safe and Healthy Children
Children's Hospital Medical Center
Cincinnati, Ohio

Acknowledgments

Writing a book requires persistence, intensity, fascination with the subject matter, and thousands of hours. It is inherently a frustrating and often lonely task. Thus, it requires a supportive environment. I am grateful to have a circle of friends who provided encouragement, as well as interludes of fun and laughter. I would like to express my special gratitude to Kay and Rick Kurz for their lasting encouragement and to Barb McIntyre for her computer expertise, library assistance, and support.

In my professional life, I have been fortunate to have had several teachers, including family therapists Carl Whitaker and Cloé Madanes, and colleagues Infant Mental Health Specialist Mary Kay Peterson and Jan Cools, who have contributed significantly to my development as a psychotherapist, educator, and developmental specialist. I also wish to acknowledge my friends and colleagues at Head Start, especially Anita Carter and Barbara Dupras. Early Childhood Educators are among the finest and most dedicated group of professionals working with children. A special thanks goes to Joyanna Silberg and Frances Waters for their intellectual friendship. Discussions with them contributed many ideas presented in this book. I am also indebted to Frances Waters for providing one of the case studies presented in Chapters 4 and 5. I am especially indebted to my clients, the children and families, who have taught me to appreciate the strength and uniqueness of every individual. Each child teaches me something new. I also wish to thank the families who openly shared their private lives so that other children may benefit from their experiences.

I gratefully appreciate Haworth's help and direction, Constance Dalenberg who provided careful editorial assistance, and Robert Geffner for his guidance. Also thanks to Heather Mlsna for her helpful suggestions, to Micheal Anderegg for his careful review of the manuscript, and to Pamela Esposito for her support and scientific advice. My special appreciation goes to Joshua Kendall, my coauthor, who made the writing of this book more enjoyment than travail.

But most of all, I owe much to my family: to my mother, Thelma Haakenson Hatlen, who instilled the intellectual curiosity; and to my father, Theodore Hatlen, who taught me the pragmatic persistence to pursue my dreams. I only wish that they could have lived to see this book. To my sisters, Norma Schwarting and Connie Romstad, I am grateful for their steadfast support and their believing in the book. My special love and thanks to my husband, Craig, for tolerating me while I struggled to write this book and for his quiet patient support, and to our three grown children, Karl, Erik, and George. They provide meaning in our lives, give us joy and inspiration, and make us so proud. Each of them holds a share in this book.—P.S.

I would like to thank the various traumatologists who have been so generous with their time over the years, including: Frank Putnam, Bessel van der Kolk, Martin Teicher, David Spiegel, Vincent Felitti, David Finkelhor, and Charles Whitfield. Your thoughtful responses to my numerous questions have proved most edifying. It has been exciting to immerse myself in a field of endeavor where the experts are typically as warmhearted as they are brilliant.

To my beloved partner, Rachel, as always, I am indebted to you for all those dollops of support.—J.K.

Introduction

> If the biochemists were able to demonstrate the physical work-
> ings of neuroses (phobias, or difficulties getting pleasure from
> life), if they could pinpoint the chemicals and impulses and
> interbrain conversations and information exchanges that consti-
> tute these feelings, would the psychoanalysts pack up their ids
> and egos and retire from the field? . . .
>   Some cooperative efforts—the sort the brain makes—would
> be useful here.
>
> Susanna Kaysen
Girl Interrupted

For the greater part of the twentieth century, mental health professionals were divided by a theoretical schism. On one side were biological psychiatrists who argued that mental illnesses were inherited
brain disorders. On the other side were psychoanalysts, psychologists, and social workers who saw the roots of psychopathology in the
environment—to wit, in childhood experiences. Because members of
the rival camps typically didn't speak the same language, most gave
up trying to communicate with one another. In short, the two theories
didn't mix. Depending on their allegiance, clinicians would focus on
trying either to fix brain chemistry with psychoactive drugs or to re-
construct the self via therapeutic talk. Anthropologist T. M. Luhrmann (2000) describes this feud in her highly acclaimed book, *Of
Two Minds: The Growing Disorder in American Psychiatry:*

> The story of twentieth-century psychiatry is that psychoanalysis
> was imported from Europe at a time when the approach to men-
> tal illness was essentially custodial. Psychoanalysis rapidly be-
> came entrenched as *the* theory that explained mental illness and
> *the* treatment that would cure it. Like most single-answer cures,
> it overpromised. When new psychopharmacological treatment

and theories emerged and successfully treated what psychoanalysis could not, the new psychiatric science claimed to win the ideological battle and to supplant its former rival. To the new adherents, psychoanalysis was charlatrany and psychiatric disorder was brain dysfunction. The psychoanalysts responded in kind. (p. 203)

In Luhrmann's analysis, the advent of managed care has led to the triumph of the brain over the mind. She laments, that with medical costs spiraling out of control, therapists now feel compelled to try to provide instant relief of symptoms. The quest for a cure has been largely abandoned.

Although biological psychiatry has recently won a crucial political victory over psychoanalysis, it has not won the war. As a matter of fact, both theories—as originally conceived a hundred years ago by their founders, psychiatrist Emil Kraepelin and neurologist Sigmund Freud, respectively—may be teetering on their last legs. Over the past two decades, a small cadre of cutting-edge researchers in neurobiology have quietly been fleshing out a revolutionary new paradigm of human development. This "third way" constitutes dialectical progress in the Hegelian sense as it synthesizes the key insights of *both* its predecessors. Surprisingly, the new neurobiology integrates the lifeblood of psychodynamic therapy—interpersonal relationships—into brain science. As it turns out, biological psychiatrists and psychoanalysts were both partially right; however, it's not genes or early experiences alone that determine the adult personality, but the interplay between these two crucial building blocks. Thus, nature and nurture are not antagonists, but rather partners in a very complex dance. From conception until death, genes and experience continually work hand in hand to determine the landscape of the brain.

What's most exciting about this "third way" is that it rests on a much more solid empirical foundation than earlier theories. Freud and his followers often relied on circular reasoning to make their claims, labeling, for example, those who challenged analytic dogma as "resistant." Thus, even refutation was often transformed into validation. Likewise, as all attempts to locate a single gene for major mental illnesses have failed, behavioral geneticists also had to rely on circumstantial evidence (Ross and Pam, 1995). "Well, the disorders must be genetic because they run in families" became the new refrain. However, since family members also influence one another via their behavior, this argument has proved hollow. In contrast, today's neurobiologists can back up their hypotheses because technological innovations now allow us to look inside the brain. For instance, scientists used to think that the physical connections between neurons that are formed during childhood are "hardwired"—that is, basically unchangeable. Now we know that brain development is an ongoing process. The connections between neurons guide our behavior, and at the same time, new thoughts and actions continue to change the pattern of connectivity between neurons. Remarkably, what we perceive, think, and feel affects the circuitry of our brain. The more activity that occurs between assemblies of neurons, the stronger the connections become. In other words, experiences can change the function of our brain and even alter its structure. Using functional imaging techniques to document their findings, neurobiologists are building new models that are forcing us to question many of the assumptions in mental health that we take for granted.

The central tenet of the new neurobiology—called the "neurobiology of interpersonal experience" by psychiatrist Daniel Siegel (1999)—is that our genetic endowment combines with experience to determine who we become as adults. In the wake of the Genome Project, many are enamored by the discovery of genes linked to conditions such as diabetes, Alzheimer's disease, obesity, and mood. Unfortunately, this has led to the false hope that mental problems can be linked to a single cause and that gene alteration will eventually cure all human maladies. But as J. Douglas Bremner (1999a), a psychobiologist from Emory University, has noted:

> Thirty years after the start of the biologic revolution in psychiatry, we still have not found the gene for schizophrenia or mania. It is clear that genetic factors do play an important role in psychiatric disorders. Most likely, a combination of genetic and environmental factors, of nature and nurture, is involved in the development of psychopathology. (p. 797)

We now know that no single gene is responsible for anything as complex as human behavior. Personality traits and patterns of behavior probably involve many genes, most of which are influenced by environment. In rare cases, a single gene does determine whether or not an individual will develop disorders, as, for example, in the case of Huntington's chorea, or phenylketonuria (PKU)—a form of mental retardation. Even when genes predispose an individual to a disease, say, type II diabetes, changes in lifestyle (e.g., diet and exercise) can be the determining factor.

If the majority of behavior problems in children are caused by the interaction between genes and the environment, then, the question becomes: What are the factors that can derail brain development? Is Johnny violent because he was exposed to alcohol during fetal development and now suffers from fetal alcohol syndrome (FAS)? (Exposure to alcohol in utero during critical periods of brain development interferes with the genes that direct the migration of neurons, causing major impairments to the developing brain.) Is Johnny violent because he lives in an abusive home? (The chronic stress of living in constant fear has altered brain development so that he overreacts to stress, has trouble inhibiting negative impulses, and distorts sensory perceptions.) Is it because he is a member of a gang that embraces neo-Nazism or other forms of racism? (Malignant belief systems have corrupted the higher centers of the brain that are concerned with reason, judgment, empathy, and impulse control, thus colluding with the lower brain centers that are generating the anger and rage.) Or is he violent because he lives in a chaotic, overly permissive home? (Continually acting out on aggressive impulses has undermined the development of the brain's inhibitory systems.)

Unraveling each factor's contribution to a child's problem is often difficult. However, as we show in this book, for many children, it is adverse experience and the stress it creates that exert a global influence on the genes that direct and regulate brain development.

This new understanding of the intimate interaction between genes and experience—or what we have referred to previously as "the third way"—sees child development in terms of a new pathway (see Figure 1). According to the old model of biological psychiatry rooted in the work of Kraepelin, the gene(s), without any influence from the environment, determines gene expression and produces the biological abnormalities associated with a particular disorder. In contrast, the

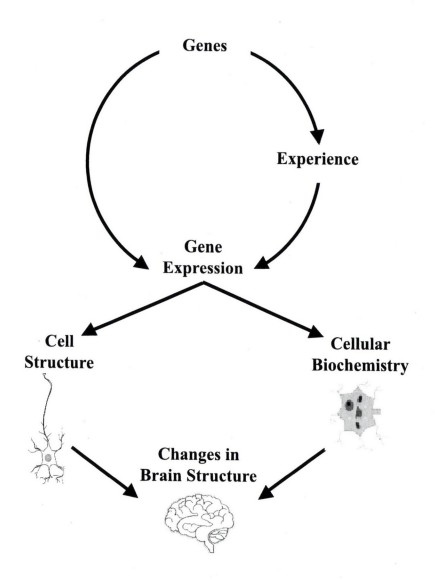

FIGURE 1. Two Pathways to Neurobiology. Some genes activate without any influence from the environment. However, many of the genes that are dedicated to the development and regulation of the nervous system depend on environmental stimulation to be activated.

new model of biological psychiatry (as reflected in the second pathway on the figures) incorporates the influence of genes and experience. According to this pathway, many of our genes have an indirect effect because the environment can modify genes. For most of the behavior problems that afflict children, the second pathway—the dynamic interaction between inborn factors and genes—is responsible for impairments in psychobiological development.

Scientists estimate that approximately one-third to one-half of our approximately 30,000 genes (Claverie, 2001) affect the development and regulation of the nervous system. In turn, at least half of these genes depend on environmental stimulation to be activated (Mack, 1996). "Most genes behind mental disorders," writes psychiatrist John Ratey (2001), "vary tremendously in the way and degree to which they are expressed in individuals, and recent research indicates that childhood stress may trigger the expression of genes that might otherwise have lain dormant throughout development" (p. 12). Experiences in childhood influence brain growth through a process called gene transcription, which affects how genes are activated.[1] Interaction with the environment can produce adaptive or maladaptive changes in gene expression. Positive experiences (e.g., nurturing from a parent) can activate genes, creating new proteins that can, for example, strengthen healthy neural connections and promote learning. In contrast, negative experiences (e.g., neglect or abuse) induce a cascade of chemical and hormonal changes in the brain that impede the development and integration of various brain systems.

In this book, we describe this new psychobiological model of child development, highlighting its implications for child psychotherapy. As it turns out, children develop disabling psychiatric symptoms when their psychobiological development goes awry. We explain how this happens, and what therapists, parents, and teachers can do to set it aright. Surprisingly, for children who suffer from "biochemical imbalances," treatments that rely solely on drugs usually don't fix the problem. Instead, these children need a new set of interpersonal experiences, and new coping skills, to realign brain circuitry. Sadly, at the very moment when scientists have marshaled mountains of evidence in support of this new approach, economic pressures are forcing many child therapists to attempt "quick fixes," even for very troubled children. We hope our book will help to reinvigorate the fields of child development and psychotherapy.

OVERVIEW OF THE NEW NEUROBIOLOGY

The new neurobiology represents a confluence of two strands of brain research. One group of developmental neuroscientists, including Allan Schore, Daniel Siegel, and ethologists such as Stephen Soumi and Myron Hofer, has been exploring the biological dimension of attachment theory and documenting that the quality, quantity, and timing of infant stimulation has enduring effects on brain development (e.g., Goldberg, Muir, and Kerr, 1995). The second group, whose prominent figures include Frank Putnam, Bessel van der Kolk, Martin Teicher, and Bruce Perry, has its moorings in traumatology, that is, the scientific study of traumatic experience (e.g., van der Kolk, McFarlane, and Weisaeth, 1996). These psychiatrists have been documenting how childhood trauma—namely, sexual abuse, physical abuse, emotional abuse, and neglect—affect the development, structure, and chemistry of the brain. Whereas traumatologists focus on *abnormal* development, attachment researchers often examine the brain under conditions of *normal* or optimal development. Thus, when taken together, these two strands of research clarify the key mechanisms behind both mental health and psychopathology in children. Whereas secure attachment produces a growth-facilitating environment that builds neuronal connections and integrates brain systems, strengthening the capacity to cope with stress; abuse and neglect induces chaotic biochemical changes that interfere in the maturation of the brain's coping systems, leading to problems with emotional regulation, relationships, and identity formation (Schore, 2001).

The Biology of Attachment

Attachment theory dates back a half century. That's when its founder, John Bowlby (1969), emerged as a leading advocate for the effect of early relationships on child development. According to Bowlby's (1965) attachment theory, "a warm, intimate and continuous relationship with his mother (or permanent mother-substitute)" (p. 13) is essential for the child's emotional and cognitive development. In a good scenario, this relationship provides a "secure base" from which the child begins to explore the world. Thus, children who are cared about learn how to regulate their emotions in healthy ways and to develop empathy for others.

Researchers a generation later began to discover that the interactions between children and their caregivers actually shape the ultimate architecture of the brain. Secure attachment promotes neuronal connections, helping to strengthen and integrate key brain structures. For example, Allan Schore (1994) (whose research we will discuss in detail in Chapter 3), shows that the development of the prefrontal cortex—the center for reasoning, problem solving, motivation, and response flexibility—is vitally dependent on reciprocal interactions with an emotionally attuned caregiver.

Sensitive parents promote brain growth through interactively regulating the infant's positive and negative states. When the infant is distressed, parents can operate on two different levels to restore emotional equilibrium. The emotionally attuned parent both experiences the infant's discomfort, and at the same time maintains a "meta" emotional state, a nonaroused state that soothes the infant. Through reciprocal interchanges, the parent actively creates in the infant a psychobiological state similar to his or her own. This early coregulation of stressful states has life-long benefits, directly influencing the development of the brain's stress response system. This early programming of the stress response becomes the biological foundation for the child's later capacity to maintain emotional balance and to cope with stressful events. These attuned interactions are critical for optimal brain development. As Daniel Siegel (1999) notes, "The experience of expressing one's emotional state and having others perceive and respond to those signals appears to be of vital importance in the development of the brain. Such sharing of primary emotions does not merely allow the child to feel 'good'; it allows the child to develop normally" (p. 129). In other words, this emotional give-and-take also helps to foster the type of neural development that allows the child to acquire the capacity for emotional self-regulation, a critical skill, given that emotion is the central organizing force within the brain. A healthy brain is one where emotions are flowing freely (Pert, 1997), and where the brain's information-processing modes (e.g., perceptions, thoughts, and sensations) are in sync.

Trauma and the Brain

Until the 1970s, most mental health professionals downplayed the effect of childhood experience on cognitive and emotional development.

Although many psychoanalysts expressed an interest in understanding themes dating back to childhood, surprisingly, they typically stressed the pathogenic power of fantasies rather than events per se. A notable exception (in addition to Bowlby) was Rene Spitz (1945), who in the 1940s demonstrated convincingly the dramatic sequelae of maternal deprivation. Spitz's study focused on two groups of infants. One group was raised in an orphanage and received minimal care. Each infant in the other group was individually cared for by a woman who was serving a prison sentence. By two years of age, the children in each group were very different. Of the twenty-six children raised in the orphanage, only two could walk and only a few could talk. In contrast, nearly all the children in the other group had reached these developmental milestones.

By 1980, several sociological currents had set in motion a renewed interest in the effects of trauma on children (Chu, 1998; Chu and Bowman, 2000). As child-welfare advocates began lobbying for laws to protect children from violence in the home, the feminist movement empowered women to begin to speak about sexual abuse, thus breaking the societywide silence on this horrible crime. At the same time, veterans returning from the Vietnam war began seeking medical help for the array of symptoms that they had developed overseas—from alcohol and substance abuse to crippling feelings of anxiety and rage. Mental health professionals began to understand that people—particularly, children—were acutely sensitive to the impact of emotionally overwhelming experiences. Countless research studies have since documented the long-term effects of abuse and neglect on adult psychopathology. A history of trauma now appears to be a critical risk factor for the onset of many leading mental health disorders, such as depression, substance abuse, and anxiety.

Within a decade after the first empirical studies on child maltreatment, psychiatrists began discovering biological correlates of its pernicious psychological effects. Thus, research on trauma and the brain is deepening our understanding of how trauma early in life derails development. For example, consider Spitz's findings on how maternal deprivation leads to cognitive and emotional delays, and contemporary studies of two-year-old institutionalized Romanian orphans, which show that their brains differ markedly from those of a healthy toddler. The orphans exhibited little or no activity both in the temporal lobes, the areas dedicated to emotions, and in the frontal lobes—the brain's thinking center (Chugani, 1997). Neurobiological studies now demonstrate that "the overwhelming stress of maltreatment in childhood is associated with adverse influences on brain development" (De Bellis, Keshavan, et al., 1999, p. 1281). Early traumatic experiences result in increased reactivity to stress and a vulnerability to stress-related psychiatric disorders (Graham et al., 1999).

Likewise, research shows that parental mental health during infancy has a significant impact on the child's brain activity and behavior. For example, electroencephalogram (EEG) studies by Dawson and colleagues (1997), found that infants of depressed mothers exhibited increased right frontal EEG activity. This asymmetry is related to negative affects, emotional reactivity, and vulnerability to psychopathology (Davidson et al., 1990, 1999). In addition, babies of depressed mothers exhibit higher levels of emotional dysregulation as evidenced by physiological changes (e.g., heart rate, vagal tone, corisol levels), immune system changes, and behavioral changes (e.g., eating and sleeping problems, affect and activity level) (Field, 1994).

As a general rule, abuse impedes brain maturation and interferes in the normal hierarchical development and integration of brain systems. The physical organization of the brain directly reflects the child's interpersonal experiences. Thus, in response to a violent and chaotic environment, he[2] is likely to develop an overactive stress-response system and an underdeveloped cortex. In such circumstances, it is highly adaptive for the child to be hyperaroused, hypervigilant, and ready to attack or defend himself (Perry, 1997). As part of this survival mechanism, extreme stress also interferes in the functioning of the cortex, especially the prefrontal cortex (Arnsten, 1998), the thinking part of the brain that is crucially involved in inhibiting the stress response. In other words, a malfunctioning family hierarchy often leads to a dysfunctional hierarchy within the brain.

Plasticity: The Window of Opportunity

Although this book focuses on the effects of experience, particularly trauma, on the developing brain, we do not mean to rule out genetic or constitutional factors. For example, most parents with more than one child will attest to the fact that differences between children are evident right from birth. In their landmark longitudinal study, begun in 1956, Chess and Thomas (1989) found that parental expectations that are compatible with both a child's mental capacities and innate disposition are vital to healthy development. But even when we are talking about constitutional factors, experience must not be left out of the equation. As we show in Chapter 2, experience can modify constitutionally related characteristics. Our hope is to help children take advantage of the positive aspects of their innate tendencies and mold less-adaptable attributes.

Though there are limits to what can be changed, the good news is that a child's brain is remarkably plastic. It continuously reacts and adapts to the environment. As Lise Eliot (1999), neuroscientist and author of *What's Going on in There? How the Brain and Mind Develop in the First Five Years of Life,* points out:

> Anyone who has ever studied nerve cells can tell you how remarkably plastic they are. The brain itself is literally molded by experience: every sight, sound, and thought leaves an imprint on specific neural circuits, modifying the way future sights, sounds, and thoughts will be registered. Brain hardware is not fixed, but living, dynamic tissue that is constantly updating itself to meet the sensory, motor, emotional, and intellectual demands at hand. (p. 4)

Thus, just as negative environments can affect the expression of genes, so too can positive ones. Our interactive treatment model is based on the principle that the environment can change brain circuitry. For example, animal research has shown that the more "enriched" the environment, the more developed the dendritic system (Camel, Withers, and Greenough, 1986; Sirevaag and Greenough, 1987). Thus, rats reared in environments containing elaborate mazes and numerous opportunities for social interaction have both thicker cortices and a higher density of synapses and increased dendritic growth in the cortex (Diamond, 1988). In principle, extensive dendritic growth facilitates performance on many behavioral tasks and decreased dendritic arborization is associated with a decline in performance (Kolb and Whishaw, 1998).

Interpersonal experiences do have the power to change the brain. Over forty years ago, researchers discovered that the periodic handling of rat pups causes long-term brain changes. Initially, scientists assumed that mild stress—being taken from their mothers and handled by humans—made the pups more resilient. However, new research points to increased maternal attention as the key factor behind the positive biological effects. Once returned to their mothers, these pups receive more attention—double the rate of licking and grooming. Likewise, pups of mothers that naturally lick at the higher rate also exhibit more brain receptors that inhibit the stress response (Liu et al., 1997) and promote relaxation (Caldji et al., 1998). New research on humans is also underlining how a secure attachment relationship can help mitigate the adverse effects of stress. In a study of seventy-seven eighteen-month-old children who were classified as having an inhibited temperament—infants who are constitutionally more reactive to stress—elevations in the stress hormone cortisol, in response to stressful situations, were found *only* in the insecurely attached group, not in the securely attached toddlers (Nachmias et al., 1996; Gunnar et al., 1996).

On the one hand, how our brain functions determines how we perceive, think, and behave. On the other hand, by changing our thinking and behavior, the organization and functioning of our brain can be retooled. In many ways, the strategies used to reshape the brain of chronically traumatized children can also serve as a guide for optimizing brain development in all children. For all children, we want to create an environment that supports the hierarchical development and integrative capacities of the brain. We want to raise children whose reasoning brain can triumph over the impulsive one. We want them to be in touch with their own feelings, have empathy for others, and to be able to use the emotions and urges arising from their experiences in ways that will enable them to live productive, creative, and interpersonally fulfilling lives.

At the present time, many child psychotherapists are under the misconception that they can ignore the brain. As John Ratey (2001), author of *A Users Guide to the Brain*, writes:

> Many wish that they could practice without having to take the brain into account at all, and a pervasive attitude in the field holds that the brain should be treated like plumbing: forget about it unless it backs up. This wish-it-away thinking is analogous to a business executive ignoring the Internet as a fad that

will soon go away. Ignoring the brain actually cripples any psychological theory. (p. 12)

However, all interpersonal interactions affect the brain. In fact, for abused children, therapeutic relationships can interactively regulate negative states and thus help buffer the effects of traumatic stress. In the final analysis, it is the brain that mediates perception, thinking, emotion, and behavior. Ultimately, to help children recover from mental disorders, we must help create an environment that enhances brain development. Given that a child's brain is much more plastic than an adult's, we can ill afford not to seize this opportunity.

ORGANIZATION OF THIS BOOK

Throughout this book we present new findings in both neurobiology and psychology, highlighting the interrelationship between these two disparate bodies of knowledge. We have tried to preserve the complexity of the critical concepts and avoid the jargon that inevitably seeps into all scholarly disciplines.

In Chapter 1, we take a step back and present some basic information about the brain. We begin by providing an overview of brain development, explaining the various growth spurts that occur throughout childhood. We move on to describe brain organization from two angles: the triune brain, the three basic brain systems that perform separate but interdependent functions, and our two brains, the left and right hemispheres. We discuss how healthy brain functioning is dependent on the close collaboration between the brain's emotional and cognitive systems, and the right and left hemispheres.

The next five chapters sketch our new psychobiological perspective on child development. Chapter 2 presents the widely accepted theory of child development of psychiatrist Stanley Greenspan. By discussing new research on the neurobiology of attachment conducted by Allan Schore and Myron Hofer, we show how biology adds a new dimension to Greenspan's developmental stages. We illustrate these new insights through a case study of a developmentally delayed toddler, Bradley. In his case, the emotionally arousing attuned interactions with caregivers appears to have led to long-term changes in brain organization and functioning. Even when constitutional factors impede integration and organization of brain functioning, experiences designed to overcome deficits, particularly if they occur early in life, can put brain development back on track.

In Chapters 3 and 4, we look at the effects of traumatic stress on brain development. Chapter 3 begins with a discussion of post-traumatic stress disorder (PTSD), covering the signs and symptoms of PTSD in children and differentiating between the two types of PTSD: single-event PTSD and complex PTSD. We then focus on the psychobiology of PTSD, beginning with a detailed explanation of the stress response—the body's automatic way of coping with a surge in the painful emotions of fear and helplessness. Next, we explain how the disorder produces long-term biological changes both in the stress response and in the brain's memory systems. We also review the two basic types of memory (explicit and implicit) before clarifying the nature of traumatic memory.

Chapter 4 addresses the effects of abuse and neglect on the developing brain. We begin by reviewing the scope of child maltreatment in our society. After characterizing complex PTSD as a distinct psychobiological syndrome, we review the specific brain impairments attributed to abuse and neglect, including: dysfunctional stress response and limbic irritability, decrease in hippocampal volume, abnormal activity in the cerebellar vermis, deficient development of the left hemisphere, deficient left-right hemisphere integration, and neuroendocrine and immune system changes. Next, we describe some of the underlying neural mechanisms, proposed by neuroscientists, whereby maltreatment leads to changes in brain structure and function. We conclude the chapter by mapping out the seven core psychological symptoms that comprise complex PTSD.

Chapters 5 and 6 focus on treatment. After explaining the neurobiological correlates that go hand in hand with clinical improvements, we clarify our new interpersonal approach to treatment. Although drugs such as the selective serotonin reuptake inhibitors (SSRIs) can influence the biochemistry of the brain by, for example, dampening the reactivity of the limbic system, they are usually not sufficient to change brain circuitry. Surprisingly, only new experiences that generate new ways of thinking, feeling, and behaving can build new patterns of connectivity between nerve cells (networks and systems) and thus reorganize the functioning of the brain. We map out the three phases of trauma therapy: (1) safety and stabilization, (2) symptom reduction and memory work, and (3) developmental skills. We illustrate the course of treatment through two case studies that were first introduced in Chapters 3 and 4. Chapter 6 describes the treatment of a child who suffers from complex PTSD and attachment disorders.

In the first six chapters, we present our new approach to child therapy from a microperspective, explaining how a particular child's development can go awry and what parents, therapists, and other significant adults can do to get him back on track. In Chapter 7, we take a macro or societywide view of these new scientific advances, linking child maltreatment to impaired brain development. The depth of this public health problem is staggering, as two million teenagers already suffer from PTSD and one million more children are abused each year. Tragically, out of all the children who experience abuse or witness domestic violence, only a handful are receiving adequate treatment. After fleshing out the shocking cost to society of child maltreatment, we offer some policy prescriptions.

Chapter 1

Brain Growth and Organization

The two minds [the cerebral hemispheres] can cooperate with each other in a deep, synergistic relationship that fosters creativity and maturity, or they can sabotage each other, leading to a plethora of psychological and psychosomatic problems.

Fredrick Schiffer, MD

Since the brain looks rather unassuming—just three pounds of grayish matter covered with convoluted ridges and valleys—it is hard to imagine that it contains so many intricately developed parts. If you made a cut through the brain, you would see a mix of gray matter, containing densely packed cell bodies 1.5 millimeters thick, and white matter, comprised of axons (see the appendix to this chapter for a definition of neurons and their component parts). Gray matter forms both the outside, called the cortex, and the discrete structures on the inside. As with any body organ, each brain structure performs distinct functions. For instance, separate areas of the cortex are dedicated to processing visual stimuli, understanding language, speaking, planning, etc. (see Figure 1.1). However, the precise boundaries are different for each of us and change over time because of environmental influences.

The brain is made up of systems or functional modules. Although it has been over fifty years since neurosurgeons initially mapped out the sensory-motor cortex, the recent discovery of functional imaging techniques, which capture the brain in action, has revived interest in the systems perspective of brain functioning. Scientists now understand that most tasks require brain activity involving several areas of the brain and that collaboration between these areas is critical to healthy brain functioning.

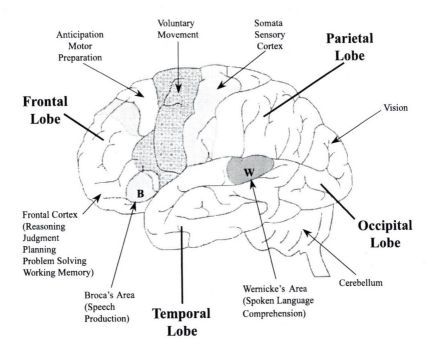

FIGURE 1.1. Functional Areas. Contemporary mapping of the mind is based on two types of studies: those using functional imaging techniques that visually record neural activity as an individual is performing a mental and/or behavioral task, and those that show the effects of damage to particular areas of the brain and the effects of stimulating specific brain regions. The brain is a complex, interactive, and dynamic system. Remarkably, functional areas can change—given the right circumstances—and one area can take over the work of another.

To produce any response, even the blink of an eye, groups of neurons must work together. As the brain develops, neurons from every part of the brain form assemblies or circuits. Local assemblies then feed into larger and larger groups until they are organized into elaborate networks, subsystems, and finally, systems. This functional linking of groups of neurons into networks and into separate systems allows us to engage in several activities at the same time—for example, thinking, driving, drinking a glass of water, and listening to music, and also experiencing various emotions such as anger, fear, and joy.

When the brain is operating efficiently, multiple assemblies of neurons are firing in unison, and information is flowing freely from one area to another. We are not born that way, however. We develop the capacity to coordinate various functional areas of the brain, such as our cognitive and emotional systems, which are located in separate areas of the brain, in childhood. In fact, neuroscience teaches that our early interpersonal experiences play a critical role in determining how well we make use of our genetic potential to integrate all these brain functions.

We begin this chapter by looking at how the brain grows. We then focus on how the brain organizes both from a vertical and horizontal perspective, explaining just how the various brain systems collaborate. As the brain develops, what it ends up looking like on the "inside" directly reflects what we have experienced on the "outside." In other words, our early relationships and experiences directly influence the ultimate architecture of the brain. In particular, securely attached children are likely to have brains that are not only *biochemically* more balanced, but also *structurally* better organized than children who grow up in chaotic or abusive environments.

HOW THE BRAIN GROWS

Mental functioning is directly related to the number of both neurons and synapses (connections between neurons) in the brain. Whereas the proliferation of *new connections* increases the *potential* for learning, new patterns of connectivity between neurons, which are strengthened and stabilized through use, result from *actual* learning. The density of synapses reaches its peak about the age of three and it remains at this level until age ten, according to Peter Huttenlocher (1994) of the University of Chicago. Generally by age sixteen, the number of synapses has dropped to adult levels. Because a child's brain is rapidly making new synapses, it is much more malleable than an adult's. Increased plasticity, or potential for change, has both advantages and disadvantages. On the one hand, adverse environments affect children much more acutely than adults; therefore, abuse or neglect in early childhood can result in long-term impairments. On the other hand, since children's brains are still in the process of being organized, they possess a remarkable ability to rebound from severe brain injuries. This scientific insight led to a new lease on life for pre-schooler Matthew Simpson (Swerdlow, 1995).

Matthew Simpson

At four, Matthew began experiencing epileptic-like seizures that neither drugs nor any other standard treatment could stop. As the interval between seizures grew shorter and shorter, doctors were concerned that he might die from a neurological disorder called Rasmussen's encephalitis, a rare form of intractable seizures that spreads only through one hemisphere and results in progressive paralysis on one side of the body, inflammation of the brain, and mental deterioration.

Lacking any other options, Matthew's parents agreed to let Benjamin Carson, a pediatric neurosurgeon at Johns Hopkins, perform a hemispherectomy—a procedure that involves removing the entire left side of the brain. Over time, cerebrospinal fluid usually settles in the areas once occupied by critical brain structures. However, there are risks to this surgery, and doctors typically recommend it only as a last resort. Only 58 such operations were performed on children at Johns Hopkins from 1968 to 1996 (Carson, 2003).

Normally, each side of the body works in tandem with the opposite hemisphere of the brain. Thus, a sound heard by the right ear is processed in the left auditory cortex. Besides controlling the movement on the right side of the body, the left brain is also critical for problem-solving and language skills.

Remarkably, the right side of Matthew's brain soon took over the functions typically performed by the left side. Within eighteen months of the surgery, Matthew showed hardly any signs of impairment in cognitive or motor functioning—except for limited use of his right arm. He performed well in school, even excelling in mathematics. If an adult were to undergo this radical procedure, transfer of functions from one side of the brain to the other would not be possible. Fortunately, Matthew Simpson was still at an age when his brain could create and reassign the neural connections needed to return him to normal functioning.

Early Growth

The human nervous system begins its development about two weeks after conception, when cells on the surface of the embryo begin to form a neural plate. Soon this neural plate thickens, and vesicles (pouches filled with cerebral spinal fluid) form at the front end of the neural tube. The formation of neurons, which evolve from precursor cells surrounding the vesicles, is complete well before birth.[1] Once produced, neurons migrate, or move to their approximate final location. By the time the fetus is twenty weeks, most neurons are already in place. Shortly after birth, neurons finish migrating, but they continue to differentiate until they start performing their specific functions (Shepard, 1994).

During the prenatal period, maternal alcohol, drug, and tobacco use, malnutrition, and other adverse experiences can have a detrimental effect on the developing brain. These prenatal insults often result in prematurity, low birth weight, or poor interactive capacities (Aitken and Trevarthen, 1997). With any toxic substance, the amount ingested and age of the fetus—the earlier, the worse the outcome—often determine the extent of the damage. For example, FAS, which is caused by heavy drinking during pregnancy, results in mental retardation along with physical deformities including a small head, thin upper lip, flattened jawbone, and poorly developed ridges between the nose and mouth.

Maternal stress also can affect fetal brain development. Martha Weinstock of Hadassah Medical School in Jerusalem, has stressed pregnant rats by exposing them to a loud buzzer. She found that the pups of the stressed mothers, when compared with controls, were more fearful and irritable, and produced more stress hormones. Apparently, their brains were less able to regulate the stress response (Weinstock, Fride, and Hertzberg, 1988; Fride and Weinstock, 1988; Weinstock, 1997). Similar research at the University of Wisconsin found that monkeys whose mothers were stressed during pregnancy had enhanced hormonal response to stressful events later in life (Clarke et al., 1994). When compared to a control group, they also appeared less interested in playing and more aggressive toward their cage mates. Further studies of other prenatally stressed monkeys suggest that stress in utero results in a wide range of impairments including neuromotor difficulties, diminished cognitive abilities, and attention problems. Symptoms were more severe when stress occurred early in pregnancy (Clarke and Schneider, 1997; Schneider et al., 1998). Researchers hypothesize that a mother's stress hormones can damage the developing brain of the fetus. Very recent research shows that maternal stress hormones released during pregnancy may adversely affect human fetal brain development (Glynn, Wadhwa, and Sandman, 2000).

At birth, all essential brain structures are present, but brain development is far from complete. During the first two years, our brains go into "fast forward," producing numerous, cyclical growth spurts. All told, in the first year of life, the brain expands two-and-a-half times—growing from 400 to 1,000 grams (Schore, 1994). By four years of age, the cortical utilization of glucose, the brain's source of energy, is twice that of an adult. This high rate of glucose metabolism, which reflects the explosion of synapses, continues until around age ten (Chugani, 1998). Myelinization, or a formation of a sheath of glial cells around the axon, is another step in the development of the nervous system. This process, which begins late in gestation and continues on into adulthood, facilitates the communication between neurons. Brain pathways myelinate at different times and at different rates. For example, whereas the ascending tracts, which stretch from the brain stem to the cortex, begin myelinating before birth, the descending tracts, which run down from the cortex to the lower brain centers, do not begin to myelinate until late infancy. Perhaps we are not wise until old age because some descending tracts, which allow us to think before we react, may not completely myelinate until the sixth decade of life (Benes, 1994).

Brain structures do not all mature at the same time. For instance, the sensory and motor areas of the cortex develop before the association areas, which respond to and integrate different types of sensory stimuli. Thus, after the primary auditory cortex takes in the specific features of a sound and the secondary areas integrate its various aspects, the association areas link it to other sensory information. One of the main association areas, Wernicke's area, is located just above the temporal lobe and is responsible for processing language. Association areas allow us to perform complex symbolic activities such as reading, writing, and mathematics, which require the integration of auditory, visual, and spatial information. If these areas develop too slowly, a child can suffer from both learning disabilities and limitations in higher-order language skills (Lyon, 1996).

The prefrontal cortex matures last. Fibers from all cortical and lower brain systems converge, ensuring communication not only between all areas of the brain but also between the brain and the visceral systems. Delayed growth here can result in a wide range of problems involving attention, inhibition of impulsive responses, planning, reasoning, judgment, self-monitoring, and the lack of creative and thoughtful responses (Lyon, 1996). Research suggests that although the prefrontal areas begin to develop as early as the latter part of the first year of life, these areas continue to mature through adulthood.

Although brain growth explodes between birth and two, growth spurts occur at other ages as well. Typically, each overproduction of neural connections is followed by the selective elimination of unused connections—a process known as pruning. This cycle of "boom and bust," in turn, results in brain reorganization or "remodeling" (Huttenlocher, 1994). This "use it or lose it" style of development allows the brain to adapt its responses to the specific needs of the environment. In addition, there is another process, an "experience-dependent" (versus an experience-expectant process), which involves the formation of neural connections in response to unique experiences (Greenough, Black, and Wallace, 1987). In this way, experience eventually determines the final architecture (i.e., circuitry) of the brain. As mentioned in the introduction, the relationship between infant and caregiver is instrumental in fostering and stabilizing these new neural connections.

Some periods of "remodeling" are referred to as critical periods because certain experiences are needed at these times in order for brain development to proceed normally. Otherwise, brain development can be derailed. As the classic studies of Hubel and Wiesel (1979) have shown, kittens can lose their sight if they are deprived of appropriate visual stimuli. When researchers covered the kittens' eyes for a few weeks, neurons associated with vision degenerated, and pathways within the visual cortex deteriorated. Similarly, if a congenital cataract blocking visual stimuli is not removed in infancy, vision in that eye will be lost forever.

Just as various subcortical and cortical regions develop at different times and at different rates, the right and left hemispheres alternate periods of rapid growth. Research suggests that a sequential growth spurt in one hemisphere is first followed by bilateral growth, and then by rapid growth in the other hemisphere (Thatcher, 1994). Between three and four years of age, a major reorganization occurs right after the brain has gone through just such a developmental cycle. Language-related processes, which up to this time occur in both sides of the brain, begin to shift predominately to the left hemisphere and visual-spatial tasks become mainly the job of the right hemisphere. As interhemispheric communication is gradually strengthened, the two hemispheres begin to perform distinct functions (Mills, Coffey-Corina, and Neville, 1994).

"In general," writes Dr. Ornitz (1996), of UCLA Medical School, "there appear to be four periods of major structural change in brain development, which punctuate the progressive increases and decreases in the size of the brain and its substructures at both the macroscopic and microscopic levels" (p. 40). The first period of remodeling takes place sometime between fifteen months and four years; the second occurs during late childhood sometime between six and ten years of age; the third is associated with prepuberty; and the fourth takes place in midadolescence. There is also some evidence that these spurts in brain growth are reflected in advances in cognitive and emotional development. For example, the major stages of brain growth and reorganization coincide with the development of the critical mental functions as defined by the famous Swiss psychologist, Jean Piaget (Ornitz, 1996). The first one overlaps Piaget's sensory-motor stage (from birth through age two), during which infants learn about the world from their sensory impressions, and the preoperational stage (two to five through seven) during which children learn to think in images. Likewise, the second period of remodeling corresponds to concrete operations (seven through eleven), during which children learn to understand logical principles. Finally, the fourth overlaps the stage of formal operations (eleven and over) when children learn to think abstractly.

Scientists used to believe that brain development slowed after the first few years of life. Current research, however, shows a dramatic overproduction of connections in early adolescence—extensive branching of axons and dendrites and a generalized thickening of the cortex—that rivals the exuberant growth observed in the first years of life (Thompson et al., 2000). During this third major wave of brain growth (which occurs around age eleven in girls and age twelve in boys), children typically build and stabilize connections between several key brain systems.

HOW THE BRAIN ORGANIZES

Looked at vertically, the brain can be divided into three parts: the brain stem, limbic system, and the neocortex (MacLean, 1990). From a horizontal perspective, the brain contains two sides: the right and left cerebral hemispheres.

The Triune Brain

The vertical or bottom-to-top (often called the triune brain) organizational perspective recognizes that the three major regions of the brain evolved over time, creating separate, but interdependent systems (see Figure 1.2). These regions mature in a hierarchical fashion that repeats the evolutionary development of the species. The brain stem—the first area to mature—is evolutionarily the oldest. The neocortex—the last area to mature—is evolutionarily the most recent.

Development begins with the *brain stem.* This structure evolved more than 500 million years ago, and is responsible for regulating basic cardiovascular functions, level of arousal, and some reflexes. Connected to the back and slightly above the brain stem is a clump called the *cerebellum,* which initially controlled movement, but now helps coordinate not just motor but social, emotional, and cognitive functioning (Schmahmann, 1997). Because the brain stem and cerebellum combine to resemble the brain of today's reptiles, this lowest region is often referred to as the reptilian brain.

The next region of the brain to develop, the *limbic system,* encompasses a group of brain structures that form a ring around the brain stem (see Figure 1.3). This area is sometimes called the mammalian brain because it first appeared in mammals, or the emotional brain, because it remains the source of our urges, appetites, and emotions. The development of the limbic structures allowed for many new functions. For instance, the hypothalamus maintains homeostasis by regulating critical functions such as blood pressure, body temperature, and glucose levels. The amygdala and hippocampus give us conditioned learning and the capacity to learn by association. With this

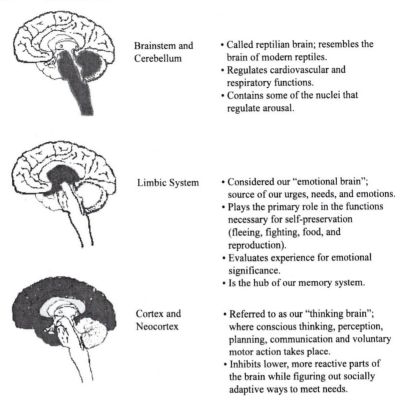

Brainstem and Cerebellum	• Called reptilian brain; resembles the brain of modern reptiles. • Regulates cardiovascular and respiratory functions. • Contains some of the nuclei that regulate arousal.
Limbic System	• Considered our "emotional brain"; source of our urges, needs, and emotions. • Plays the primary role in the functions necessary for self-preservation (fleeing, fighting, food, and reproduction). • Evaluates experience for emotional significance. • Is the hub of our memory system.
Cortex and Neocortex	• Referred to as our "thinking brain"; where conscious thinking, perception, planning, communication and voluntary motor action takes place. • Inhibits lower, more reactive parts of the brain while figuring out socially adaptive ways to meet needs.

FIGURE 1.2. Triune Brain. An evolutionary perspective of brain development, by Paul MacLean, which emphasizes that the human brain evolved from the bottom up. Each new layer added new functions that helped in the struggle to survive and dominate. As the fetal brain develops, it repeats the evolutionary development of the species—the primitive lower layers mature first and the cortex develops last. The cerebellum also evolved from an area that initially controlled movement to a structure that plays a significant role in thinking, emotional regulation, and communication.

primitive memory system, animals could begin to defend themselves by linking sensations—whether pleasurable or painful—to context. For example, a watering hole may represent either food or danger.

The third region of the brain to develop, the *cortex* or thinking brain, is where planning, reasoning, and cognition take place. About 100 to 150 million years ago, the frontal lobes expanded consider-

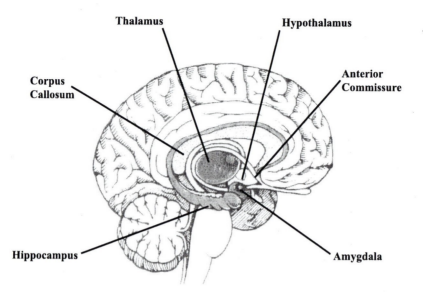

FIGURE 1.3. Structures of the Limbic/Hypothalamic System.The limbic system is dedicated to survival. The thalamus, a walnut-sized structure at the center of each hemisphere, acts as the relay station for incoming sensory stimuli and permits the senses to be used in combination. The hypothalamus, a pea-sized structure that lies just below the thalamus, works to maintain homeostasis and is the main center for information exchange between the brain and body. The amygdala, an almond-shaped structure, stores memories of fearful experiences, monitors incoming stimuli for anything threatening, and activates the fight- or-flight stress response when danger is detected. The hippocampus, finger-sized clusters of neurons, is the hub of memory and learning because all conscious memories must be processed through this structure. The corpus callosum, the huge fiber tract that connects the cortical areas of the two hemispheres, allows for conscious information to be exchanged between hemispheres. The anterior commissure, an older pathway that lies beneath the corpus callosum, carries unconscious, emotional information between the two hemispheres. Figure adapted from Sylwester (1995). Used with permission.

ably, creating the capacity for symbolic language and conscious awareness. The neocortex gives us both cognition and metacognition (the ability to think about our thoughts, emotions, and behavior).

Although the neocortex made intellectual achievement possible, it did not render the limbic system and brain stem obsolete. These lower regions of the brain continue to have a profound impact on our functioning because the brain's central pursuit is survival. The urges and emotions generated in the limbic system are relayed through nerve pathways to the cortex where they can be consciously registered. Then, the cortex must figure out what to do to satisfy these urges.

Unless the limbic system and neocortex are in synch, the consequences are dire. Antonio Damasio (1994), a neurologist at the University of Iowa, found this out in the mid-1970s when he saw a patient named "Eliot," who had just had an orange-sized tumor removed from the ventral area of his prefrontal lobe (an area just above the eyes). After the surgery, Eliot's behavior suddenly became erratic, even though his cognitive abilities remained intact. No longer able to hold down a steady job, he left his wife and children, remarried, and then divorced again. According to Damasio, having lost the ties between his limbic system and neocortex, Eliot could no longer rationally assess options. Emotions are critical to reasoning because they help us to evaluate the significance of our experiences.

Just as we need emotions to help us sort out our thoughts, we need thinking to process our emotions. Normally, as the brain develops, the cortex begins to assume control over the reactive lower parts of the brain. Behavior problems are inevitable if the cortex isn't able to perform this job. For instance, if a child lacks experiences that develop the cortex, such as interactions with parents or caregivers that encourage impulse control along with language and problem-solving skills, she may be prone to temper tantrums. Likewise, if a young child is abused, he may also have difficulty regulating his emotions due to the increased excitatory activity in the limbic region. As psychologist Daniel Goleman (1995) writes, "In a very real sense, we have two minds, one that thinks and one that feels" (p. 8). Of course, we really don't have two minds because all brain systems are parts of the whole. Ultimately, human development depends greatly on how these two systems—the cognitive and emotional—work together.

Our Two Minds

When Fredrick Schiffer (1998) uses the metaphor of "our two minds" to describe brain functioning, he refers not to the cognitive and emotional systems, but to the two cerebral hemispheres or half-brains. As noted earlier, the left hemisphere controls the right side of the body, and the right hemisphere the left side. Although the two hemispheres are mirror images of one another, each has its own style of thinking, patterns of motivation, and behavior. According to Schiffer, the hemispheres form distinct personalities and the relationship between them explains a whole host of psychological disorders from depression to psychosis. In his book, *Of Two Minds*, Schiffer writes:

> Many psychological insults of both childhood and adulthood can injure one hemisphere more than the other. Such damage will often enhance or corrupt the power of the troubled side and can often leave the more mature side underdeveloped, which can lead to a destructive struggle between the two minds and to psychological problems. (p. 15)

Just as the thinking and emotional brain need to be in balance, so, too, do the two cerebral hemispheres.

The so-called "split-brain" studies carried out in the 1960s and 1970s have identified some of the key functional differences between the hemispheres. Until then, neuroscientists did not understand the asymmetry of the human brain. For instance, the two main language areas of the brain—Wernicke's area and Broca's area—are located in the left hemisphere, just above the left ear (see Figure 1.1). Whereas Wernicke's area aids in the comprehension of spoken language, Broca's area generates speech. In split-brain studies, a procedure known as a commissurotomy, which cuts the corpus callosum, the huge fiber tract connecting the hemispheres, was performed on patients with uncontrollable seizures who were not responding to standard treatments. This surgery prevented electrical activity from crossing from one hemisphere into another.

Roger Sperry, who was later awarded a Nobel Prize, carried out the first psychological tests on split-brain patients. Research participants sat in front of a screen while pictures were flashed to the left or right visual field. Normally, images on the right side of the visual field are sent to the left hemisphere, and images on the left side are sent to the right. The information is then instantaneously communicated to the other hemisphere via the corpus callosum. However, split-brain patients, "W. J." for example, could process images on only one side:

W. J. easily named the visual stimuli flashed into the right visual field; that is, to the left, speaking hemisphere. That half-brain performed just as well as it had before the surgery. When stimuli were flashed to the left visual field, however, W. J. said nothing after each trial. When questioned, he denied seeing the stimuli. The right hemisphere, now disconnected had no way of transferring information to the left, which would engender a spoken response. It had become an independent mental system. (Gazzaniga, 1985, p. 42)

These early studies underscored earlier observations from brain-injured patients, demonstrating that the left hemisphere is generally responsible for speech and language, and the right hemisphere for specific sensory and spatial information. For instance, in one experiment, a spoon was flashed to the left visual field. When the subject was asked to name what she had seen, she said, "nothing," because the mute right hemisphere is separated from the speaking left hemisphere. Next, she was asked to select with her left hand the item she had just seen. By feel she was able to select the spoon from among a number of concealed objects. However, she was still unable to name the object because the information could not be shared with the verbal left hemisphere. Instead, her left hemisphere could only guess that it was a "pencil" (Sperry, 1968).

Although these studies showed that a severed corpus callosum precludes the exchange of cognitive information between the hemispheres, emotional information is able to cross via a lower route—the anterior commissure, which lies below the corpus callosum and connects the unconscious limbic structures in both hemispheres (see Figure 1.3). For example, when a picture of a nude woman was mixed in with neutral words and flashed to the left visual field (right hemisphere), the patient began to laugh. Asked why she was laughing, the subject said that the "machines" were funny. Her right hemisphere had communicated the appropriate feeling to the left hemisphere, even though she did not consciously know why. In another study, a split-brain patient reported feeling sad and uncomfortable when his right hemisphere was shown the picture of a funeral procession. Again, the patient could not figure out why he felt sad (Schiffer, 1998).

Perhaps the strangest condition to occur after patients had their corpus callosum severed is known as "alien hand." For a short time after surgery, patients often found their left hand (which is controlled by the right hemisphere) acting independently and in opposition to the left hemisphere. For example, one woman found it hard to put on her clothes. Whenever she would reach for a dress with her right hand, her left hand would put it back and grab a brighter colored dress. Another patient's left hand grabbed food from the refrigerator that he did not want and changed the television channel even though he was enjoying the show. Likewise, a male patient would light a cigarette only to find his left hand grab it and put it out (Joseph, 1990, as cited in Schiffer, 1998).

Alan Parkin (1998), who has studied many of these cases, explains the phenomenon as follows:

> The supplementary motor area (SMA)—the area that, in addition to the corpus callosum, is implicated in alien hand—springs into action when the brain prepares to execute complex volitional bodily action. . . . The activation on the side that is not actually going to move is pretty weak, but it may be enough to cause movement unless it is stopped. Normally, this inhibition comes from the SMA on the side that is actually meant to move—it sends a message to its opposite number that effectively reads: "Do not carry through . . . leave this one to me." This message passes through the corpus callosum, so in split-brain patients it does not get through. As a result both SMAs send "move it" messages to their respective limbs even though the conscious brain had plans to move only one. (p. 52)

Thus, in split-brain patients, the "alien hand"—which is directed by the nondominant hemisphere—is fighting for control in a system that only allows for one hemisphere to be in charge.

Further insight into the possibility that the two hemispheres may have distinct preferences comes from two split-brain patients who had exceptional language abilities in their right hemispheres. One of these patients could write with messages from his right hemisphere, spelling out words using scrabble letters. An interesting example is P.S., a fifteen-year-old boy from Vermont, who was asked what he wanted to do after finishing school. When this question was flashed to his left hemisphere, he said "a draftsman." However, when the same question was flashed to his right hemisphere, he spelled out, "automobile race[r]" (LeDoux, Wilson, and Gazzaniga, 1977).

Initially, the finding of two separate minds or two separate mental systems was revolutionary because it challenged the common assumption of mental unity, the theory of "mass action" that assumed that all neurons acted in unison to perform mental functions. Brain imaging studies have provided further evidence that the hemispheres do indeed have special skills.

Functions and Characteristics Associated with the Right and Left Cerebral Hemispheres

Left Hemisphere

- Positive, optimistic emotions (e.g., happiness)
- Motivational tendency to approach, explore, and take action
- Involved in the processing of verbal communication, words, and numbers
- Has the capacity to analyze, problem solve, and process information sequentially
- Allows for elaboration and provides detailed perspective

Right Hemisphere

- Negative, pessimistic emotions (e.g., fear or despair)
- Motivational tendency to withdraw and avoid
- Involved in the processing of nonverbal, emotional communication, imagery, and visual-spatial information
- Limited capacity to think analytically
- Provides global perspective

The left hemisphere, usually the dominant one, specializes in analytical and sequential thinking. Although language functions are distributed throughout the brain, most of the specialized language areas are located in the left hemisphere. The right hemisphere is more involved with spatial information, body awareness, and socioemotional information, and specializes in visual and metaphorical thinking. As with language, music areas are located throughout the brain. However, most specialized music areas are located in the right hemisphere. Whereas the left hemisphere focuses and elaborates on details, the right provides a global perspective (Werry, 1996; van der Kolk, Burbridge, and Suzuki, 1997; Ratey, 2001). The asymmetry is also strongly linked to particular emotions and motivations. Studies indicate that basic emotions, such as happiness, sadness, and fear, represent distinct patterns of brain activity. Research suggests that the left hemisphere mediates positive emotions such as joy and happiness, and the motivational tendency to seek solutions and take action. In contrast, the pessimistic, wary right hemisphere, is associated with negative emotions such as despair and fear along with the urge to avoid (Davidson, 1994).

Because of this emotional asymmetry, serious damage to either hemisphere (e.g., a stroke) often results in a distortion of reality. If the damage involves the left hemisphere, the right hemisphere will likely paint the world with its view of doom and gloom. If the injury is to the right, the patient may have an overly optimistic view of reality. Surprisingly, optimism that is not balanced by a keen look at reality creates its own set of problems. For example, Damasio (1994) describes a neurological condition known as anosognosia, which refers to the inability to recognize one's own disease or disabilities. It occurs in a group of patients who have left-side paralysis (damage to the right hemisphere). He writes:

> Imagine a victim of a major stroke, entirely paralyzed in the left side of the body, unable to move hand and arm, leg and foot, face half immobile, unable to stand or walk. And now imagine that same person oblivious to the entire problem, reporting that nothing is possibly the matter, answering the question, "how do you feel?" with a sincere, "Fine." (p. 62)

It is not just the disregard for the paralysis, but the emotional incongruity that these patients show for their condition that is striking. When an individual's self-image is so distorted, decision making is bound to be severely impaired. As Damasio (1994) says, "Paralysis is perhaps the least of their troubles" (p. 64). He cites, for example, the case of the late Supreme Court Justice William O. Douglas, who suffered a right hemispheric stroke in 1975:

> Later, after renewed efforts at rehabilitation had proved fruitless, Douglas replied to a visitor who asked about his left leg,

"I've been kicking forty-yard field goals with it in the exercise room," and ventured that he would sign up with the Washington Redskins. When the stunned visitor politely countered that his advanced age might put a damper on the project, the justice laughed and said, "Yes, but you ought to see how I'm arching them." (p. 68)

Given that the right hemisphere generally mediates negative emotions, it is not surprising that the memories associated with traumatic experience seem to be stored there. Using EEGs, Harvard researchers Schiffer, Teicher, and Papanicolaou (1995) found that when traumatized patients recalled a neutral event, their left brains were more active. In contrast, when these same patients recalled a traumatic memory, their right brains were more active. In his book, *Of Two Minds,* Schiffer (1998) reports on another split-brain patient, A.A., whose left and right hemispheric responses to trauma-related memories were also significantly different. His right brain remained distressed by events that had occurred years earlier, whereas his left brain was nonchalant and undisturbed by these memories. Subsequent studies have also shown that the right hemisphere is much more involved in the experiencing and recall of traumatic events (e.g., Rauch et al., 1996).

Flow: The Optimal Collaboration Between Different Parts of the Brain

Circuits, including nerve pathways such as the corpus callosum (the huge fiber tract that joins the left and right hemispheres) and the cingulum (the fiber tract that delivers information from the limbic system to the neocortex), integrate brain systems. Normally, these fiber tracts almost instantaneously relay information from one system to another and from one side of the brain to the other, allowing the parts of the brain to work together.

Most of the time, the conscious, verbal hemisphere plays the dominant role in speaking for the unconscious parts of the brain. However, to be an effective leader, this area must be in constant communication with every other part of the brain. Thus, positron-emission tomography (PET) scans show that most tasks activate multiple areas. Ideally, each system, with its own special talents, is constantly interacting with other parts of the brain. These intimate conversations are critical to higher-order thinking, creativity, problem solving, and emotional processing.

University of Chicago psychologist Mihaly Csikszentmihalyi (1990), who for decades has studied the positive aspects of human experience, hypothesizes that what makes experiences truly satisfying is a state of consciousness called flow. Surprisingly, flow does not always happen in moments of relaxation, but rather during tasks that challenge our physical and mental abilities to the utmost. As he writes in *Flow: The Psychology of Optimal Experience:*

> [Flow] usually occur when a person's body or mind is stretched to its limits in a voluntary effort to accomplish something difficult and worthwhile. Optimal experience is something we *make* happen. For a child, it could be placing with trembling fingers the last block on a tower she has built, higher than she has built so far; for a swimmer, it could be trying to beat his own record; for a violinist, mastering an intricate musical passage. For each person there are thousands of opportunities, challenges to expand ourselves. (p. 3)

Csikszentmihalyi goes on to say that flow involves a defined goal, riveted attention, intentional movement, and immediate feedback. The working relationship that develops between brain modules is so natural that tasks are carried out without an overwhelming sense of exertion. You're in a groove, yet, at the same time, you feel a sense of excitement and discovery. Flow is a harmonious state of consciousness that brings brain waves into synchrony and all the important resources of the mind to bear on a task. It creates a physiological calmness, combined with an intense alertness and a readiness to shift and respond to challenges within the environment.

Flow—the fluid and synchronized movement of information throughout the brain and body—taps the natural healing capacities of the mind. When information moves from one area of the brain to another, we are actually processing experience through different modalities— sensory perceptions, images, thoughts, behavior, and sensations (see Figure 1.4). When these various modalities—areas of the brain— work cooperatively to synthesize experience, intellectual and emo-

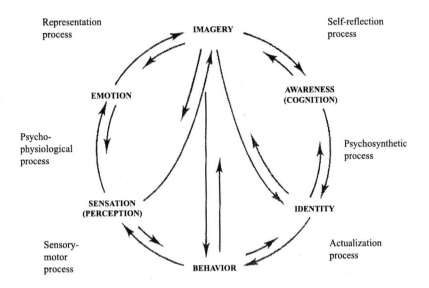

FIGURE 1.4. Modalities of Human Experience: Going with the Flow. Typically, symptoms are state-bound in one modality. The essence of symptom resolution involves the processing of information through all modalities of human experience. From *The Psychobiology of Mind-Body Healing*, Revised Edition, by Ernest Lawrence Rossi. Copyright 1993 by Ernest Lawrence Rossi. Used by permission of W. W. Norton and Company, Inc.

tional capacities flourish and consciousness expands. In contrast, when modalities splinter off and function independently, we feel at war within ourselves. As psychotherapist Ernest Rossi (1993) says, "Each modality has its own genius . . . people have symptoms and problems when their experience is *stuck or state bound* in one modality or another so they cannot use the natural geniuses of the other aspects of their nature" (p. 93).

When psychotherapists help clients process experiences, they are often working to move internalized experiences from one modality to another and enhance the integration of modality-specific information. For example, the Swiss psychoanalyst Carl Jung had patients draw a picture of their feelings when they were unable to put them into words. As thoughts began to flow, the patients reframed their own internal lives and became unstuck (Rossi, 1993). Whenever we use touch to calm a child, suggest she draw a mad or sad picture, imagine a safe place, or practice using words instead of actions to resolve conflicts, we are encouraging flow. We are helping a child to access her own internal resources by modulating and integrating emotion. Encouraging a child to process experience through the various modalities builds self-awareness, promotes problem-solving skills, and develops self-control.

Given the importance of early experience on brain development, some children can much more readily achieve flow than others. A securely attached child, calm and self-confident, will grow up with a brain that is designed to process experience. Early positive experiences have built in the capacity to integrate modality-specific information. In contrast, an abused or neglected child is more apt to get stuck in one mode (e.g., negative emotions, sensations, or self-destructive patterns of behavior) because the fear and helplessness caused by abuse blocks the collaboration among brain systems. The neurochemicals that are released during extreme stress interfere with brain functions that are involved in integrating experience. As Candace Pert (1997), a professor of physiology and biophysics at Georgetown University Medical Center, writes: "When stress prevents the molecules of emotion [neuropeptides/peptides] from flowing freely where needed, the largely autonomic processes that are regulated by peptide flow, such as breathing, blood flow, immunity, digestion, and elimination, collapse down to a few simple feedback loops and upset the normal healing response" (pp. 242-243).

In some children, constitutionally based differences in the nervous system—problems responding to stimuli, processing information, and/or organizing behavior—contribute to the lack of flow and collaboration between key areas of the brain. Bradley, the case study presented in the next chapter, illustrates how nature and nurture can conspire to derail development. In the final analysis, to help troubled children tackle their myriad behavioral problems, therapists must strengthen the circuitry in their brain—the working relationship between the various areas of the brain. We will explain how this process works as we tell Bradley's story.

Chapter 2

Birth to Five: Factoring in Biology

In the half-century since psychoanalyst John Bowlby first articulated attachment theory, numerous experts in child development have attempted to clarify the precise course of psychological development. According to one of the most widely accepted theoretical models, first put forth by child psychiatrist Stanley Greenspan over fifteen years ago, maturation occurs in six stages. For Greenspan, securely attached children are usually able to meet the challenges of each stage, but the offspring of less-attentive caregivers are likely to miss some key milestones. To treat emotional and developmental problems, Greenspan advocates a form of therapy that enables children to go back and master needed developmental skills. A seven-year-old with temper tantrums thus might need to work on emotional regulation—a capacity normally acquired during Stage 6 (between the ages of three and five).

In this chapter, we show how the new psychobiological research expands the current understanding of the maturation process in children from birth to five. Since psychological development and brain development actually represent two sides of the same coin, they can no longer be seen in isolation from one another. As noted earlier, the attachment relationship—namely, emotional interchanges between infant and caregiver involving touch, talk, and eye contact—shapes the growth of brain structures and pathways, which, in turn, affect the child's mental capacities. As Myron Hofer (1995) writes, "mutual homeostatic regulation characterizes our first relationship" (p. 227), meaning that through the coregulation of emotional states parents create in children a sense of emotional equilibrium and security. In a good scenario, parents thus induce a physiological state that promotes optimal brain growth. Furthermore, research by Allan Schore demonstrates that the emotions generated by these social interactions shape cognitive development.

We begin by briefly discussing how the psychological milestones characteristic of each stage of development also reflect growth in specific brain structures and circuitry—involving, for example, the integration of the emotional, motor, and cognitive systems. We illustrate these abstract principles—the development of mental capacities and their biological counterparts—through the case of a preschooler named Bradley whose development has gone awry. Having failed to develop critical mental capacities at the appropriate stages, at three years of age Bradley had severe difficulties in both communicating and relating to others. Both his cognitive and emotional development were lagging. He could barely talk at all. By reaching out to him at a critical period in his development, his treatment team was able to improve his psychobiological functioning. We surmise that this new form of interpersonal therapy helped Bradley become more connected to others and his environment by actually rewiring his brain, promoting and strengthening neural pathways between key brain systems. Since relational interaction is necessary to get the brain working in the first place, it's also the key to fixing it.

INTERACTION, BRAIN MATURATION, AND THE STAGES OF DEVELOPMENT

According to neuroscientist Antonio Damasio (1994), the basic function of the brain is to be well informed about its own activities, its body, and the environment, in order to make appropriate adjustments between the self and the environment. Echoing this perspective, Allan Schore (2001) writes:

> Development . . . represents an increase of complexity of the maturing brain systems that adaptively regulate the interaction between the developing organism and the social environment. (p. 4)

In a layered way, each stage builds on previously acquired capacities. "A principle of organizational theory," writes Jerome Kagan (1994), a developmental psychologist, "is that as one ascends from fundamental components to larger entities that combine the former, the stability of the increasingly complex structure is enhanced" (p. 271).

However, as mental processes interconnect, they may lead to new abilities and functions, which may not have any clear antecedents, but, instead, represent the synthesis of older ones (Kagan, 1986).

Although all children go through the same stages of development (see appendix at the end of this chapter), they do so in their own unique way. For example, the individual differences in a child's nervous system determine how an infant will react to stimuli, process information, and organize behavior. Whereas some infants are overreactive to stimuli, others are underreactive. Infants also show distinct preferences for the various sensory modalities. Some infants and children seem drawn to auditory input, others seem to have talent for understanding complex visual patterns. Some like low sounds, others like high-pitched ones. One infant might like a light feathery touch, and another might prefer deep massage. Along with preferences for certain sensory modalities, young children also develop a unique way of processing sensory information. For instance, some infants have trouble integrating multisensory input. By twelve months, we can easily observe how children organize their behavior. Whereas some toddlers have no difficulty planning to achieve a goal, others have difficulty translating desire into action. Often these children have trouble with routines as well as with more complex social interaction (Greenspan and Paulson, 1998).

Understanding a child's preferences and style of interacting with the world enables caregivers to individualize their interactions in order to help him master the skills of each stage. More specifically, caretakers need to respond appropriately to a child's emotional states; interactions need to generate "high levels of positive affect, in co-shared play states, and low levels of negative affect" (Schore, 2001, p. 4). This dyadic regulation of emotion allows an adult both to challenge a child to attempt things that may be difficult for her and, at the same time, provide support and validation.

Case Study: Bradley

Bradley was just three years old when his teacher referred him to one of the authors (P.S.) two weeks after the start of school because of concern about developmental delays. Bradley did not talk nor did he use gestures to indicate what he wanted. When the group sang songs, he would just babble. Lacking initiative, he would stare into space, sometimes oddly flapping his arms.

Bradley appeared lost in his own fantasy world. Only when physically guided did he comply with routine requests such as washing his hands. His play was repetitive. For example, he would line up toys in the same position over and over again. He was intrigued by puzzles and would carefully remove the pieces, turn them upside down, and assemble the puzzle face down beside the frame. This was repeated endlessly until interrupted by an adult. Avoiding eye contact, he paid little attention both to the other children and to the adults who attempted to engage him.

Bradley crawled at seven months and walked at fourteen months. His motor development and self-help skills were both more or less on target. He was toilet trained, although he still required adult help to go to the bathroom.

Bradley is the oldest of three children. He has two brothers: at the time, one brother was two years old and the other nine months. His mother was pregnant. Bradley's mother and her family had emigrated from Southeast Asia. Bradley's parents lived in student housing. His mother stayed at home and his father attended school and worked to support the family.

Bradley's mother described him as an "exceptionally good baby, who did not cry and liked to be by himself." He made few demands. She said that he always liked letters and numbers. When he was two, his favorite "toy" was the telephone book. He would sit for two or three hours looking at the pages. In reference to feeding and diapering, she said, "I would do it before he would let me know. I've always done a lot for him." Although he never expressed a desire to be picked up, he appeared to like being held.

As is customary for parents from her country, Bradley's mother adopted a laissez-faire style of parenting. If he seemed contented, she left him alone. She was, however, concerned that Bradley, in contrast to his younger brother, was not yet talking. Bradley had babbled at around eight to ten months, but then his vocalizations stopped. On those rare occasions when he used words, he did not seem to attach any meaning to them. For instance, for a while he frequently said "money," but after a few weeks, this word suddenly disappeared from his vocabulary. Bradley then said "maow," which means mother, and "nah," meaning stop. Attributing his language delay to his bilingual upbringing, Bradley's physician had suggested that he be enrolled in Head Start.

In this initial interview, Bradley's mother interacted with her three children in an affectionate manner. She spoke about her isolation and how she missed the support of her family. In contrast to Bradley, the two younger children were constantly seeking her attention. According to his mother, what little time her husband could spend with the children, he devoted to playing with the younger two boys because Bradley rarely seemed interested.

Stage 1. Birth to Three Months:
Focusing Attention and Regulating Arousal

A PET scan of a healthy newborn shows no activity in the prefrontal cortex and minimal activity in the sensory and motor areas of the cortex. In contrast, lower centers of the brain, such as the thalamus and the amygdala are very active as is the brain stem (Chugani, Phelps, and Mazziotta, 1987; Chugani, 1997). In addition, the brain has matured sufficiently to enable the newborn to use all her senses and to respond to those sensations with emotions such as pleasure and disgust.

The newborn faces two challenges: to regulate arousal (i.e., to be calm rather than overwhelmed) and to focus on external stimuli. These abilities generally go hand in hand. Many parents and skilled caregivers instinctively use a baby's interest in the environment—faces, voices, a favorite toy, soothing touch, rhythmic movements—both to help him maintain calm and to stimulate his mind.

"The outside world," as Ronald Kotulak (1993) writes, "is the brain's real food." However, in order to take in the outside world, the brain needs the appropriate state of arousal. Arousal is regulated by a group of nuclei in the brain stem. New or novel stimuli activate the neurons in these nuclei, which, in turn, issue a wake-up call to the sensory neurons in the cortex. This allows the mind to focus on the interesting stimuli while simultaneously blocking out irrelevant sensory input. In essence, the appropriate level of arousal organizes the nervous system. Too little, *underarousal,* and the sensory signal does not even register because the neurons are not awake. Too much, *overarousal,* and the neurons become overly excited, and the system disorganizes because the signal is drowned out by "static."

Although the newborn's arousal system is functional, it is not well developed. According to Allan Schore (1994), the positive emotions generated in the attachment relationship promote the sprouting of axons that deliver vital neurotransmitters to the cortex. These neurotransmitters, produced by nuclei located deep in the brain, in turn, activate sensory and motor systems in the cortex that awaken an infant's interest in the world. In the typically circular fashion of brain development, by looking, listening, feeling, and moving, the infant literally causes her cortex to expand, because the more a neural system is activated, the more it develops.

An infant can become appropriately aroused and interested in the world by noticing both the sensations he finds pleasurable as well as the ones he finds disturbing. Do bright lights seem to irritate? Is he soothed by light touch or firm pressure? Does he enjoy being bounced on your knee? Does rocking calm him or is the movement too stimulating? Are low tones or high tones more intriguing? What rhythmic patterns does he enjoy? Greenspan reminds us that the proper development of the nervous system depends on exercising all sensory modalities. In other words, the infant needs to be emotionally aroused and tuned-in to sight, sounds, smells, and touch during about half of his waking hours (Greenspan and Paulson, 1998).

Over the course of development, the emotions and level of arousal that are initially regulated by the significant caregiver become increasingly self-regulated. Even young infants soon learn to use their senses to calm themselves—by concentrating on a specific object (e.g., a rattle). The capacity for self-regulation—the ability to control internal emotional states and level of arousal—is the very foundation of mental health. Feeling calm translates into feeling secure and capable of coping with challenges in a person's environment. Helping a child learn to regulate her emotions and arousal is, perhaps, a parent's most important job. Learning this skill is a slow step-by-step process that begins in early infancy and continues into adulthood.

When an infant is able to concentrate on specific stimuli, and her experience is consistent and predictable, she will begin to recognize patterns.[1] She starts to recognize visual images as familiar people and things. Sounds have a common rhythm and tone, and smells have a characteristic sameness. As John Ratey (2001) explains:

> Neurons are generally firing all the time, but in a random manner; stimuli merely cause them to fire faster and to do it in an organized, synchronized way. The neurons are like members of an orchestra, warming up and tuning in a chaotic fashion until the conductor suddenly signals the first downbeat, at which point they immediately sound the harmonious opening note. (pp. 57-58)

Repetition and patterned sensory experience establish the neural organization that allows babies, at three or four months, to begin to recognize their mother's voice, the family dog, their cribs, or various rooms in the house. As Ratey (2001) writes: "The more often a specific pattern is fired in response to a stimulus, the more firm the nerve assembly becomes. Hence the axiom: Neurons that fire together wire together" (p. 55). Getting all the sensory areas of the cortex activated and working together leads to more complex pattern-recognition. Helping the infant coordinate input from all five senses in an emotionally meaningful way is what Greenspan and Paulson (1998) call a whole team workout. A baby that is tuned in to a predictable world is prepared for the next stage of development—falling in love.

Unfortunately, some babies don't master all the challenges of the first few months of life. Some are either over- or underreactive to stimuli. For instance, the hyperaroused baby all too readily disorganizes and becomes irritable and begins to cry. Incoming stimuli may not be able to fire in a synchronized and ordered way because the random activity of the neurons is too intense. There may be too much background noise. In contrast, the underaroused baby—such as Bradley—is quiet and less responsive to stimuli. In this case, perhaps there is not enough background noise—the signal cannot get through because the neurons are not primed and ready for action, or, the signal, itself, is distorted because the sensory information comes in too fast, too slow, or in bits and pieces. In a majority of cases where a child fails to achieve developmental milestones, both nature and nurture typically play a role. Bradley's tendency to not respond to outside stimuli was reinforced by his mother's depression, which limited her ability to provide the extra stimulation or the type of stimulation needed to encourage his interest in the outside world.

Case Study: Bradley

Bradley seemed to be very disconnected from his environment. He was particularly unresponsive to auditory and tactile stimuli. Once, when his baby brother grabbed and twisted his hair, he apparently didn't even notice. In addition, he often ignored complex visual stimuli, preferring to focus on simple shapes and lines rather than on human faces. Even pictures seemed to make him uncomfortable as, if you recall, he always turned his puzzle pieces upside down.

Often, children who have severe difficulty communicating and relating cannot process information quickly. Information comes in too fast or it comes in fragments. Thus, the information they take in from the environment is often distorted and inaccurate (Ratey, 2001). For example, Bradley had a hard time picking up facial expressions that change quickly and sounds such as the letter "c," which last only milliseconds. These visual and auditory processing difficulties put Bradley at high risk for developing lifelong communication problems.

Stage 2. Two to Seven Months: Falling in Love, Learning to Relate

By age three months, PET scans show considerable activity in several areas of the limbic system, including the hippocampus. Although the prefrontal cortex remains dormant, the cingulate cortex is now active (Chugani, 1997; Chugani, Phelps, and Mazziotta, 1987). Strategically located between the limbic structures and the prefrontal cortex, the cingulate region is the driving force that guides goal-directed behavior. It functions as the gatekeeper, deciding which of the urges generated in the limbic system and bits of sensory information should be delivered to frontal lobes and what—if anything—the cortex should do to satisfy these urges.

By four months, however, PET scans show some activity in a region called the orbitofrontal cortex (see Figure 2.1). This region of the prefrontal cortex seems to be responsible for the processing and regulation of emotion, the ability to emotionally connect with another person, and to feel the pleasure of interpersonal communication (Schore, 1996). The attachment relationship underlies the development of this area of the prefrontal cortex. Schore's (1994) research suggests that the emotionally arousing reciprocal interactions between infant and care-

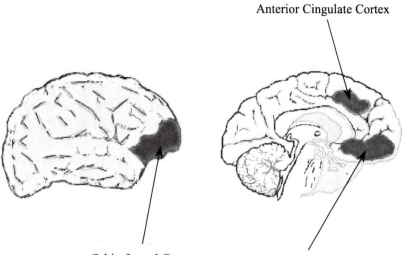

FIGURE 2.1. Orbitofrontal Cortex, Ventromedial Cortex, and Anterior Cingulate Cortex. The orbitofrontal and ventromedial corteces are responsible for regulating and processing emotion. For example, the orbitofrontal area mediates functions such as attachment/social bonding, emotional regulation, and empathy. It inhibits urges arising from the limbic area, allowing us to control our impulses in support of the advantages that can be gained by waiting. The ventromedial cortex is also involved in inhibiting lower centers and interpreting emotions. The anterior cingulate, according to van der Kolk (1997), is the last stop before consciousness. It helps decide what emotional information to pass on to the cortex, recruits areas of the cortex to help process emotions and urges arising from the limbic system, and helps focus attention on thinking.

giver lead to increases in the neurotransmitter, dopamine, which in his words, "trigger a local growth spurt in the blood vessels, neurons, and glia of the prefrontal cortex especially in the early maturing right hemisphere" (p. 134). Endogenous opioids also mediate this process. According to Schore (1994), the infant's perceptions of positive emotion such as the positive facial expression of the caregiver, stimulate the production of opioid peptides, thereby activating dopamine neurons.

An emotionally attuned caregiver also shapes the growth of the infant's emotional systems. Newborns are capable of experiencing a variety of emotions such as pleasure, distress, disgust, and protest, though these emotional states are not well developed. However, it does not take long for emotions to begin to differentiate themselves from one another. By four months of age, an infant will look distinctly sad if she is suddenly separated from her mother. Around four to six months, real expressions of anger begin to appear, and by seven or eight months, we can see the classic facial expressions of fear when the infant is exposed to unfamiliar situations or people. At this age, the frontal cortex has already developed enough to enable the infant to recognize familiar faces and to compare the present with the past.

Through the sharing of emotional states, often referred to as *mirroring,* babies use adults as extensions of themselves to reflect and enhance distinct emotions and associated behavior. For example, each time a baby's smile is reciprocated or his expressions of delight are met with a smile and a hug, these emotions are reinforced. Thus, the emotional circuitry organizes itself as it strengthens and stabilizes a circumscribed network of neurons dedicated to a particular emotion. If, however, the infant's emotions are met with indifference or rejection, emotional as well as cognitive development will be stymied. Without adequate mirroring, critical circuitry, including pathways that integrate the cognitive and emotional systems, will fail to develop.

Mirroring also helps infants learn to regulate their emotions. Every infant has an optimal level of stimulation. When underaroused, the infant typically seeks more stimulation, and an attuned mother will match the infant's behavior and then exaggerate it. In contrast, when the infant looks away, a sensitive mother will recognize that he is overstimulated and will respond accordingly. If, however, the mother does not disengage and continues to excite the infant, he eventually disorganizes.

Attuned caregivers also know how to use *emotional reciprocity,* or the sharing of emotional states, to help infants shift emotional states. For example, if an infant is, by nature, easily excited or overloaded, a parent will need to both entice and soothe. After empathizing with the infant's distress, a sensitive parent might assume the lead and through a series of emotional interchanges move the infant to a calmer state. Likewise, with a withdrawn infant, such as Bradley, more persistence and playfulness will be required to stimulate reciprocal interaction and emotion. Babies differ in how long they can remain engaged. At first, interactions may need to end after only two or three minutes, but soon, they can last five or ten minutes. Keep in mind that babies need periods of quiet to recover, and they just look and listen. In this coregulation of states, an attuned caregiver will work to expand positive emotions and modulate negative emotions.

The attachment relationship soon evolves beyond shared emotional states to shared attention, in which an infant begins to communicate about something specific. When an infant looks at a rattle and her mother shifts her attention to the object and responds, "Do you want the rattle?" and hands it to her, the mother and infant are sharing an experience.

A secure attachment relationship, based on the coregulation of states, also spawns feelings of empathy. Children who do not experience an intense, loving relationship with at least one person may never feel a shared sense of humanity and are at risk for developing antisocial behaviors. This feeling of belonging is essential for the development of morality and altruism. Research indicates that children who never develop trust and lack a secure attachment relationship are at risk for developing antisocial behaviors (Galvin et al., 1997).

Case Study: Bradley

Although Bradley occasionally related warmly to others, he often tuned people out, preferring to focus his attention on geometrical patterns. The typical interaction between Bradley and his parents took the form of a single exchange. He could not engage in any give-and-take. He had no interest in communicating, either verbally or with gestures. As Greenspan might put it, there were no "circles of communication." Bradley's mother was easygoing, but she also appeared emotionally drained as she struggled to take care of three young children without much social support. Unfortunately, Bradley was the type of child who needed particularly attentive parents in order to break out of his detached state and start engaging with others. The interactions between Bradley and his mother were not generating sufficient emotion to foster the development of the distinct emotional states of sadness, joy, anger, and fear, which normally develop in the first year of life.

Thus, Bradley's lack of emotion was beginning to wreak havoc with his long-term psychobiological development. After all, emotion is critical in fostering the growth of the cortex, especially the frontal cortex. We can hypothesize that a PET scan of Bradley might have shown considerably less activity in the orbitofrontal cortex than one of a better-adjusted infant.

Stage 3. Three to Ten Months: Developing Intentional Communication

By three months, most infants begin to develop intentional communication. They start using gestures, facial expressions, and sounds to indicate what they want. This ability depends on the growth of both the ascending pathways from the limbic system to the cortex and the frontal lobes. For example, before an infant can voluntarily reach for an object, the urge that emerges from the limbic system must be communicated to the motor cortex of the frontal lobes where it can then be translated into action. This communication within the brain not only allows for the capacity to express intentions, but also fosters the growth of the cortex and encourages exploratory behavior and interest in special people (Schore, 1994).

By seven to ten months, most infants are crawling. This new motor capacity offers an array of new possibilities of self-assertion. The infant is typically thrilled with her new abilities to set a goal (e.g., to get that brass carving on the coffee table), and carry out the action needed to reach it (crawl to the table, pull herself up, and grab the carving). Over and over again, desire and emotion get transformed into action, stimulating and reinforcing pathways linking the emotional, cognitive, and motor systems. These multiple circles of communication along with expanding sequences of action and reaction, in turn, build neural connections throughout the entire brain.

Purposeful action is also what helps an infant learn about cause and effect. He begins to sense that his actions can elicit certain behavior from others. At two or three months, he may look intently at a toy, prompting a familiar caregiver to offer it to him. At four months, the infant will take the toy and then signal his pleasure at being understood. These first experiences with cause and effect represent the beginnings of logical thinking (Greenspan and Greenspan, 1985).

When an infant does not engage in purposeful action, or what is called *motor planning and sequencing,* brain development suffers. As Greenspan points out, one of the biggest challenges infants with cerebral palsy face is learning to move in some purposeful way, even if simply moving an arm, tongue, or just eyes to communicate intent (Greenspan and Paulson, 1998). Although it is impossible to understand every signal an infant sends, caregivers should at least try to figure out what the infant is trying to communicate, even if she decides not to indulge the desire. By communicating with responsive adults, the infant begins to develop a strong sense of self.

Case Study: Bradley

Bradley had considerable difficulty communicating his needs and engaging in purposeful behavior. Transforming urges and desires into goal-directed behavior requires collaboration between the emotional and motor systems in the brain. Children who have trouble relating to others have difficulty making these connections. We can speculate that for Bradley, these anatomical pathways had not matured.

In contrast to most babies, Bradley rarely used gestures and facial expressions to express himself. At home, his intentional behavior was limited to moving near his mother or standing passively in front of the refrigerator when he was hungry. In school, he would simply stand next to the teachers to indicate he wanted something.

Stage 4. Nine to Eighteen Months:
The Emergence of an Organized Sense of Self

Between nine and eighteen months—the transition from infancy to toddlerhood—various new cognitive and emotional capacities emerge, including problem solving, self-control, conceptualization, and language (Greenspan and Greenspan, 1985). These capacities correspond to the nascent sense of self—an evolving system of belief about the integrity of a person's mind and body. By engaging in complex interactions, such as extended conversations with caregivers, the infant/toddler creates an image of herself and others. She learns to anticipate reward, punishment, pleasure, and disapproval. Depending on the child's experiences, she may have a picture of the world as safe and caring or as dangerous and hurtful. How she views herself reflects the responses that she has evoked from others. She may see herself as a person to be respected and loved, or as a person to be rejected and humiliated.

Emotion continues to motivate goal-directed behavior. No longer crying or using simple gestures to indicate a desire, the toddler is capable of organizing a complex series of actions. For example, if he wants a specific toy, he may seek out a parent who is in another room. He might also take the parent's hand and pull her toward the bedroom and eventually to his closet. Through a series of interactions—the parent asking questions and the toddler babbling and pointing—the parent finally discovers it is the toy on the shelf that he wants.

Along with the ability to carry out a series of actions comes the ability to imitate (Greenspan and Paulson, 1998). The toddler pretends to cook, talk on the phone, or feed and comfort her doll. The toddler soon begins to conceptualize as well. She becomes curious about the purpose of things, what they are called, and how they function. People and the roles they play also pique her interest.

By the end of this stage, most toddlers also begin to develop a sense of self that extends across all emotional states (Putnam, 1997). Although a year-old infant feels like a different person when he experiences different emotions such as joy or anger, at eighteen months, toddlers are often able to experience themselves as embodying two different emotions at one time (Greenspan and Greenspan, 1985). It is through interactions with caretakers that young children begin to integrate emotional states. For example, the capacity to feel ambivalence, to experience both hate and love at the same time, develops as the toddler internalizes the loving image of his significant caregiver. Although anger may make him feel as though he wants to destroy others, the loving image begins to temper the all-consuming negative emotions.

The development of ambivalence adds an entirely new dimension to the toddler's problem-solving capabilities. He now faces two competing alternatives: what he wants to do and what he is allowed to do. This is the dilemma of a toddler who would love to tear books off a shelf but refrains from acting on these impulses for fear of disapproval from his mother.

Thus, toddlers achieve what is often referred to as *object permanence* or *object constancy.* In other words, he understands that his mother still exists even when she is out of sight. This new conceptual ability not only fosters the capacity to inhibit impulses, but also spawns new games. For example, the toddler may toss food from a high chair, and then peek over the edge to try to see it, look for hidden objects, or play peekaboo and hide-and-seek.

This stage depends on the maturation of the prefrontal cortex and the collaboration of the various brain systems, including the sensory, emotional, cognitive, and motor. Let's consider the problem solving of an assertive sixteen-month-old who is hungry. The message "I'm hungry" first registers in the hypothalamus, then is relayed to the prefrontal cortex. Because of object permanence, the toddler can now generate an image of food—say, a container of yogurt. Keeping this goal in mind, she carries out a plan of action by coordinating information from cognitive and sensorimotor systems. She finds her mother, drags her to the refrigerator, and points to the yogurt. When all brain systems are working together, we say that the child's behavior is organized. In contrast, aimless, disorganized behavior is literally an external manifestation of poorly integrated brain systems.

At eight months, PET scans show activity in just the basal part of the prefrontal cortex called the orbitofrontal area. By twelve months, however, the entire prefrontal cortex is active. Surprisingly, a one-year-old's scan looks remarkably similar to an adult's (Chugani, 1997). The prefrontal cortex, especially the orbitofrontal cortex, plays the central role in integrating information from all areas of the brain. It is the region where axons from the cortex and lower-brain regions come together. Consider, for example, *object permanence.* Biological research suggests this mental capacity begins as a part of the imprinting process. The visual information about an attachment figure, especially facial expressions, is processed in an area of the right anterior temporal cortex, which is specifically dedicated to faces. Around twelve months, a pathway emerges between this area, the limbic system, and the prefrontal cortex that allows the infant to identify familiar faces. Eventually, the prefrontal area stores this information making it available for retrieval as needed (Schore, 1994).

According to Allan Schore (1994), the growth of the prefrontal cortex is mediated by the neurotransmitters dopamine and norepinephrine. Dopamine spurs the initial development of the prefrontal cortex by increasing blood flow and stimulating the growth of neurons and glial cells. At about fourteen to eighteen months, in contrast, norepinephrine starts playing a dominant role. In each case, experience drives neurochemistry. Schore suggests the shift from dopamine to norepinephrine coincides with changing expectations of parents.

Whereas one-year-olds receive mostly positive responses from parents, toddlers receive more prohibitions (Fagot and Kavanagh, 1993). This demand for impulse control—not allowing the child to tear pages in a book, poke at eyes, pull hair, etc.—creates mild stress, causing an increased delivery of norepinephrine, a neurochemical associated with the stress response, to the prefrontal cortex.

Norepinephrine, Schore (1994) postulates, helps to form descending pathways from the prefrontal cortex down to lower regions of the brain. These descending pathways eventually allow the prefrontal cortex to override the desires that are generated in lower centers of the brain. Because the ascending tracts mature first, unbridled expressions of emotion (such as temper tantrums) are common among toddlers aged eighteen to thirty-six months. The so-called "terrible twos" can't end until an efficient inhibitory system has been laid down. (It's important to remember that it takes far longer for the descending or inhibitory tracts to mature than it does for the ascending or excitatory tracts.)

Schore (2001) argues that the attachment relationship directly impacts the infant's ability to cope with stress:

> In attachment transactions of affective synchrony, the psychobiologically attuned caregiver interactively regulates the infant's positive and negative states, thereby co-constructing a growth facilitating environment. . . . The efficient functioning of this coping system is central to the infant's expanding capacity for self-regulation, the ability to flexibly regulate stressful emotional states through interactions with other humans—interactive regulation in interconnected contexts, and without other humans—autoregulation in autonomous contexts.

He goes on to say that emotional development depends on the capacity to adaptively shift between interpersonal and intrapersonal regulatory modes. (p. 2)

In the next stage, we will see how the onset of imagination and language both strengthens *autoregulation,* the ability of the cortex to override the urges of the emotional systems, and encourages the harmonious cooperation between the emotional and cognitive systems.

Case Study: Bradley

At three, Bradley's development was severely lagging. Barely able to engage in reciprocal interactions, he couldn't yet pursue goal-directed actions. For the typical nine- to eighteen-month-old, urges and desires are constantly being transformed into images and organized movements, a process that stimulates and reinforces brain pathways. Since Bradley wasn't reaching this milestone, his problems were in danger of snowballing.

Stage 5. Eighteen to Thirty-Six Months: Creating Thoughts and Using Language

Until about eighteen months, the urges arising from the limbic system and relayed to the cortex inevitably lead to action. As Ames and Ilg (1976a) of the Gesell Institute of Human Development put it, toddlers "bumble along . . . and almost seem to think with their feet" (p. 1). Thinking and language then come to the forefront. Sometime between eighteen and twenty-four months, toddlers begin to create images in their minds and to translate them into words. The internal representations, as Greenspan and Paulson (1998) point out, are multisensory images. For example, when a child thinks of a banana, he can picture its shape and color, and imagine its taste. These images feel real because they are connected to emotionally arousing memories. Both language and imagination can now be used to organize behavior. Let's take the example of the hungry two-year-old. Rather than just point, grab, or squeal, the toddler can imagine a banana and actually say the word "banana." As time goes on, he can put two ideas or images together, saying, for example, "mama, banana."

Children reveal their mental images through language. If a child asks for a favorite doll or truck that she has not seen for a while, she clearly has a construct for that object. Fantasy or pretend play can also demonstrate that the child is beginning to conceptualize. For example, when a two-year-old puts a doll into a high chair and pretends to feed it, she probably has some abstract understanding of nurturing. Drawing, painting, and sculpting are other ways toddlers represent internally generated images. By encouraging children to transform images into language, art, and pretend play, adults help them build a symbolic world, which becomes basis for all future creative thinking (Greenspan, 1997).

Language also provides the child with an invaluable tool for coping with emotions. Because an eighteen-month-old toddler can't yet express his emotions and desires in words, he is often frustrated. When language comes on the scene, the toddler can talk about his emotions (e.g., anger) rather than acting on them (e.g., having a tantrum). Adults help young children learn to express emotion through words by labeling their emotions, "You look mad, sad, or hungry."

Because development does not proceed in a straight line, progress is usually followed by periods of regression. For example, a two-year-old may be fairly content to meander around his surroundings. But within a short period of time, most toddlers usually become bossy, demanding, emotional, and conflicted. For instance, if she chooses one outfit, within seconds, she will want to wear a different one (Ames and Ilg, 1976a). Child-development experts describe development as involving alternating periods of progress and regression. In the words of Ames and Ilg (1976a),

> Stages, or ages, when things are fine and in good equilibrium, seem to need to break-up and to be followed by stages when things are not so fine, equilibrium is not as steady. We call this manner of growing, *interweaving*. *Good* seems to interweave with *bad; equilibrium* with *disequilibrium*. The good, solid equilibrium of any early age seems to need to break-up into disequilibrium before the child can reach a higher or more mature stage of equilibrium, which again will be followed by disequilibrium. (pp. 4-5)

The neurological mechanism underlying this pattern of organization, disorganization, and reorganization, involves the overproduction of synapses, followed by selective pruning of unused connections until new neural networks emerge. Behavioral changes—two steps forward, one step back—correspond directly to these neurobiological changes. A growth spurt—the proliferation of synapses—has a disorganizing effect on the child's brain and behavior. For instance, a normally easy-going child may become demanding and conflicted. New skills emerge when reorganized circuitry becomes reinforced and stabilized. Ultimately, development follows the basic biological principle that "there can be no reorganization without disorganization" (Scott, 1979, p. 233).

New capacities may also cause problems in the short run. Fears generated in the limbic system can now be transformed into frightening mental images. The toddler who was going to bed without a fuss may suddenly balk due to worries about monsters lurking in the closet.

At two-and-a-half to three years of age, children begin to make connections between the mental images in their minds. They begin to build a network of associations that become the basis for problem-solving skills. They start imagining alternatives, considering consequences, and developing elaborate plans of action (Greenspan, 1997). Although children eventually move from thinking in images to thinking in words, imagery remains an essential component of creative thought as attested to by Nobel prize-winning physicist Albert Einstein (1956): "The words of language, as they are written or spoken, do not seem to play any role in my mechanism of thought . . . elements [of thought] are, in my case, of visual and some of muscular type. Conventional words or other signs have to be sought for laboriously only in a secondary stage" (pp. 25-26).

Case Study: Bradley

Normally, between eighteen and thirty-six months, children begin to use language and develop imagination. At three, Bradley still had virtually no expressive language or pretend play. Movement, such as gestures and facial expressions, organizes thinking and spawns language because areas of the brain that coordinate physical movement also help coordinate the processing of thoughts (Ratey, 1999). Language areas of the brain, such as Broca's area, which lies adjacent to the motor cortex, are also closely allied to the movement centers. Unfortunately, Bradley rarely used nonverbal forms of communication. He did not point or grab adults by the hand, and his facial expressions showed little emotion.

Designing an Intervention Strategy for Bradley

Following the initial assessment, P.S. met with Bradley's parents. We agreed to schedule an appointment at a local speech and language clinic. Bradley was enrolled in a Head Start class that met four times a week for three-and-a-half hours in addition to speech therapy twice a week in the classroom and once a week at the university's speech and language clinic. The classroom teachers were experienced in helping children with special needs tackle the regular preschool curriculum. As a mental health consultant, P.S. helped the teachers design and implement a treatment plan for Bradley.

In Bradley's case, the developmental milestones associated with each stage of development had been only partially attained. Because the stages build on one another, we had to begin by going back to Stage 1. We first focused on generating emotion before turning to more complex skills, such as building a symbolic world.

Stimulating Emotion. We began by trying to find ways to heighten emotion and energize Bradley. This task proved challenging, as he was not very responsive to touch or sound. To tap into his emotions, we needed to engage with Bradley in activities that interested him. He liked to play outdoors, so we made sure there was opportunity for lots of rough-and-tumble play. We also encouraged movement indoors by providing him with toys such as large, bouncy balls. Noticing that music seemed to energize him, we also encouraged his active participation in the group sing-along. Daily, during large group time, songs that involved gestures and movement were sung. Soon Bradley was not only vocalizing, but also gesticulating to the words of the songs.

The teachers observed that words were more interesting to Bradley when they were spoken slowly and accompanied by animated gestures and facial expressions. He also paid more attention to melodious sounds similar to the universal "parentese" spoken to infants and young children. In light of the research on auditory and visual processing disorders, which suggests that some children have difficulty picking up quick sounds and fast moving stimuli, it is not surprising that Bradley was more responsive to the slower, exaggerated sounds and images.

Mutual Engagement. In order to teach Bradley how to engage with others, teachers began shadowing him throughout the day. They did not allow him to spend time alone engaging in a monotonous activity. They began playing with him the games of infancy such as peekaboo, tickling, and tag. Since movement seemed to stimulate emotion and interaction, they were more successful in engaging him when these games were part of vigorous physical activity. Whenever Bradley found an activity he enjoyed—be it putting together puzzles or blowing bubbles—the teachers would join in, often gently teasing him until he engaged with them. They also tried to face him in order to make him more comfortable with eye contact.

Encouraging Intentional Communication. The next goal was to teach Bradley to express his needs directly. The staff began by treating all his behavior as purposeful. For instance, when Bradley approached the teachers but just stood there passively, they would scoop him up into their arms, assuming that he wanted a big hug. Sometimes they would play "dumb," or do things the "wrong" way. When he stood by the refrigerator, the staff acted as if they didn't know what he wanted. Likewise, they would line things up the wrong way, put the puzzle pieces in the wrong place, or put his mittens on his feet. These situations usually stimulated an animated response.

Working with Parents. At the same time, the teachers and P.S. were meeting regularly with Bradley's parents to share information and teach them how to interact with him in new ways. His father began playing with Bradley in the park. His mother learned to be more engaging and not to be so quick to anticipate Bradley's needs, making him work a little harder to get what he wanted, such as food from the refrigerator. Both parents were encouraged to spend considerable one-on-one time with Bradley. In addition, the support services available through Head Start were able to help the family cope with a variety of social and economic stressors.

Evaluating Progress. After just four months of treatment, Bradley had moved up the development ladder. For the first time, he was obviously experiencing the joy of interpersonal interactions. At the same time, he was also actively expressing his displeasure when frustrated by kicking and throwing himself onto the floor. P.S. had to convince the preschool staff that his temper tantrums were really a sign of progress, indicating that his emotional systems were developing. Intense desires were being shunted to the cortex for action. Whenever Bradley got angry, the teachers were sympathetic and found ways to comfort him, though they were careful not to reward his temper tantrums by indulging him. When he was calm, they had him practice alternative ways of solving the problem. Or, if he lapsed into a temper tantrum because he did not want to do something that was requested of him, they made sure, after he calmed down, that he followed through with their original request.

Over time, Bradley learned more adaptive ways of expressing himself. For instance, earlier in the year, a classmate, Kelly, had "adopted" him, dragging him around the room, hugging him, etc. At first, he was passive and compliant. But as the year went on, he began to protest. As the teacher described in her notes: "I put my hands on either side of his head and moved it from side to side and told him to tell her 'No.' Awhile later, he put his *own* hands up to his head and said 'No' to her while shaking his head."

Bradley also moved from passively watching the other children to initiating interactions. He began by bringing toys such as dinosaurs and action figures to other children. The teachers provided an ongoing narrative to describe his actions: For example, "Bradley is bringing Jessica some dinosaurs. He wants to be her friend. I guess Aaron doesn't want to play with the Power Rangers. Maybe Kelly does." And Bradley would look at the teacher and smile.

At other times, his approach was much less graceful, such as when he approached the girls who were having a tea party and tipped over the table. Bradley's teacher recognized his behavior as an awkward attempt to join in. Gently, but firmly, she asked him to put everything back where it was. The tea party resumed; this time with Bradley happily participating.

There are many ways to foster peer relationships. Having a special friend often facilitates the process. In Bradley's case, Kelly, the class "mother," was a natural candidate for the role. As Bradley began mastering more developmental skills, their relationship evolved from one solely based on caregiving to friendship. Joining in a child's play and expanding on it to include other children helps promote peer relationships. Also, just talking about what a child is doing draws the attention of the other children. For example, "Bradley is lining up all the dinosaurs . . . there is tyrannosaurus rex and brontosaurus." Soon other children are watching, and some usually join in the play.

Stage 6. Three to Five:
Developing Organized Thinking

The mental images of two-year-olds lack internal organization. Watching a toddler in a preschool classroom is similar to surfing the television networks. The scenes are disconnected. First, the child picks up a paintbrush. After making a few strokes at the easel, she heads for the doll area. Picking up a doll, she puts her into a high chair, looks toward the plastic play food, but then notices a group of children playing with water at the sand table. Soon she is absorbed with sand and water, making mounds of wet sand and creating rivers of running water.

Over the next eighteen months, thinking becomes less chaotic. As Greenspan (1997) notes, "The child begins to form bridges among his ideas and between his own thoughts and those of others" (p. 85). By age four, play is far more sequential, logical, and organized. Now she may put a doll in the high chair, find a bib, and announce that she is the mommy cooking breakfast. As she stirs the eggs, the child may see the teacher nearby and invite her to have some food.

This cognitive shift occurs because children begin to develop an internal model of the world, sometimes called a *mental schema,* and to organize ideas into categories. Three-year-olds are capable of categorizing experience according to time, space, and quantity. Although they may be unsure about their exact meaning, children at three use words such as "yesterday," "last night," "last year," and so on. Time of day is usually linked to the daily routine: snack time, dinnertime, and when mom comes home from work. The understanding of spatial relationships also continues to expand. The typical three-a-half-year-old can understand words such as "under," "on," "in," "beside," "over," "back," and "next to" (Ames and Ilg, 1976b).

At this age, children also begin to see language as a means to understand the world. They want to know "How?" "When?" "What?" and of course, "Why?" At the same time as the mind tries to fit all new experiences into existing schemas, it also seeks to find new ways to organize and categorize. Putting things together in novel ways can create new meaning. Piaget called these two basic mental activities *assimilation* (the integration of new experience into existing schemas) and *accommodation* (the creation of new schemas).

As in the other stages, emotion continues to be the driving force, giving meaning to particular experiences and determining how memories get filed—as something good, bad, joyous, mad, sad, or frightening. Emotion is also the cohesive force that underlies the sequence of behaviors and thoughts. In the example mentioned previously of the four-year-old playing with a doll, nurturing structures the flow of thoughts and activity.

The mental connections between perceptions, images, words, and actions reflect the actual physical connections between neurons that are being organized and strengthened. Between the ages of three and four, the brain undergoes a growth spurt involving both hemispheres, followed by a major reorganization of functioning (Thatcher, 1994). Prior to this growth cycle, language-related processes occur in both hemispheres, but afterward, they begin to shift to the left hemisphere, as the right hemisphere begins to focus on visual-spatial tasks (Mills, Coffey-Corina, and Neville, 1994). By age five, in 95 percent of children, language is firmly located in the left hemisphere, with the speech areas of the right hemisphere taken over by other things such as gesture (Carter, 1998, p. 155). This lateralization of some functions proceeds hand in hand with improved interhemispheric communication and behavioral organization.

There can, of course, be no reorganization without disorganization. As opposed to the three-year-old, the three-and-a-half-year-old no longer approaches the world with equanimity. In the words of Ames and Ilg (1976b):

> We may fairly and in all friendliness, describe the three and a half year old boy or girl as being characteristically inwardized, insecure, anxious, and above all determined and self-willed. One might assume that his strong-willed self-assertiveness, which is so conspicuously evident, might be rooted in a strong personal security. Not so! In fact, the very opposite seems to be the case. (p. 6)

Ames and Ilg go on to describe the motor disorganization evident in the behavior of the three-and-a-half-year-old:

> He stutters, he stumbles, he trembles. A child who six months earlier may have walked a proud one foot to a step up the stairs may now go back to a more babyish two feet to a step. Quite steady at three, he may now express fear of falling. Steady handed at three as he built a sturdy tower of blocks, his hand may now tremble as he adds blocks to his tower. Handedness may even shift at this age, and it may seem as if the child actually does not know which hand to use. (p. 6)

Many three-and-a-half-year-olds respond to this internal disorganization by becoming oppositional. Routine often becomes a battleground. They resist getting dressed, eating meals, and going to bed. In this "nothing pleases me mode," Ames and Ilg (1976b) suggest that mothers should not hesitate using the services of a young baby-sitter. "[A] three and a half [year-old] is amazingly sensitive to the reactions of others. He *knows* that the sitter really doesn't *care* whether he eats or goes hungry, gets his rest or becomes exhausted" (p. 8). Even the most skilled parent can benefit from assistance during this period.

As in the earlier stages of development, the period of disorganization is immediately followed by reorganization. By four, children are usually self-assured and expansive, eager for new and exciting adventures (Ames and Ilg, 1976c). The reorganized brain of the four-year-old resembles a beehive, as a swarm of interconnecting circuitry is buzzing around inside. This biological activity produces an endless imagination. At four, a picture that starts out as a house may become a boat, a pirate ship, and then an island where pirates can bury their treasures.

Greater self-assurance stems from an increased capacity for self-reflection and self-awareness. The developing metacognitive processes make it possible for the child to form an integrated identity that spans all emotional states, consolidate personality (ego) strengths such as impulse control, reality testing, and concentration, and be able to choose which aspect of the self to emphasize (Putnam, 1997). Self-awareness also helps a child develop empathy: "What I said hurt her feelings," or "I was mean." He learns to control his impulses because he recognizes that his behavior causes a reaction in others. In addition, he can now differentiate between reality and fantasy, and between self and not self. Self-awareness also prevents us from projecting our own thoughts and emotions onto others, from thinking that others are angry, when, in fact, we are experiencing the anger. The meta-self also expands a child's capacity for fantasy, allowing him to become someone else while at the same time knowing that he is just pretending to be a fireman, policeman, or evil warrior. The child can also experiment with different emotions as he simultaneously maintains a distinct meta mood.

The continuing maturation of the prefrontal cortex underlies the development of self-monitoring capacities. As the integration area for the entire brain, the prefrontal region contains elaborate networks of ascending, descending, and lateral pathways that ensure contact with all other cortical and subcortical systems. Though the development of the prefrontal cortex begins in infancy, many areas probably do not become fully functional until around age four (Lyon, 1996). As previously noted, this maturational process continues through adulthood with other major periods of rapid growth occurring somewhere between six and ten, prepuberty, and midadolescence (Ornitz, 1996).

What can caregivers do to encourage complex thinking and self-awareness? Ultimately, intellectual development is dependent on an enriched, loving environment, in which adults talk with and read to children, share ideas, and ask about their opinions. Stories excite the imagination and link ideas into larger themes and concepts. In addition, children need adults to take them places, to discuss the meaning of their experiences, and to broaden their logical thinking by asking lots of questions. Adults must also accept and encourage the entire spectrum of emotions, including negative emotions such as anger and jealousy, and at the same time teach children appropriate ways of expressing their feelings.

Greenspan reminds us that there is no effective substitute for enthusiastic participation in a child's play. He suggests that each parent spend thirty to forty-five minutes per day, or every other day, alone with the child. During this unstructured playtime, the adult should follow the lead of the child, and simultaneously help her link ideas, look for patterns, and group information into categories. This playtime not only expands cognitive abilities, but also can help the child to experience understanding, closeness, and security. As the child elaborates on his concerns, parents can help in the search for solutions as well as introduce new issues. For example, if the play involves nurturing—taking care of the "baby"—the adult can introduce the independence-dependence conflict by suggesting that maybe the "baby" may want to do things for herself. Subplots can be added, such as "good guys versus bad guys." As always, questions need to be asked. The little prince does not just fly off to another planet. Is he going off to visit "Haly-Bop," to get more food to feed his hungry people, or to find more soldiers to fight "The Evil Empire?" Play offers the chance to both develop and practice new skills.

Case Study: Bradley

Bradley's goal-directed behavior helped spawn his imagination. The anatomical linking of the emotional and motor systems—translating desire into action—fostered new cognitive capacities. Soon, he was both labeling the pictures on his favorite puzzles—such as Big Bird—and naming the objects he was pointing to. His play became much more complex. As his teacher wrote: "I joined Bradley who was playing with the Fisher-Price airplane and airport. He had two figures, a boy and a girl, but he wanted to look for Ernie and Bert. After he found them, he went back to the airplane, loaded them on the plane, and took everyone on a ride."

Fascinated by letters and numbers, Bradley could surprisingly name them all. Considering the delay in total language development, this suggested "hyperlexia," the condition where the ability to recognize words is better developed than either the ability to comprehend them or the child's overall level of verbal functioning (Aram and Healy, 1988). Although he could sound out words, they had little meaning for him. Being hyperlexic is similar to being able to read music without knowing what melodies sound like. On the one hand, this obsession with letters, numbers, and words provided a vehicle for animated interaction. On the other hand, it stymied his ability to find meaning in his experiences. When an adult tried to read a story to him, he was interested only in naming the letters and page numbers, not in comprehending the text.

To promote symbolic thinking, we sometimes used picture books. At first, he resisted looking at them, but he soon became absorbed in one that showed baby animals turning into adults. The transformation amused him, and books without words eventually became a great source for conversation.

At other times, we used his interest in letters and numbers to stimulate interaction and symbolic play. For instance, one of Bradley's favorite toys was a cash register. He would repeatedly push the buttons in a pattern such as 1111, 2222, 3333, 4444, 5555, etc., and say the numbers. On one occasion, P.S. added the wrong number at the end of the sequence. He thought that was funny, so he began to add "wrong numbers" and the interaction continued as new sequences and patterns were added. By adding other props, we created a script for Bradley. The teachers set up a grocery store complete with boxes and cans of food, grocery cart, and cash register. Bradley became the "checkout man," reading the prices and ringing up items as the other children shopped. He, too, shopped for his favorite foods. The teachers also encouraged him to "cook" the food that he had purchased.

Thus, in the "grocery store" script, we ended up both stimulating intentional behavior and helping him to build logical associations between ideas. As with all preschoolers, we continued to work with Bradley on developmental skills associated with each stage all at once.

Collaborating with Parents and Other Professionals. Supporting and mobilizing Bradley's parents continued to be a high priority. In working with very young children, mental health professionals may need to nurture the nurturers, helping parents find ways to feel loved and cared for. At the same time, the child always comes first. Ultimately, parents must feel the needs of the child as if they were their own.

We focused on helping Bradley's parents reframe the meaning that they assigned to his behavior. Bradley's father was encouraged to stop by the classroom as often as possible because it is an ideal environment in which to teach parents about their children. They can watch, ponder, practice, and grow to understand their child's behavior.

Evaluating Progress. Bradley attended Head Start's summer day care program. The following fall, he was enrolled in a four-year-old Head Start/Preschool program four days a week. The following is an excerpt from a report that P.S. wrote after Bradley had been in the program for about eighteen months:

> Bradley has demonstrated remarkable growth in his social and language development. It appears as if the gap in functioning between expected development and his chronological age is narrowing.
>
> In September, most of Bradley's communication was done through gestures, including hand and finger movements that spelled words such as "No," or "Liz" (his teacher's name). Also, about eighty percent of his language was echolalic. Now, however, spontaneous, meaningful speech, in contrast to the rote repetition of words, accounts for most of his language. He uses language to express his needs and desires. For example, he has learned to say "open the door" (when he wants to go outdoors), and "No." Because he can protect himself verbally, it makes it unnecessary for him to object to things by crying, fussing, or behaving disruptively. His ability to initiate and maintain a conversation with another person, however, remains limited.

In the fall, most of his play was repetitive, stereotyped, and focused on shapes, letters, and numbers. He still tends to ignore the content of stories, and attend only to the letters and numbers. However, about a week ago, the teacher read the story about the gingerbread man. She used cardboard figures to act out the drama. Afterward, Bradley reenacted the entire story using the figures. We are pleased that, at the present time, over half of Bradley's play is representational. He imagines he is flying airplanes, driving trucks, taking trips, cooking food, etc. His thoughts, however, remain disjointed with little coherence between the scenes.

Chronologically, Bradley is four and a half years old. However, his language skills still correspond to those of a two-and-a-half to three-year-old, even though his visual/motor skills have reached the level of a five-and-a-half-year-old.

By the end of the school year, Bradley was looking and acting more like a typical five-year-old. He was talking and playing with his friends, creating elaborate scenarios, reading, laughing, riding bikes, and jumping off climbers. Bradley's family moved from the area shortly afterward. Although they were pleased with his progress, they also realized that he still faced some challenges ahead. There was no doubt, however, that intensive treatment had affected both his behavior and his brain. Intervention presumably not only stimulated the maturation of key parts of the emotional, cognitive, and motor systems, but also strengthened the pathways that integrated these systems. His brain growth back on track, Bradley's once dim future appeared much brighter, as he had begun developing the internal resources necessary to engage more fully in the world around him.

CONCLUSION

Mental capacities and their behavioral counterparts reflect the maturation of key brain structures, systems, and the pathways that join them. Attachment research over the last few decades has demonstrated how the quality of the child's bond with her significant caregivers affects mental health. It is well documented that the attachment relationship has a lasting influence on a child's ability to experience and process feelings, and on future relationships. We now understand that early relational experiences also shape brain growth and organization, including the capacity for higher-level cognitive processing. Although children with behavioral difficulties similar to Bradley's may suffer from constitutionally based disorders, drug treatment alone rarely provides a cure. Whatever the source of the biological abnormalities, interpersonal approaches can often lead to the needed psychobiological changes.

Interventions that enable children to go back and master the development skills that they never learned can lead to significant long-term improvement. Furthermore, therapy must often focus on helping the child establish healthy interpersonal connections with family members and peers. By addressing the child's specific needs early enough, treatment can get development back on track. Once the child's brain reorganizes, he can begin to access more of his inner resources. Thus, intensive interventions can actually change biology and rebuild lives. This prudent form of social investment can prevent children from being saddled with mental disabilities in adulthood—at which time treatment is much more onerous.

APPENDIX:
CHARTING YOUR BABY'S EMOTIONAL MILESTONES

From *First Feelings* by Stanley Greenspan and Nancy T. Greenspan, Copyright ©1985 by Stanley Greenspan, MD and Nancy Thorndike Greenspan. Used by permission of Viking Penguin, a division of Penguin Putnam Inc.

I/Self-Regulation and Interests in the World—Birth to 3 Months

Increasingly (but still only sometimes):

- Able to calm down
- Sleeps regularly
- Brightens to sights (by alerting and focusing on object)
- Brightens to sounds (by alerting and focusing on your voice)
- Enjoys touch
- Enjoys movement in space (up and down, side to side)

II/Falling in Love—2 to 7 Months

When wooed, increasingly (but still only sometimes):

- Looks at you with a special, joyful smile
- Gazes at you with great interest
- Joyfully smiles at you in response to your interesting facial expressions
- Vocalizes back as you vocalize

III/Developing Intentional Communication—3 to 10 Months

Increasingly (but still only sometimes) responds to:

- Your gestures with gestures in return (you hand her a rattle and she takes it)
- Your vocalizations with vocalizations
- Your emotional expressions with an emotional response (a smile begets a smile)
- Pleasure or joy with pleasure
- Encouragement to explore with curiosity (reaches for interesting toy)

Increasingly (but still only sometimes) initiates:

- Interactions (expectantly looks for you to respond)
- Joy and pleasure (woos you spontaneously)
- Comforting (reaches up to be held)
- Exploration and assertiveness (explores your face or examines a new toy)

IV/The Emergence of an Organized Sense of Self—9 to 18 Months

Increasingly (but still only sometimes):

- Initiates a complex behavior pattern such as going to refrigerator and pointing to desired food, playing a chase game, rolling a ball back and forth with you
- Uses complex behavior in order to establish closeness (pulls on your leg and reaches up to be picked up)
- Uses complex behavior to explore and be assertive (reaches for toys, finds you in another room)
- Plays in a focused, organized manner on own
- Examines toys or other objects to see how they work
- Responds to limits that you set with your voice or gestures
- Recovers from anger after a few minutes

- Able to use objects like a comb or telephone in semirealistic manner
- Seems to know how to get you to react (which actions make you laugh, which make you mad)

V/Creating Emotional Ideas—18 to 36 Months

Increasingly (but still only sometimes):

- Engages in pretend play with others (puts doll to sleep, feeds doll, has cars or trucks race)
- Engages in pretend play alone
- Makes spatial designs with blocks or other materials (builds a tower, lines up blocks)
- Uses words or complex social gestures (pointing, sounds, gestures) to express needs or feelings ("me, mad" or "no, bed")
- Uses words or gestures to communicate desire for closeness (saying "hug" or gesturing to sit on your lap)
- Uses words or gestures to explore, be assertive and/or curious ("come here" and then explores toy with you)
- Able to recover from anger or temper tantrum and be cooperative and organized (after 5 or 10 minutes)

Later in stage and throughout next, increasingly (but still only sometimes):

- Uses your help and some toys to play out pretend drama dealing with closeness, nurturing, or care (taking care of favorite stuffed animal)
- Uses your help and some toys to play out pretend drama dealing with assertiveness, curiosity, and exploration (monsters chasing, cars racing, examining doll's bodies)
- Pretend play becomes more complex, so that one pretend sequence leads to another (instead of repetition, where the doll goes to bed, gets up, goes to bed, etc., the doll goes to bed, gets up, and then gets dressed, or the cars race, crash, and then go get fixed)
- Spatial designs become more complex and have interrelated parts, so that a block house has rooms or maybe furniture, a drawing of a face has some of its parts

VI/Emotional Thinking: The Basis for Fantasy, Reality, and Self-Esteem—30 to 48 Months

Increasingly (but still only sometimes):

- Recognizes what is real and what isn't
- Follows rules
- Remains calm and focused

- Feels optimistic and confident
- Realizes how behavior, thoughts, and feelings can be related to consequences (if behaves nicely, makes you pleased; if naughty, gets punished; if tries hard, learns to do something)
- Realizes relationship between feelings, behavior, and consequences in terms of being close to another person (knows what to do or say to get a hug, or a back rub)
- Realizes relationship between feelings, behavior, and consequences in terms of assertiveness, curiosity, and exploration (knows how to exert willpower through verbal, emotional communication to get what he wants)
- Realizes relationship between feelings, behavior, and consequences in terms of anger (much of time can respond to limits)
- Interacts in socially appropriate way with adults
- Interacts in socially appropriate way with peers

Chapter 3

PTSD: Biology Impinging on Behavior

I don't want to go to that bad building. The one where there was thunder and lightning and fire.

Claudia Denny, who, at age two,
survived the Oklahoma City bombing

Though traumatic events—such as natural disasters and wars—have plagued human beings since prehistoric times, they remained outside the scope of medical science until about a century ago. That's when a neurologist named Sigmund Freud began noticing that a number of women suffering from the mysterious condition then known as hysteria had endured sexual assaults—often at the hands of a family member. In 1895, Freud published these revolutionary insights on the health effects of interpersonal violence in his *Studies on Hysteria,* cowritten with Josef Breuer (Freud and Breuer, 1966). However, within a few years, Freud abandoned this stance, also held by French psychologist Pierre Janet, in favor of a new scientific theory—psychoanalysis, which saw internal conflict as the primary source of psychological suffering.[1] Ultimately, this early work on trauma and dissociation ended up going underground for a generation because, as Harvard psychiatrist Judith Herman argues, this intriguing, but disturbing knowledge base lacked a political movement to sustain its development.

World War I brought trauma back into public awareness as soldiers suffering from "shell shock" flooded veterans' hospitals. Many physicians sensed that the horrors of war were connected to disabling

Material in this chapter was initially presented by Phyllis Stien as part of a training session—Bio/Psycho/Social Approach to the Treatment of Childhood Dissociative Disorders—given by Francis Waters for The Center for Child Protection, Children's Hospital San Diego, January 1998.

symptoms such as mutism and motor paralysis, but they lacked an established mode of treatment. A punitive stance was commonplace. For example, British psychiatrist Lewis Yealland, author of the 1918 treatise, *Hysterical Disorders of Warfare,* advocated shocking soldiers to help snap them out of their condition (Herman, 1997). In contrast, a handful of psychiatrists, such as the psychoanalytically trained American Abram Kardiner, author of *War, Stress, and Neurotic Illness: The Traumatic Neurosis of War,* published in 1947, empathized with the painful plight of the battle-scarred soldier. "Soldiers are not hysterical . . . nor are [they] suffering from some persistent form of wickedness, perversity or weakness of will" (p. 406). Unlike prior researchers who often saw a soldier's preexisting character flaws as the cause of symptoms, Kardiner hypothesized that trauma had a direct physiological impact on the nervous system.

By the 1970s, researchers noticed a common set of symptoms among veterans and survivors of violence on the home front, particularly rape victims and battered women. In 1980, the American Psychiatric Association formally recognized PTSD as a distinct diagnostic entity in the third edition of the *Diagnostic and Statistical Manual for Mental Disorders* (DSM-III). Today's psychiatrists echo Kardiner when they describe PTSD as a normal reaction to an abnormal experience. Trauma, as opposed to everyday stresses or what Freud once called common unhappiness, produces feelings of terror and helplessness, which overwhelm normal psychological defenses. Events such as earthquakes, plane crashes, and sexual abuse typically lead to changes in biological functioning that, in turn, affect how we think, feel, and behave. In general, acts of intentional interpersonal violence are likely to cause more severe symptoms than natural disasters.

Only after PTSD was officially recognized did mental health professionals begin to abandon the naïve assumption that children were somehow immune to the disorder. We now know that children are even more vulnerable to violence and disaster because they are still developing a sense of self. In fact, children lack both the cognitive understanding and coping capacity of adults. The victim's age, support system, the intensity of the event (whether, for example, a child witnesses or actually experiences violence), and its significance for the child, typically determine the precise constellation of symptoms. Research suggests that a childhood history of maltreatment is the most powerful risk factor for developing PTSD in response to a stressful event (Shalev, 1996; Yehuda, 2002).

Tragically, one single traumatic experience is enough to alter brain functioning. Memory problems, ranging from amnesia to intrusive memories or flashbacks, are considered the hallmark of PTSD. PTSD also creates a state of heightened arousal that disrupts the usual collaboration between the emotional and cognitive parts of the brain— the limbic system and the neocortex. These biological changes in the brain often lead children to develop an emotion-based coping style aimed at managing overwhelming feelings rather than thoughtfully tackling the challenges at hand (van der Kolk, 1997).

PTSD remains a serious public health problem, affecting millions of children, according to the most conservative estimates. In the most recent national epidemiological survey conducted by Ronald Kessler of Harvard Medical School, the lifetime prevalence rate for PTSD stands at about 8 percent, meaning that one in twelve Americans is at risk. Among adolescents ages fifteen to twenty-four, Kessler found the prevalence rates at 2.8 percent for males and 10.3 percent for females. The gap between the sexes is presumed to result from the correspondingly higher rates of sexual abuse among females (Kessler et al., 1995). Children who grow up in troubled communities are even more vulnerable. In a study of inner-city children entering foster care in Baltimore, Maryland, researchers found that an astounding 33 percent met the diagnostic criteria for PTSD (Dale et al., 1999).

In this chapter, we begin by looking at the signs and symptoms of PTSD in children. After describing the two basic types of PTSD, we illustrate each one with a case example. We include a rather detailed discussion of the stress response before we explain exactly how traumatic stress impairs both the stress response and memory. We conclude with a section on how to help children cope with a traumatic event so that they do not develop PTSD.

IDENTIFYING PTSD IN CHILDREN

The diagnostic criteria for PTSD continue to evolve. The latest diagnostic manual, DSM-IV, published in 1994, divides the main symptoms of PTSD into three categories: *reexperiencing* of the traumatic event, persistent *avoidance* of stimuli associated with the event, and a persistent state of *heightened arousal.* Unfortunately, in the DSM classification system, children are still lumped together with adults. Since the current criteria derive from research conducted on adults, they do not necessarily capture the clinical picture for children (Putnam, 1997). Some children who do, in fact, suffer from PTSD may not meet the current criteria. Likewise, some children who meet the criteria may, in fact, be suffering from another disorder. Researchers hope to correct this problem in future editions of the DSM.

Signs and Symptoms Chart

In addition to the four ways of reexperiencing trauma (nightmares, traumatic play, behavioral reenactments, and psychophysiological reenactments), children with PTSD derived from a single, overwhelming event, usually manifest several of the following symptoms:

- Somatization (e.g., headaches)
- Intensification of normal fears (e.g., fear of being alone)
- Depression or sadness
- Impaired concentration and hyperactivity
- Aggressive behavior or temper tantrums
- Irritability and exaggerated startle response
- Pessimism
- Magical (egocentric) thinking

Although traumatized adults are typically troubled by intrusive thoughts and images, children tend to reexperience trauma differently. Children can relive traumatic events through images, and their flashbacks often take the form of terrifying dreams, replaying the disturbing event with all the accompanying feelings of terror and despair. Normally, children's dreams pivot around a vast web of associations that reflect current fears and hopes. In the wake of trauma, however, dreams often become very literal and repetitive (Pynoos and Nader, 1988). Most children have scary dreams from time to time that might involve, for example, being chased by an animal, but they usually wake up before being caught. By contrast, in posttraumatic dreams, children may end up being killed (Terr, 1990). Children also reexperience trauma through play that reenacts elements or themes of the event. This type of play is a telltale sign of PTSD. Normal play is three-dimensional, as children experiment with creative new ways of interacting with others as well as with their environment. By playing and playacting, children can expand their minds, explore their emotions, and discover new ways to solve problems. Traumatic play, in contrast, is two-dimensional or monotonous, and leads to stagnation rather than growth. The same themes keep resurfacing: helplessness, unpredictability, terror, and death (Terr, 1981).

Child psychiatrist Lenore Terr first defined traumatic play in her pioneering study that focused on the victims of the 1976 kidnapping in Chowchilla, California. In all, twenty-six preschool and school-age children were forcibly removed from their school bus, put in two darkened vans, and buried alive in an underground tractor trailer. After spending over twenty-eight hours in enclosed, dark spaces, they escaped when the roof of the trailer collapsed. Noticing that for years afterward many of the child survivors played games that involved burying vehicles, Terr began to realize that they were compulsively replaying elements of the original trauma in a vain attempt to process their experiences. Terr (1981) eventually labeled eleven characteristics of traumatic play, including its compulsive repetitiveness and its failure to alleviate anxiety. In fact, this kind of play increases anxiety because, "the child perceives that she or he cannot find effective mechanisms to deal with the trauma even in retrospect" (p. 757).

Behavioral reenactments closely resemble traumatic play, although the child experiences each activity differently. Terr (1990) says that children "will define their post traumatic play as 'fun' even when it looks grim and joyless to the outsider . . . They will describe their behavioral reenactments as 'how I acted' or 'something weird I did' or even 'how I am as a person'" (p. 265). In contrast to traumatic play, behavioral reenactments involve patterns of everyday behavior that incorporate aspects of the trauma. For example, sexually provocative behavior can be a way of reenacting sexual abuse, even though the youngster may explain the sexualized behavior as "just me." As a matter of course, some of the children kidnapped in Chowchilla felt compelled to bury things while acknowledging that this behavior was "weird."

Terr calls a fourth common way of reexperiencing trauma *psycho-physiological reenactments,* or body memories, because they involve somatic or physical discomfort. For example, under stress, the child may experience the same uncomfortable sensations associated with the trauma—such as tightness in the chest or nausea. In fact, a host of physical health problems including headaches, backaches, stomachaches, and skin rashes along with shortness of breath can be traced back to traumatic experience.

Not surprisingly, trauma creates feelings of anxiety that can last for years. Traumatized children often worry that the horrible event will happen again in just the same way. Thus, they learn to avoid anything that dredges up thoughts of the initial trauma. As Terr (1990) notes, most of the Chowchilla survivors were afraid of being kidnapped again and of the vehicles similar to those involved in the kidnapping. Besides inducing literal and concrete fears, trauma intensifies normal childhood fears—e.g., many of the Chowchilla kidnap victims were extraordinarily frightened by strangers.

Heightened arousal can manifest itself either in internalizing symptoms, such as poor concentration and sleep problems, or in externalizing ones, such as irritability or temper tantrums. Children also develop an exaggerated startle response (Pynoos et al., 1997). Trauma wreaks havoc on the normal range of emotions. During an overwhelming event, children often "freeze" in order to protect themselves emotionally. As one of the Chowchilla children said, "[I was] too scared to cry" (Terr, 1990, p. 35). As children return to safety, the initial feelings of helplessness and terror typically turn to anger, rage, and shame—all normal responses to interpersonal violence. Shame, as Terr says, arises from being violated, of feeling less than human. Children may try to push away these painful emotions, preferring to see themselves—and not the perpetrators—as the guilty party because it gives them an illusory sense of control. "Often children would rather put together some made-up reasons for tragedies . . . than experience the humiliation of being victims to the world's randomness" (p. 113).

The behavioral changes that accompany PTSD can lead to deep shifts in the child's emotional makeup and personality. Overwhelming emotions may also cause changes in the child's attitude toward life itself. If left untreated, traumatized children can lose their faith in the future. Unlike most children, victims can no longer imagine exciting scenarios for themselves; they cannot pretend, for example, that they will get married, and become an astronaut, an athlete, or a ballet dancer (Terr, 1990).

THE TWO TYPES OF PTSD

In her pioneering work on PTSD in children, Lenore Terr distinguished between Type I, which results from a single overwhelming event, and Type II, which typically emerges after repeated traumas. Though clinicians and researchers have adopted these concepts, other terms—simple PTSD and complex PTSD—are now more common. Type I often leads to simple PTSD, and Type II to complex PTSD. Complex PTSD typically involves repeated child abuse and neglect at the hands of caregivers over a period of years.

Brittany exemplifies simple PTSD and Larry complex PTSD.

Case Study: Brittany

When the fire started, Brittany, age four, and her twelve-year-old brother, Sam, were playing cards with their father in the family room. As her mother was beginning to prepare dinner in the kitchen, she suddenly screamed. Brittany, her brother, and father ran into the kitchen where flames were leaping from the top of the oven. Brittany's mother tried to snuff it out with an oven mitt, but it, too, caught fire, as did the curtains. Rushing out of the apartment, the stunned family watched as fire fighters stormed into the building, dousing the flames with water hoses. The damage was significant, however, and they had to evacuate the premises. Fortunately, no one suffered any physical injuries.

The youngest family member, Brittany, did not seem to recover from the terrifying event as quickly as everyone else. Normally easygoing, she became irritable and clingy. In fact, she was afraid to leave her grandmother's house where the family was now living. She also sometimes had trouble sleeping because of nightmares. Brittany's parents weren't surprised when her preschool teacher mentioned other worrisome behavior. Every day, she would go to the play area, build a house out of blocks, yell "Fire," and then demolish the house. Brittany also startled easily, hiding under a table whenever she heard a high-pitched loud noise. After discussing Brittany's behaviors with the teacher, her parents decided to contact a mental health professional.

Analysis

Brittany's PTSD symptoms cover all three clusters of the disorder: avoidance, heightened arousal, and reexperiencing. Her unwillingness to leave her grandmother's house constitutes avoidance. Her irritability, sleeplessness, and enhanced startle reaction are signs of heightened arousal. Brittany is reexperiencing the fire through nightmares and traumatic play, which continues to evoke feelings of helplessness and fear.

Case Study: Larry

One evening, while watching a television show about sexual abuse, Larry, age sixteen, told his mother that he had been victimized by his uncle—her brother, Mike—from the ages of six to ten. Each summer, Larry's mother, her sister, Sally, and Mike would all take their kids to their parents' farm in Maine for two weeks. Mike would ask Larry to accompany him on long walks and then force him to perform oral sex. According to Larry, when the abuse first started, he was so stunned that he didn't seem to register any feelings. After a couple of years, he started resisting, but Mike would convince him to continue by buying expensive gifts. Only after the farm was sold did the abuse stop.

For years, Larry felt guilty, as if he had caused Mike to seduce him. He also felt shame and never told anyone about what had happened. Once his mother found a therapist for him, Larry began to understand just how much the abuse had affected his life both at home and in school. By the time he reached high school, he had become a loner. Distrustful of most men, he would become very argumentative with his male teachers. From time to time, he would harm himself, burning his arms with a cigarette lighter—a behavior that provided him some temporary relief from overwhelming feelings of anxiety and rage. He sometimes complained of not being able to take in what was going on around him and of losing track of time. Larry also had frequent nightmares of being molested and murdered.

Analysis

Larry suffers from the PTSD symptoms of avoidance, heightened arousal, and reexperiencing. As in most cases of complex PTSD,

Larry experienced repeated abuse by an adult in a caregiving role. Thus, because of this interpersonal dimension, in contrast to Brittany who suffered from simple PTSD, Larry struggled with deep feelings of shame. In general, complex PTSD involves profound changes in personality, such as isolation and impaired ability to form relationships, alterations in consciousness and memory, damaged self-image, and severe problems regulating disturbing emotions. Perhaps Larry's symptoms might not have developed into complex PTSD if someone could have intervened shortly after the abuse first started.

The rest of this chapter focuses on simple PTSD. In the next chapter, we look more closely at children who, similar to Larry, suffer from complex PTSD.

THE PSYCHOBIOLOGY OF PTSD

In other words: Experience can become biology.

Bruce Perry, MD

Though it may be difficult to believe, one traumatic event—say, an earthquake—in anyone's life, but especially in a child's, can alter both the structure and chemistry of the brain. Trauma both disrupts the normal functioning of the stress response and causes memory disturbances such as amnesia and/or the intrusive reliving of painful experiences. Before we explain how trauma causes the stress response to go out of whack, we first need to explain what the stress response is and how it works. To help frame our discussion of the overwhelming emotions associated with trauma, we also provide some background on emotional processing in general.

The Stress Response: The Body's Way of Coping with Fear

Designed to help us mobilize ourselves to cope with danger, the stress response prepares us to engage in one or more of the following behaviors: *withdrawal (flight); immobility (freezing); aggression (fight);* and *appeasement (submission).* Typically, our first reaction to danger is to freeze, to stop all movement. From an evolutionary perspective, this is remarkably adaptive because predators react to movement. Furthermore, the biological mechanisms that produce immobility also prepare the body to attack or escape (LeDoux, 1996).

Imagine you are home alone and hear the sound of a door slowly creaking open. You automatically stop what you are doing and become immobile (freezing). You turn toward the sound to determine what it means. You decide it must be an intruder, quickly look around for some place to hide, and head for a nearby closet (flight). If you are discovered hiding in the closet, you may tell the burglar to take what he wants (submit). If you are actually attacked, you may choose to fight back—hit, kick, bite, scratch, etc. (fight).

The processing of fear, as with all of our emotional reactions, involves three steps: the unconscious *evaluation* of a stimulus, a *bodily response,* and a *conscious experience.* Although psychological research focuses primarily on the conscious part of emotion, neuroscience believes that most of what happens takes place out of awareness. According to LeDoux (1996), feelings are best viewed as the end result of an unconscious process. "The brain states and bodily responses are the fundamental facts of an emotion, and the conscious feelings are the frills that have added icing to the emotional cake" (p. 302). In other words, our minds and bodies are constantly processing emotions, even if we are not attuned to what is going on.

Masking experiments offer insights into the unconscious emotional mind. For instance, when researchers flash a fearful or angry face for a few milliseconds followed by a neutral or happy one, although subjects report seeing only the neutral or happy face, physiological changes such as an increased heart rate show that subjects are unconsciously reacting to the negative pictures. This masking technique is also used when imaging the brains of subjects. When a fearful face is subliminally presented, subjects display increased activity in the amygdala, the limbic structure that detects danger. When a happy face is flashed, the amygdala quiets. Thus, unconscious emotional structures react even though the images have not been consciously recognized (Mlot, 1998).

Emotional evaluation or appraisal is happening every time we experience something. Our senses—sight, hearing, smell, taste, and touch—deliver information to the thalamus, a structure in the center of the brain where the sensory information is simultaneously relayed to the cortex and the amygdala. LeDoux (1996) explains that our brains can use two routes to process experience: the high road and the low road.

The low road, the short route from the thalamus directly to the amygdala, allows for virtually instantaneous reaction. Without the capacity to respond automatically and immediately to danger—avoiding the path of a swerving car, for example—we would not survive. The first wave of information coming directly from the thalamus provides a quick but crude assessment of the incoming stimuli. Experiences are judged to be good or bad, threatening or nonthreatening. At the same time, the sensory information is also delivered to the cortex for more detailed recognition and analysis—e.g., It's a car. We automatically compare the present situation with similar experiences. This second wave of information is then communicated to the limbic system.

Both routes—the high road to the cortex and the low road to the limbic system—involve unconscious brain processes (Damasio, 1994). The automatic processing of emotion continues as structures within the limbic system assign an emotional importance (meaning) to the experience. At the heart of the fear circuitry lies the amygdala, an almond-shaped cluster of nuclei located in the limbic area, which registers danger. The left amygdala seems more sensitive to vocalization, whereas the right seems to respond more to facial expressions. Different parts of the amygdale may, in fact, trigger the various survival responses of withdrawal, immobility, aggression, and appeasement (Carter, 1998).

The emotional message from the amygdala is then relayed to the hypothalamus and motor centers within the brain, where it gets transformed into a *bodily response*. The hypothalamus sends *neural signals* to the body via the autonomic nervous system (ANS) and releases *hormones* into the blood. Immediately after the amygdala sounds the alarm, the parasympathetic division of the autonomic nervous system momentarily suppresses blood pressure, heart rate, and other internal functions so that incoming stimuli can be more effectively assessed. However, within seconds, sometimes milliseconds, the sympathetic part of the autonomic nervous system kicks into high gear, producing *a generalized activation of the entire body*. Heart rate and breathing increase, blood pressure rises, and the lungs expand to take in more air. Blood is diverted to skeletal muscles and the arteries of the heart dilate. Other arteries, such as those in the skin, constrict to lessen any bleeding that may have occurred. The spleen releases more blood cells. Stimulation of the inner part of the adrenal glands that sit on top of the kidneys release adrenaline into the blood stream, augmenting the body's response.

Ordinarily, the parasympathetic division of the ANS is less involved in the stress response. However, a particularly frightening experience may stimulate the parasympathetic nervous system fibers that activate the muscles of the bladder and rectum, causing involuntary emptying of these structures (Gilman and Newman, 1992). In addition, generalized activation of the parasympathetic nervous system may contribute to the dissociative symptoms that are sometimes observed in individuals exposed to overwhelming stress. As a part of this process, the increase in vagal tone reduces both the heart rate and blood pressure, and endogenous opiates, which are linked to the dopamine system, are released. This reaction to extreme stress has been observed mostly in very young children and girls. Unable to escape, the body responds by dissociating, mentally and emotionally disconnecting from the reality at hand. The child moves from mobilizing to combat the stressor to a state of resignation called "defeat" in animal models (Perry, 2000a).

During the stress response, the amygdala also sends a message to a group of neurons in the brain stem called the locus coeruleus, which results in the release of norepinephrine. As the brain floods with norepinephrine, attention narrows. The neurons become more sensitive to incoming stimuli that relate to the source of danger. The amygdala also signals certain motor areas of the brain, including the basal ganglia and brain stem, which produce the automatic responses such as the startle reflex, facial expressions of fear, and freezing.

How do emotions, such as fear, reach *consciousness?* Feelings, the conscious representation of unconscious emotional processes, are created by direct and indirect pathways. The direct neural pathways go from the limbic system, where emotions are generated to the frontal cortex, where emotions are consciously registered. The indirect path involves the physical and chemical changes in the body such as muscle contractions, heart rate, breathing, and the release of hormones and peptides from glands and tissues of the body. These chemical signals are fed back to the brain and eventually to the cortex, which interprets the bodily changes (see Figure 3.1).

At this point, we can move from automatic pilot to conscious control. Although we may think the noise we hear signals a dangerous intruder, and our body is revved for action, we don't necessarily need to reach for a gun and start shooting. Our prefrontal lobes allow us to stop and consider options. In the case of the intruder, we may decide to grab a baseball bat, lock the door, call 911, or slip out the back door to a neighbor's house.

Normally, the cortex holds in check the emergency reactions triggered by the stress response. However, problems can easily occur because the connections flowing from the emotional to the cognitive areas are far stronger than those going in the other direction (LeDoux, 1996). To further complicate matters, moderate stress interferes with the functioning of the prefrontal cortex; we become distracted, disorganized, and our working memory worsens (Arnsten, 1998). Any significant brain injury to the prefrontal cortex will further limit its capacity to modulate the stress response, resulting in emotional behavior that is unchecked by rationality (Lewis, 1998).

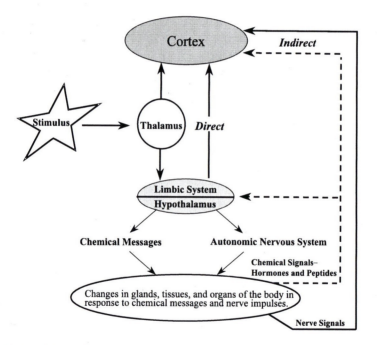

FIGURE 3.1. The Processing of Emotion: Direct and Indirect Pathways. Emotions are consciously registered via direct and indirect pathways. The direct route involves pathways from the limbic system to the cortex. The indirect route involves the hypothalamus, which transforms the emotional information into nerve signals and chemical messages. These changes are fed back to areas of the cortex (e.g., somatosensory cortex and insula cortex) before being registered as emotions in the frontal cortex.

Fortunately, the prefrontal cortex is not the only system to put the brakes on the stress response. Even as the body is being called to action, the brain is already sending out hormones to turn off the stress response. Responding to the amygdala's danger message, the hypothalamus also converts the neural signal into a hormonal response.[2] The hypothalamus releases a chemical called CRF, corticotropin-releasing factor[3], which causes the nearby pituitary gland to release another chemical ACTH, adrenalcorticotrophic hormone. ACTH flows through the bloodstream all the way to the outer layer of the adrenal glands where it leads to the release of the steroid hormone cortisol (see Figure 3.2).

Cortisol, which converts fats to glucose and is thought to suppress the immune response, helps to calm down the brain. When cortisol is released into the blood, it travels back to the brain where it locks onto cortisol receptors in the hippocampus, amygdala, and prefrontal cortex. The hippocampus, as LeDoux (1996) explains, counteracts the amygdala:

> When the hormone binds to receptors in the hippocampus, messages are sent to the hypothalamus to tell it to tell the pituitary and adrenal glands to slow down the release. In the face of stress, the amygdala keeps saying "release" and the hippocampus keeps saying, "slow down." Through multiple cycles through these loops the concentration of the stress hormones in the blood is delicately matched to the demands of the stressful situation. (p. 240)

The "endorphins," the brain's own internally produced painkillers, the benzodiazepines (similar in composition to the antianxiety drug Valium) and the inhibitory neurotransmitter, GABA (gamma-aminobutyric acid), also help to quiet the brain and restore the body to its natural balanced state.

Thus, the brain has its own way of increasing arousal and calming down. Though these defensive spurts can be lifesaving, if relied on too often, they can also wreak havoc on your mind and body. As Robert Sapolsky (1998) explains in his book, *Why Zebras Don't Get Ulcers,* "If you are that zebra running for your life, or that lion sprinting for your meal, your body's physiological response mechanisms are superbly adapted for dealing with such short-term physical emergencies . . . but they are potentially a disaster when provoked chronic-

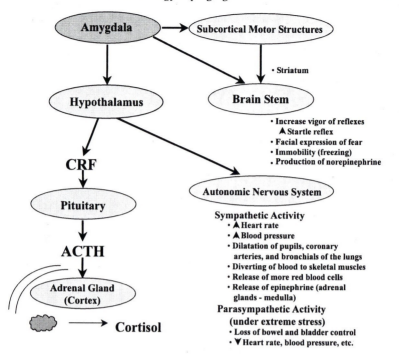

FIGURE 3.2. The Fight-or-Flight Stress Response. In response to a threatening event, the amygdala triggers the fight-or-flight stress response and voluntary muscles are readied for action. The hypothalamus, responding to the message from the amygdala, activates the sympathetic nervous system. Heart rate and blood pressure increase, pupils dilate, blood is shunted to skeletal muscles, more blood cells are released, and epinephrine is released by the adrenal glands. Under conditions of extreme stress, the parasympathetic division of the autonomic nervous system may also be activated, resulting in dissociative symptoms and possible loss of bowel and bladder control. As part of the stress response, the HPA axis is activated—a slower process because it involves hormones that are released into the bloodstream. The hypothalamus releases CRF, which causes the release of ACTH from the pituitary gland. In turn, ACTH causes the adrenal glands to secrete cortisol, which converts fats to glucose. inhibits the immune response, and helps the mind/body return to a calm state.

ally" (p. 6). For example, when the stress response is switched on, some normal life-sustaining processes, such as digestion, growth, socialization, and reproduction, may be put on hold. These "optimistic processes," as Sapolsky refers to them, are only needed if we survive the threatening situation.

Impairment of the Stress Response

Prolonged or overwhelming stress endured at any age can impair the stress response, making it more reactive and less adaptive. The body begins to react as if danger is always around the corner, no matter what the presenting stimulus actually is. According to neuroscientists Armony and LeDoux (1997), the amygdala, the brain structure that regulates fear, reorganizes itself as it registers circumstances that are dangerous. The neurons reassemble, reconnecting in a new and different pattern. With this trauma now encoded in the amygdala, the threshold for reacting to threatening stimuli is lowered. Furthermore, as LeDoux (1996) hypothesizes, trauma may change the brain's preferred mode of processing stimuli, leading to a greater reliance on the short route of appraisal—with its inferior power to discriminate—than on the long route. "Later exposure to stimuli that even remotely resemble those occurring during the trauma would then pass like greased lightening over the potentiated pathways to the amygdala, unleashing the fear reaction" (p. 258). Though experts in child development have long known that some children are constitutionally more reactive to stimuli than others, we can no longer be so sure that an inhibited child was simply born that way. In fact, for some of these children, environmental stressors—physical or verbal abuse—may be responsible for these biological differences.

Chemical Changes Linked to Trauma

- Elevated levels of norepinephrine/epinephrine, which contributes to core PTSD systems such as hyperarousal, flashbacks, intrusive memories, and nightmares.
- Changes in the hormones of the hypothalamic-pituitary-adrenal (HPA) axis, which impairs the adaptability of the stress response, including the body's ability to return to a calm state.
- Altered concentrations of neuropeptides (e.g., endogenous opioids) which contribute to bodily and emotional anesthesia.
- Changes in related neurotransmitter systems (e.g., dopamine, serotonin, and central amino acids) and in the receptors for stress-related neurotransmitters and hormones, which further intensifies the dysregulation of the stress response.

Trauma also seems to alter brain chemistry, leading to abnormally high levels of the catecholamines (epinephrine, norepinephrine, dopamine)—the chemical marker behind the major PTSD symptoms, including hypervigilance, exaggerated startle response, irritability, panic attacks, and intrusive thoughts and images (Southwick et al., 1997; DeBellis, Baum, et al., 1999). In the aftermath of the Branch Davidian crisis in Waco, Texas, Dr. Bruce Perry (2000a,b) examined a number of the traumatized children. Five days after the raid, all had significantly elevated catecholamine levels and the group average resting heart rate was 134. (Average heart rate for children is eighty beats/minute.) For the next six weeks, the resting heart rates of the Davidian children never fell below 100.

Extreme stress can also produce *changes in the hormones of the hypothalamic-pituitary-adrenal (HPA) axis*. As you may recall, the HPA axis is the pathway that produces cortisol, a crucial part of the feedback mechanism that curtails the stress response. The dysregulation of the stress response—altered levels of stress hormones and neurotransmitters—can also involve changes in the density and type of the receptors on nerve cells in the brain. For instance, when norepinephrine and epinephrine levels rise, alpha-2 receptors are supposed to initiate a reaction to slow down the release of these substances. However, traumatic stress seems to reduce the number of alpha-2 receptors (Perry, 1994). Fewer alpha-2 receptors mean higher levels of norepinephrine and epinephrine and, thus, more PTSD symptoms.

Structural changes (a more excitable amygdala, the bias toward the short route, and changes in receptor concentrations), as well as alterations in brain chemistry (higher levels of catecholamines and changes in the stress hormones), keep the stress response locked in overdrive. This heightened arousal also renders circuits in the hippocampus and prefrontal cortex—the very brain structures that are supposed to put the brakes on the amygdala and hypothalamus—less functional. Similar to a runaway locomotive, the brain thus enters a vicious cycle of escalating arousal and dysfunction of the stress response.

The Two Memory Systems

> We weave our memories into narrative, from which we construct our identities.
>
> Leonard Shengold

Before discussing how trauma disrupts memory, we need to step back for a moment and review the nature and function of memory. Memory allows us to register the world outside ourselves. Our autobiographical memory, which files our experiences according to time, place, and their personal meaning, gives us both a foundation for a unified identity as well as a framework for integrating new experiences. However, the human brain is not simply a camera that produces objective snapshots. Each of us possesses a unique bias that affects how our brain processes new experiences.

Memory is essentially a reconstructive process, requiring the coordination of many brain circuits. Our mind first breaks down a given experience into components—such as the location, time of day, emotional tone, and the physical characteristics of the people involved—which are then filed away in separate areas of the brain. Normally, the conscious memory system (also known as *explicit* or *declarative memory*), and *the unconscious* memory system (also known as *implicit* or *procedural memory*), work together. The conscious memory system, which is mediated by the hippocampus, contains experiences that we can readily retrieve and talk about. In contrast, we actually possess several different unconscious memory systems, all of which affect behavior without our awareness. For instance, procedural memory, which involves the motor areas of the brain, allows us to learn and remember skills such as riding a bike or playing a musical instrument. Another example of implicit memory involves the recall or reexperiencing of emotions and bodily sensations. Fear conditioning, the amygdala's automatic responses to circumstances that might herald danger, is this kind of emotional memory.

Case studies of brain injury patients suggest that the unconscious and conscious memory systems use different brain structures and circuits and that the conscious memory system requires a fully functional hippocampus. In the famous case of H.M. back in the 1950s, doctors removed the patient's temporal lobes, including the hippocampus, to alleviate intractable epileptic seizures. After surgery, although H.M. could not lay down new long-term, conscious memories, he could learn new manual skills and retain emotional memories (Squire and Kandel, 1999). For example, in a mirror drawing task— copying a picture while viewing only the reflection—H.M. improved his performance with practice. In addition, he retained this ability over time. H.M. also learned how to read mirror images of words and solve complex puzzles even though he had no conscious memory of ever having mastered these skills (LeDoux, 1996).

LeDoux (1996) tells the story of a strange experiment performed on another amnesia patient who resembled H.M. As expected, the doctors had to reintroduce themselves every time they saw her. One morning, Dr. C. reached out to shake the patient's hand as he typically did. But this time, Dr. C. had hidden a sharp tack in his hand. Grasping the doctor's hand, the patient was startled by a nasty prick. Thereafter, she refused to shake that doctor's hand. The patient could not explain why she would not shake Dr. C.'s hand, only that she felt uncomfortable. (Although this experiment proved the hypothesis, one wonders if the doctors could have chosen a less painful procedure.)

Just as the hippocampus is in charge of the conscious-memory system, the amygdala is critical to the functioning of the unconscious-memory system. Whereas the amygdala is reasonably well developed at birth, the hippocampus doesn't mature (isn't fully myelinated) until about age three or four (van der Kolk, 1994). Thus, the unconscious-memory system predates the conscious-memory system. Though infants and toddlers do not have conscious memories, their unconscious-memory systems record early emotional experiences.

The conscious- and unconscious-memory systems are both independent and interdependent, as most stimuli typically activate both systems. Whereas conscious memory retrieves contextual details, the unconscious memory elicits emotions. Consider an example. Picture yourself walking to work. Perhaps you are daydreaming about an upcoming vacation, or planning an important meeting with your boss. You arrive at a street corner, glance left and right, and step into the street. At that moment, a horn blares and tires screech. You react almost instantaneously by leaping back onto the curb, just as a car careens past and crashes into the car parked directly in front of you. Your heart pounds, you feel short of breath, and your legs begin to tremble as adrenaline rushes through your body. Now, whenever you hear the sound of a horn or squealing tires, both memory systems are activated. The sound immediately triggers the implicit or unconscious-memory system so that the amygdala activates your body's stress response, increasing your heart rate, blood pressure, muscle tension, etc. At the same time as you are registering the changes in your mind and body, your hippocampus is directing the activity of your conscious-memory system. You start remembering the accident: exactly where you were and what you did. As LeDoux (1996) says, eventually, "the awareness of fear comes to rest side by side in consciousness with your explicit memory . . . actually these two events [the past memory and the present emotion] are seamlessly fused as a unified, conscious experience of the moment . . . this unified experience of past memory and arousal [emotion] can then potentially get converted into a new explicit, long-term memory" (pp. 201-203).

The simultaneous activation of the two memory systems allows for the development of conscious emotional memories, which become part of our autobiographical memory. The process that integrates all aspects of an experience—thoughts, emotions, and actions—into conscious memory, also allows us to remember our feelings without reexperiencing the full-blown emotional reaction. Integrating implicit emotional memories into the explicit/conscious memory system and reframing those memories is at the core of trauma therapy.

Trauma and Memory Problems

J. Douglas Bremner from Emory University School of Medicine calls PTSD a "disease of memory." He (1999a) writes:

> PTSD patients demonstrate a variety of memory problems including deficits in declarative [explicit/conscious] memory . . . and fragmentation of memories (both autobiographic and trauma related). PTSD is also associated with alterations in nondeclarative memory (i.e., types of memory that cannot be willfully brought up into the conscious, including motor memory such as how to ride a bicycle). These types of nondeclarative memories include conditioned responses and abnormal reliving of traumatic memories following exposure to situationally appropriate cues. (p. 798)

Traumatic memories are themselves fragments. Disconnected from autobiographical memory, they are usually stored as images, sounds, smells, and bodily sensations such as nausea and numbing cold. Initially, trauma survivors typically have few if any thoughts associated with the memory. Unlike normal memories, traumatic memories generally remain the same over time. Furthermore, as previously discussed, in children they typically emerge in the form of traumatic play, behavioral reenactments, or body memories. Perhaps, most distressing of all to trauma survivors, particularly children, is that traumatic memories are not under voluntary control. Instead, they intrude into awareness whenever the traumatized person is exposed to reminders of the event(s) or whenever he or she is in the same emotional state as during the trauma. During flashbacks, people experience memories of traumatic events as if they are still happening in the present and are often unaware of what is happening in the here and now (van der Kolk, Burbridge, and Suzuki, 1997; van der Kolk, 1996b; Putnam, 1997).

Trauma also interferes with the usual integrative processes of memory. Consider for a moment the case of four-year-old Brittany, who developed PTSD in the aftermath of the fire in her home. Any loud, grating noise, similar to a helicopter flying overhead, terrified her, leading her to scream, cover her ears, and hide under the table. For Brittany, anything sounding similar to a fire engine triggered powerful unconscious emotional memories, which heralded danger. Before her conscious-memory system could evaluate the real external stimulus, her body had already registered the fear, causing her to start panting and trembling. An important part of trauma therapy is to get the two memory systems to begin to work in sync again.

Sometimes the overwhelming nature of trauma causes survivors to lose access to a conscious memory of the event—a process referred to as *dissociative amnesia.* As Richard Kluft (1993) points out, survivors may then forget that they have forgotten something—that is, develop amnesia for their amnesia. However, although they may temporarily lack explicit or conscious memories that can be described in words, the implicit or unconscious memories always remain in operation. Dissociative amnesia is not necessarily permanent. If and when the amnesia dissipates, the memory of the traumatic experience tends to return as sensory fragments often without any context, which tend to be triggered in nontreatment settings such as home and school (Putnam, 1997; Chu et al., 1999).

The Biology of Traumatic Memory

Most researchers believe that memory processes fail because high levels of stress-related chemicals impair the functioning of critical brain structures, especially the hippocampus (Bremner, 1999a). When the hippocampus cannot properly encode memories of an event, that is, integrate and organize modality-specific information—e.g., sensory, motor, visual, and auditory—research suggests that the memory can only be retrieved as fragments. According to van der Kolk, Burbridge, and Suzuki (1997), when the hippocampus cannot do its job, instead of becoming integrated, memories are laid down and later retrieved as images, body sensations, smells, and sounds that feel alien and separate from other life experiences" (p. 107).

Research continues to link extreme stress with a breakdown in the functioning of the hippocampus, the prefrontal cortex (especially the medial and orbitofrontal cortex) and the anterior cingulate. Several imaging studies suggest that dysfunction of *the medial and orbitofrontal cortex* also play an important role in the abnormal reexperiencing of traumatic memories and in the long duration of fearful responses. For example, a person who was attacked in an elevator may continue to experience overwhelming fear of elevators years after the experience. Ordinarily, the medial and orbitofrontal cortex can modulate and inhibit the amygdala's response to fearful stimuli. However, neuroimaging studies of individuals who suffer from PTSD—in contrast to subjects who do not have PTSD—indicated atypical functioning in the medial and orbitofrontal cortex (Bremner, 1999b; Bremner et al., 1999). As Bremner explains:

> The orbitofrontal region is the part of your brain that evaluates the primal feelings of fear and anxiety which come up from the brain's deeper recesses. It's the part that tells you that you're in a hospital watching a slide show of the Vietnam War, not in Vietnam living through the real thing. The vets with PTSD weren't using that part of their brain. That's why every time a truck backfires or they see a war picture in a major magazine they are forced to relive their wartime experiences: they can't tell the difference. (as quoted in Gladwell, 1997, p. 17)

Imaging studies (Bremner et al., 1999; Shin et al., 1999) also suggest that PTSD symptoms are associated with reduced activity in the *anterior cingulate,* which acts as a gatekeeper for emotions arising from the limbic system and recruits areas of the cortex to respond to the emotional need.

A considerable body of research also points to the critical role played by state-dependent learning in recalling and reexperiencing traumatic memories. This concept refers to how memories encoded in a certain emotional state are more accessible when one is in that same emotional state. Thus, on the one hand, it may be difficult to access traumatic memories unless one is in a hyperaroused state—contributing to the phenomenon of dissociative amnesia. On the other hand, traumatic reminders are likely to create fearful states that can trigger flasbacks, reenactments, body memories, and other intrusive traumatic memories.

Most researchers agree that the severity of the precipitating event is the most critical variable in determining whether a child will develop full-blown PTSD. Though early intervention may not be able to prevent the disorder, it can certainly reduce the intensity of the symptoms. As soon as a child has experienced trauma, say, right after the fire in Brittany's case, parents need to begin to plan a course of action. According to studies by developmental psychologist James Garbarino (1992) on children in war zones, and by social worker Beverly James (1997) on child survivors of a hurricane in Hawaii, close proximity to parents during a traumatic event significantly alleviates long-term distress. Children also fear that trauma will somehow overturn their entire world, causing their parents to abandon them. Once reassured of their parents' love, children are better able to cope with whatever may have happened to them.

What Parents Can Do

- Stay in *close proximity* to the child.
- Start developing a plan of action *immediately* after the traumatic event.
- Provide additional *nurturing.*
- *Validate* the child's feelings, particularly those of anxiety, sadness, and anger.
- Reassure the child about his or her *competence.*
- If a child doesn't seem to be getting any better after a few weeks, parents should try to find a child therapist with a specialty in trauma.

CONCLUSION

Over the last generation, mental health professionals have made great strides in understanding and treating PTSD. The symptoms of simple PTSD fall into three main categories: reexperiencing of the traumatic event, heightened arousal, and avoidance. Tragically, children are particularly vulnerable, so that one overwhelming event can disrupt long-term brain functioning, impairing both the stress response and memory processing. Equally unfortunate is that, of the millions of children who are at risk for the disorder, only a small percentage is currently being properly diagnosed and treated. Though treatment models specifically geared for children remain in their infancy, timely interventions can be quite effective in preventing simple PTSD from derailing a child's emotional and cognitive development. However, in cases where children undergo repeated stress over a period of years, undoing this snowball effect is much more challenging. In Chapter 4, we focus on the more severe form of PTSD commonly referred to as complex PTSD. Specific therapeutic interventions for both simple and complex PTSD will be addressed in Chapter 6.

Chapter 4

Complex PTSD in Children:
Brain and Behavior

Children are not resilient, children are malleable.

Bruce Perry, MD

If a single overwhelming event is sufficient to alter the course of a child's development, what about the effects of chronic traumatic stress? Not surprisingly, the clinical picture for children with histories of severe abuse and neglect is disturbing. As mental health professionals, educators, foster parents, and those in the juvenile court system have long observed, these children often develop self-defeating, provocative, and destructive patterns of behavior. Temper tantrums are common. They tend to have difficulty expressing and receiving affection and may blame others for their problems. Many are hyperactive, inattentive, and learning disabled. Mood changes are often rapid so that a child may seem like a different person, depending on the context. Sexually abused children also consistently demonstrate inappropriate sexual behaviors, including abuse of their peers (Friedrich, 1990). Socially, traumatized children may be excessively withdrawn or, alternatively, they may resort to bullying and intimidation. Children with histories of maltreatment thus may meet the diagnostic criteria for a number of psychiatric disorders, including eating disorders, anxiety disorders, attention-deficit hyperactivity disorder (ADHD), substance abuse, mood disorders, and dissociative disorders.

Information in this chapter was outlined by Phyllis Stien in a workshop presented at the San Diego Conference on Responding to Child Maltreatment in January 1998. In this two-part workshop, co-presenter Francis Waters presented videotaped case examples of the psychological and developmental problems associated with maltreatment.

Interpersonal stressors, research shows, are far more detrimental than nonsocial traumatic events (Sgoifo et al., 1999). So the bad news is that abusive childhoods can lead to a host of psychiatric symptoms. However, the flip side is that clinicians are much better able to treat the disorders afflicting children. Now that the mystery behind what used to be called simply "bad" or "mad" behavior is gone, the prognosis for troubled children is much brighter. Researchers have identified stress-induced neurological deficits as the bridge between trauma and many psychiatric disorders. Maltreatment leaves deep scars on the brain itself, which then manifest themselves in behavioral difficulties. Armed with this new knowledge, clinicians have developed an array of new interventions to help children heal from these psychobiological wounds.

In this chapter, we argue that chronic abuse typically leads to a psychobiological syndrome associated with a spectrum of symptoms and maladaptive behaviors. The biological profile of complex PTSD bears some resemblance to PTSD, except that the changes in brain structure and functioning are much more profound. After briefly sketching the scope of the problem, we describe the preliminary research linking neurological abnormalities to maltreatment, including dysregulation of the stress response and limbic irritability, underdevelopment of the left hemisphere, hemispheric lateralization, dysfunction of the cerebellar vermis, changes in the hippocampus and corpus callosum, as well as neuroendocrine and immune system dysfunction.

CHILD MALTREATMENT:
THE SCOPE OF THE PROBLEM

Child maltreatment is usually subdivided into the five categories of neglect/deprivation of necessities, physical abuse, sexual abuse, medical neglect, and emotional/verbal abuse. Until recently, reported cases of maltreatment typically rose by 10 to 25 percent per year—from 60,000 substantiated cases in 1974 to almost 3 million in 1994 (U.S. Department of Health and Human Services, 1996). This steep increase had two sources: a greater recognition of child abuse in our society and an actual increase in its prevalence. Since 1994, according to the U.S. Department of Health and Human Services (2000), the number of child victims has started to level off, dropping to about

900,000 in 1998. However, most experts continue to maintain that these HHS figures, culled from the states, do not capture the full extent of the problem. One problem with this database is that most of the children who are reported to state child protective services agencies are indigent. This demographic bias accounts for why more than half of the 900,000 children included in the 1998 report fell under the "deprivation of necessities" category, 100,000 under "sexual abuse," and 50,000 under "emotional abuse." If one could take a snapshot of child maltreatment across all social strata, the overall numbers would no doubt be much higher and the composition of the cases would be quite different. For example, according to one national survey, for children ages ten to sixteen, only 25 percent of all abuse cases are actually reported (Finkelhor and Dziuba-Leatherman, 1994).

Although abuse and neglect remain the most common cause of chronic traumatic stress in children, losses, repeated separations, and exposure to family violence can have a similar impact on psychobiological development. Probably the most unrecognized group of chronically traumatized children are those exposed to domestic violence. It is estimated that over three million children witness battery, stabbing, and shootings between their parents (Thormaehlen and Bass-Feld, 1994). According to Bessel van der Kolk (1997), "Boys who witness violence by their fathers have a 1,000 percent greater likelihood of growing up to abuse their partners than men who were not exposed to marital violence when they were young" (p. 83). As with the men who abuse, many battered women (estimated between 30 and 80 percent) have also witnessed violence between their parents. It is also well documented that domestic violence and child abuse often go hand in hand, with scholars finding an overlap 30 to 50 percent of the time (Elders, 1999).

Do all abused children develop pervasive developmental problems? A growing body of research indicates that the severity, type, and chronicity of the abuse determine the malignancy of its effects. In the case of sexual abuse, for example, the earlier it starts, the longer it lasts, and the more intense the contact (e.g., intercourse as opposed to fondling), the greater the effect will be on the child. Likewise, the prognosis for the child is also typically much worse if the perpetrator is a parent rather than a stranger. Thus, children who have been terrorized by repeated assaults, especially within the family, or those who have experienced severe neglect are likely to suffer the most. Even

worse is the combination of abuse and neglect. In cases of mild or circumscribed abuse, prompt emotional support can often prevent any
long-lasting effects. However, because of the deep neurobiological
wounds associated with prolonged abuse, recovery for these children
is a far more arduous process.

COMPLEX PTSD:
A PSYCHOBIOLOGICAL SYNDROME

As discussed in Chapter 3, child psychiatrist Lenore Terr (1994)
was one of the first to distinguish between the two kinds of traumatic
stress which she called Type I, resulting from a single event, and Type
II, resulting from repeated trauma. As with PTSD itself, advances in
the assessment and treatment of complex PTSD have so far been
driven by adult therapists rather than child therapists. In *Rebuilding
Shattered Lives,* psychiatrist James Chu (1998) captures the painful
inner world of abuse victims:

> Severe and long-standing trauma introduces a profound destabil-
> ization in the day-to-day existence of many survivors. . . . They
> experience symptoms that alter their perceptions of their envi-
> ronment, disrupt their cognitive functioning, and interfere with
> a sense of continuity in their existence. . . . They wish for com-
> fort and security, but find themselves caught up in a world of
> struggle, hostility, disappointment, and abandonment that reca-
> pitulates their early lives. (p. 17)

Chu's characterization is indebted to Judith Herman's (1997) theoretical reformulations of a decade ago when she introduced the syndrome of complex PTSD in adults. In her words, "Attempts to fit the
patient into the mold of existing diagnostic constructs generally result, at best, in a partial understanding of the problem and a fragmented approach to treatment" (pp. 118-119). The hallmark of complex PTSD, whether in children or adults, is the use of primitive
"defensive operations" such as, to use Terr's (1990) words, "denial,
splitting, self-anesthesia, and dissociation" (p. 183). These defenses
do not involve a conscious choice, but rather are generated automatically as a way for survivors to cope with overwhelming feelings of

anxiety and rage. Subsequent research indicates that nearly all the psychological symptoms wrought by trauma are associated with neurological impairments. We thus define the psychobiological syndrome caused by chronic traumatic stress as consisting of the following seven core symptoms:

1. Problems regulating emotion and arousal
2. Alterations in consciousness and memory
3. Damage to self-concept and identity
4. Disruptions in cognitive capacities
5. Hyperactivity and attention problems
6. Relationship problems
7. Alterations in systems of belief[1]

BRAIN IMPAIRMENTS
ASSOCIATED WITH COMPLEX PTSD

Each child with complex PTSD develops his own particular set of symptoms in response to his own unique trauma history. For example, Larry, whom we discussed in Chapter 3, suffered from memory lapses and attention problems in the aftermath of sexual abuse by an uncle. He also began burning himself to cope with overwhelming feelings of anxiety and rage. Another child with a similar history of sexual abuse might not engage in self-harming behavior, but develop, say, an eating disorder. Although the same traumas do not always lead to exactly the same symptoms, we can say that all children with complex PTSD share similar developmental disturbances and a range of symptoms that are associated with stress-induced neurological deficits. In other words, their brains are all malfunctioning in much the same way.

Dysregulation of the Stress Response System and Limbic Irritability

Repeated stress may impair the stress response even more than a single event due, in part, to a mechanism known as *kindling* (Post et al., 1997). The amygdala, for example, becomes so reactive that it no longer takes much of a stimulus to set it off. Animal experiments have shown how this happens. In one study, for example, a rat was given a tiny electrical stimulus once a day for about twenty days. After five days, the rat started to twitch and after about twenty days, it had full-blown seizures. Afterward, whenever the rat endured any kind of unpleasant experience—such as being exposed to cold water—it would have a seizure. This effect lasted for years! Repeated physical or sexual abuse seems to have a similar effect on a developing child. In a study of 115 children admitted to a child and adolescent inpatient unit, the children with a history of abuse showed a marked increase in symptoms suggestive of temporal lobe epilepsy along with clinically significant EEG (brain wave) abnormalities, especially on the left side (Ito et al., 1993). Another study measuring limbic irritability in 253 adults found that patients with a history of both physical and sexual abuse had more than twice as many symptoms suggestive of temporolimbic seizures than patients without a history of childhood abuse (Teicher et al., 1993).

The overwhelming stress of maltreatment also seems to alter the neurotransmitters (epinephrine and norepinephrine) and hormones (CRF, ACTH, cortisol) of the stress response systems (De Bellis et al., 1994; De Bellis, Baum, et al., 1999). In addition, maltreatment can throw out of whack other neurotransmitter systems, such as serotonin, dopamine, neuropeptides (e.g., endogenous opioids, neuropeptide Y), and the central amino acids (Ladd, Owens, and Nemeroff, 1996; Perry, 1994; van der Kolk, 1987; Lewis et al., 1990; Volavka, 1995). Finally, on top of all this, critical brain structures that are involved in inhibiting the stress response may also be adversely affected. These include areas of the prefrontal cortex and hippocampus, as well as the anterior cingulate (the area that recruits other parts of the brain, especially the thinking parts, to help cope with conflict). Net result: emotional dysregulation and a global deterioration in brain functioning.

Chronic maltreatment also leads to some paradoxical findings. Normally, under stress, the sympathetic nervous system is activated, leading to a hyperaroused state. Under conditions of overwhelming and repeated stress, however, the parasympathetic division of the autonomic nervous system may also be activated, along with the endogenous opioids and dopamine systems (and the inhibiting influence of cortisol), resulting in a state of apparent calm. Due to an increase in vagal tone, heart rate and blood pressure actually decrease, despite the high levels of circulating catecholamines (epinephrine, norepinephrine, and dopamine). This parasympathetic dominated state allows a child to disengage from current reality, and the endogenous opioids induce a soothing numbness, a bodily and emotional anesthesia (Perry, 2000a). The intensely high state of sympathetic plus parasympathetic arousal, writes Allan Schore (2001), "is like 'riding the gas and the brake at the same time', and the simultaneous activation of hyperexcitation and hyperinhibition results in the 'freeze response'" (p. 31). Over time, this primitive psychic defense mechanism to dissociate from bodily sensations and current reality may become a child's primary adaptation to stress (Perry, 2000a).

Decrease in Hippocampal Volume and Abnormal Activity in the Cerebellar Vermis

The hippocampus, located deep inside the temporal lobes, is the hub of conscious memory and learning (Squire and Kandel, 1999). Evidence suggests that information (auditory, sensory, visual, motor) destined for long-term memory is delivered to the hippocampus from the cortex where it is registered, integrated, and eventually encoded into long-term memory—a process that can take up to a year or more. Rita Carter (1998), author of *Mapping the Mind,* explains a current perspective on how the hippocampus works to encode experiences into long-term memory:

> During this time, they [memory traces of the experience] are frequently brought together by the hippocampus and replayed. This happens largely during [dream] sleep. . . . Every replay sends messages back up to the cortex where each element of the scene was originally registered. This regeneration of the original neural patterns etches them deeper and deeper into the cortical tissue, protecting them from degradation until eventually the memories are more or less permanently embedded. They also become linked together independently of the hippocampus. (p. 165)

Until memories become fully consolidated into long-term memory, the hippocampus is needed for retrieval—to bind and organize the various elements of a memory—especially with regard to context (Bremner and Narayan, 1998). In addition, the hippocampus, working with the cortex, assesses current experience to help determine whether it involves reward, punishment, or is basically neutral (van der Kolk, 1996a). If circumstances are judged to be nonthreatening, the hippocampus sends a message to the amygdala to turn off the stress response (LeDoux, 1996).

Whereas a single overwhelming event can interfere in the functioning of the hippocampus but not cause structural damage (Bonne et al., 2001), chronic stress or the chronic stress of PTSD (related to traumatic reminders and continuously reexperiencing the event) may result in actual damage to neurons of the hippocampus. Several researchers—including Murray Stein and J. Douglas Bremner—have found a decrease in hippocampal volume to be a by-product of physical and sexual abuse. (Decreased volume means loss of cells as a result of death, reduction in length of dendrites, and/or suppression of neurogenesis.) For example, Bremner and colleagues (1997) found the left side of the hippocampus to be 12 percent smaller in a sample of seventeen adults with a history of childhood abuse. The study also found a correlation between the decrease in hippocampal volume and deficits in verbal memory (e.g., the ability to recall a paragraph). In another study (Bremner, 2001)—comparing women with PTSD related to early childhood abuse, women with a history of maltreatment without PTSD, and women without abuse or PTSD—this same group reported a 16 percent reduction in hippocampal volume (both right and left) in women with childhood abuse and PTSD. Further measurements, involving hippocampal blood flow, showed the failure to activate the left hippocampus during a verbal memory task, suggesting a failure in hippocampal functioning in addition to structural damage. Stein and colleagues (1997) also found a decrease in left hippocampal volume in twenty-one sexually abused women compared to twenty-one nonabused women. In Stein's study, the degree of hippocampal shrinkage was positively correlated with the level of dissociative symptoms in the abused group.

Consistent with these findings, a group of researchers from the Netherlands (Nijenhuis, Ehling, and Krikke, 2002) report that hippocampal volume in a group of patients with dissociative identity disorder was approximately 21 percent smaller than hippocampal volume in healthy women. The decrease in hippocampal volume was related to the severity of reported abuse and intensity of the symptoms. In another study (Vythilingam et al., 2002), an 18 percent smaller left hippocampal volume was found *only* in depressed women who had a history of severe child abuse. The hippocampal volume in depressed women without abuse was similar to the control group of healthy adults.

Cortisol, many researchers believe, appears to be responsible for much of the damage to the hippocampus. Released from the cortex of the adrenal glands, cortisol has multiple effects on the organs and tissues of the body, including stimulating the release of glucose, suppressing the immune system, and inhibiting the stress response. In times of stress, the body produces more cortisol as a protective mechanism. Though substances such as cortisol, norepinephrine, and epinephrine are essential for responding to acute stress, too much cortisol can eat away at the neural networks in the brain. In particular, high levels of cortisol, combined with such factors as glutamate (McEwen and Magarinos, 1997) and stress-induced reduction in the growth-producing neuropeptide BDNF (brain-derived neurotrophic factor) (Smith et al., 1995), damage dendrites in the hippocampus, eventually causing nerve cells to die (Sapolsky, 1996). Other areas of the brain that have a high density of cortisol-sensitive receptors, such as the prefrontal cortex, the anterior cingulate, and the cerebellar vermis are also likely to suffer the toxic effects of cortisol. Even moderate levels of cortisol can make neurons in the hippocampus more vulnerable to environmental stressors such as physical trauma, lack of oxygen, and toxic substances. Under stress, the hippocampus also becomes less able to regenerate neurons (McEwen, 2002).

Research on child abuse survivors points to dysregulation of the HPA axis (Putnam and Trickett, 1997) and higher concentrations (urinary) of cortisol (De Bellis et al., 1999a; Lemieux and Coe, 1995). A study by a group of researchers from the Emory University School of Medicine found that adult women with a history of childhood sexual abuse were shown to have a heightened HPA axis response to stress—including a profound dysregulation of CRF—compared to controls. The researchers concluded that the hyperreactivity of the HPA axis and autonomic nervous system stemming from childhood abuse may be an important predisposing factor for adult psychopathological conditions (Heim et al., 2000). In this ongoing study, researchers (Nemeroff et al., 2002) now report that the variations downstream in the baseline levels of cortisol seem to predict depression: Individuals with a history of childhood abuse and PTSD *without* major depression showed subnormal levels of cortisol, whereas those individuals *with* major depression and early trauma had abnormally high levels of cortisol. Other studies have also shown that chronic PTSD is associated with lower *baseline* levels of cortisol (Yehuda, 1997), presumably due to the sensitization of the HPA axis. Thus, it appears that in chronic forms of PTSD, the dysfunction of the hypothalamic-pituitary-adrenal axis can be characterized by the tendency to overreact in both directions, upward and downward. This dynamic tendency to overreact is supported by studies that reveal that even individuals who exhibit "hypocortisol" show a pattern of exaggerated cortisol response to stress, e.g., a three-fold increase in cortisol in response to trauma-specific reminders (Mason et al., 2002; Bremner, 2002). Bremner (1997) and his colleagues have hypothesized that the high levels of cortisol released at the time of the original trauma (and later with exposure to traumatic reminders) results in damage to the neurons of the hippocampus that eventually leads to a decrease in hippocampal volume.

A damaged hippocampus may account for increased levels of cortisol (because the hipppocampus has an inhibitory effect on the HPA axis), as well as all kinds of memory problems, including specific deficits in short-term (verbal) memory (Bremner et al., 1995). Furthermore, as Bremner (1999a) hypothesizes, a "dysfunctional hippocampus . . . may represent the anatomic basis of the fragmentation of memory" in patients with complex PTSD (p. 802). A biological "triple whammy"—abnormal activation of the parasympathetic nervous system, a malfunctioning hippocampus, and a dysfunctional medial and orbitofrontal cortex—may thus be a key force behind many dissociative symptoms, including depersonalization, amnesia, and flashbacks. According to Bessel van der Kolk, abused children are likely to become more symptomatic in the face of present stresses because their hippocampus has already been damaged. These children are less able to process current experiences into normal memory networks. Instead, they tend to isolate memory fragments from autobiographical memory (van der Kolk, Burbridge, and Suzuki, 1997). In other words, hippocampal damage may account for a multitude of memory problems. Speculating that short- and long-term memory problems translate into learning problems, Bremner (1999a) urges public health officials to study the connection between interpersonal violence and low academic achievement.

The cerebellar vermis (part of the cerebellum), located in the back of the brain just above the brain stem, also has a remarkably high concentration of cortisol receptors. Thus, it comes as no surprise that research also points to abnormal activity in this part of the brain in abused children. Although neuroscientists used to think that the cerebellum's only function was to coordinate movement, it actually also helps with emotional and cognitive functions. For example, the vermis helps regulate the electrical activity in the limbic system. In studies of abused children, Teicher has found that the vermis is not able to perform this job adequately. As Teicher notes, "If indeed, the vermis is important not only for postural, attentional, and emotional balance, but in compensating for and regulating emotional instability, this latter capacity may be impaired by early trauma" (2000, p. 57). According to Teicher, a malfunctioning vermis can contribute to a myriad of psychiatric disorders, including depression, ADHD, bipolar disorder, schizophrenia, and autism.

Underdevelopment of the Left Hemisphere and Communication Problems Between Brain Hemispheres

Maltreatment appears to impede normal development of the left hemisphere. In a series of studies comparing children with documented histories of abuse or neglect with a control group (Teicher et al., 1997; Ito et al., 1998), Teicher and his colleagues looked at MRI scans, studied EEG coherence tests (which provide information on brain maturation), examined medical records, and administered neuropsychological tests to measure left and right brain capacities (evidence that may suggest better visual-spatial ability than verbal performance). They found that the cortex of the left hemisphere was not as well-developed in children who were maltreated. These results were supported by the neuropsychological tests that showed left-hemisphere deficits to be six times more common in the abused group. Left-hemisphere deficits were greatest in the patients with a history of psychological abuse. Teicher (2000) speculates that interference in the myelinization of nerve fibers, another adverse brain development linked to maltreatment, may also contribute to the lack of development in the left hemisphere.

Teicher also noticed that the abused group was less able to use both brain hemispheres to process experience than normal. In particular, children with complex PTSD relied more on their left hemispheres during neutral tasks and more on their right hemispheres during more emotionally charged activities. Abnormalities in the corpus callosum, the large fiber tract that connects the left and right hemispheres, may help explain why this tendency called *lateralization* appears in abused children, but is absent in nonabused children. Teicher and colleagues (1997) evaluated MRI data on children with trauma histories who were subdivided into four categories, depending on whether they had endured (1) physical abuse, (2) sexual abuse, (3) psychological abuse (involving domestic violence or verbal abuse), or (4) neglect. Data analysis revealed that the size of the corpus callosum was abnormal across all categories and that these regional variations (the corpus callosum contains several regions) differed by gender and type of abuse. Physical abuse and neglect produced the greatest effect perhaps because they tend to occur earlier in life.

Likewise, MRI studies of abused children conducted by De Bellis, Keshavan, and colleagues (1999) also documented abnormalities in the corpus callosum. In this groundbreaking study, De Bellis and his colleagues also measured the size (i.e., volume) of the brains of forty-four maltreated children with PTSD. Compared to the control group of nonabused children, the maltreated children had brains that were approximately 7 percent smaller. The findings indicated that the longer a child was abused, the smaller the cerebral volume and the more symptoms (e.g., intrusive thoughts, avoidance, hyperarousal and/or dissociation) the child exhibited.[2]

Research thus suggests that abused children may be doomed to have smaller brains that work less efficiently. IQ and brain size are positively correlated; thus the smaller the brain, the greater the potential for cognitive deficits. The underdevelopment of the left hemisphere can impede the development of language and reasoning skills and interfere in the development of *metacognition* (i.e., the capacity to think about our thinking or to monitor ourselves) and in the ability to regulate negative emotions. For example, patients with reduced activity in the left hemisphere are at high risk for developing depression (Davidson, 1994). Furthermore, when the two hemispheres aren't in sync, both higher-order thinking and emotional processing are also impaired (Hoptman and Davidson, 1994).

The lack of cooperation between the two hemispheres can also create other symptoms. Generally, negative emotions such as fear are processed in the right hemisphere, and positive emotions such as affection and happiness in the left. If the hemispheres are not operating in concert, these emotions can't be experienced at the same time. Perhaps that's why maltreated children often divide people into the categories of "all good" and "all bad," rather than developing a more balanced view of others. Teicher (2000) suggests that diminished right-left hemispheric integration may help explain the shifting moods observed in borderline patients (a trauma-related personality disorder):

> With less well integrated hemispheres, borderline patients may shift rapidly from a logical and possibly overvaluing left-hemisphere state to a highly negative, critical, and emotional right hemisphere state. (pp. 63-64)

According to Teicher, brain fragmentation may be the hallmark of mental illness. As a rule, psychiatric disorders arise whenever the brain is failing to access key areas to process experience. For example, the lack of integration between hemispheres may contribute to dissociative ego states and symptoms such as trance states and depersonalization. When activity in the left hemisphere is diminished, perceptions may seem timeless and disconnected because the emotions that are generated in the right hemisphere cannot be transformed into words, placed in context, and assigned meaning (Rossi, 1993).

Neuroendocrine and Immune System Dysfunction

Abuse and neglect also influence growth-related hormones and possibly sex hormones. For example, in cases of severe neglect, puberty is often delayed, and physical growth is stunted. Johns Hopkins psychologist John Money (1992) has coined the "Kaspar Hauser syndrome of psychosocial dwarfism" to characterize the plight of children who endure unimaginable torture and suffer from statural, emotional, and intellectual impairment as a result. For example, Money recounts the case of a boy who had never attended school until he was rescued at sixteen. Besides beating him routinely, his parents also periodically denied him food and locked him in a closet. At age sixteen, he was about fifty-one inches tall—the normal height of an eight-year-old. As with most psychosocial dwarfs, once rescued, this boy experienced some catch-up growth, but he never attained a normal height. Fortunately, these horrific cases of abuse are rare, but they still tell us something about how the endocrine system works. Bonding seems to be crucial to healthy brain development as touch initiates a cascade of biological reactions responsible for turning on the genes that promote growth. A group of researchers at Duke University has discovered a biological chain of events that links the lack of touch to the suppression of growth (Wang, Bartolome, and Schanberg, 1996). More research is needed to pinpoint the precise effects on the endocrine system of maltreatment seen in a significant segment of the children who end up with complex PTSD.

Chronic stress also contributes to an increase in infections, autoimmune disorders, and multiple other diseases (Moyers, 1993; Sapolsky, 1998; McEwen, 2002). Not surprisingly, Putnam (1996) reported that sexually abused girls had higher rates of infection than a comparison group. Abuse-related immune dysfunction may also increase susceptibility to autoimmune diseases (e.g., acute glomerial nephritis, rheumatic fever, ulcerative colitis, rheumatoid arthritis). In a longitudinal study of sexually abused girls, Putnam and his colleagues (De Bellis et al., 1996) found a significant increase in plasma antinuclear antibodies (a general term for autoantibodies that attack the body—cellular proteins) in abused subjects when compared with a control group. Thus, the abused girls showed evidence of a malfunctioning immune system. Some new research suggests that these effects carry over into adulthood. In a study that Bessel van der Kolk calls "ground-breaking" (personal communication), Vincent Felitti and colleagues (1998) found a direct link between adverse childhood experiences (ACEs) such as physical, psychological, and sexual abuse along with parental mental illness and incarceration, and the leading causes of death in adults. The greater the number of ACEs, the greater the likelihood of adult diseases such as heart disease, cancer, lung disease, and diabetes. For example, the presence of four or more such risk factors in childhood increased the likelihood of stroke nearly two and a half times.

Summary

The developing brain is acutely sensitive to the negative effects of chronic stress (e.g., abuse, neglect, and exposure to family violence). Most researchers support the theory that stress-induced neurological damage underlies many of the symptoms in complex PTSD. However, they use a number of different models to explain how stress damages the brain. Sapolsky, Bremner, McEwen, and Teicher, for example, emphasize the deleterious effects of cortisol, especially on the hippocampus, as well as the mechanism called *sensitization.* This mechanism refers to an increase in reactivity (behavioral and biological) with repeated exposure to adverse stimuli at the same or lower level. Bruce Perry (1997) notes that early trauma can sensitize the brain's fear system, alter metabolism, and enhance neuronal irritability, causing the system to turn on with very little provocation. The resulting state of hyperarousal and/or dissociation can, in turn, interfere in the functioning of the prefrontal cortex (Arnsten, 1998), hippocampus (LeDoux, 1996), and left hemisphere (Rauch et al., 1996).

Furthermore, intense, unregulated stress induces a chaotic biochemical environment that impedes brain maturation (Schore, 2001), especially in brain areas that have important integrative functions, such as the hippocampus and prefrontal cortex. Brain development may be further compromised because stress inhibits the flow of information from one part of the brain to another. When the flow of information is constantly short-circuited, brain pathways—such as those linking the cognitive and emotional systems and the left and right hemispheres—fail to mature adequately.

Bruce Perry (1997) reminds us that any combination of factors such as neglect, malnutrition, physical injury, stroke, and abuse, which increase the reactivity of lower-brain centers and/or decrease the functional capacity of the cortex to inhibit the lower more reactive parts of the brain, "will necessarily result in persistence of primitive, immature behavioral reactivity" (p. 129). In other words, maltreatment not only increases the reactivity of the lower-brain centers, but can also weaken the ability of the cortex to control these subcortical systems.

Mounting evidence suggests that chronic traumatic stress damages specific areas of the brain (especially those concerned with inhibition and integration), fragments overall brain functioning, and creates an imbalance of power between the emotional and cognitive systems. Instead of guiding thoughtful action, emotions simply generate the automatic, conditioned reactions of the stress response. The dysfunction in key areas of the brain leads maltreated children to develop chaotic patterns of relating to others and the environment. Saddled with overwhelming emotions whose source they rarely comprehend, these children are often ill equipped to tackle the daily challenges of life.

THE EFFECTS OF MALTREATMENT ON A CHILD'S PSYCHE

> Thus for me the usual childhood reality was reversed. Inside my own house, among people I knew, was where danger lay. . . . My world was a photographic negative of my playmates' world: for white, read black.
>
> Sylvia Fraser
> *My Father's House: A Memoir of Healing*

Case Study: Jessica

At age thirteen, Jessica told her mother that she had been sexually abused by an uncle who had been living with the family.[3] The abuse began when she was four and lasted for three years. Jessica never told her mother about the abuse because the uncle had threatened to harm the family if she did. Jessica's father had also terrorized the whole family; he had beaten his wife—in front of Jessica—on numerous occasions and had once nearly killed Jessica's younger brother when he threw him against a wall. Jessica said she had forgotten about these incidents after her uncle had moved out.

Though disturbed by Jessica's revelations, her mother also felt relieved because with the help of Jessica's new therapist, she could now make sense of Jessica's odd behavior. Jessica had had frequent nightmares of being raped and murdered. She kept away from all contact with any adult men; she had once told her mother that she was afraid that their neighbor—a bachelor in his sixties—would kidnap her. She was withdrawn, socially isolated, and would not go outside alone at night. In addition, Jessica's academic work suffered; she almost failed the sixth grade. Sometimes during a class at school, she would tune out completely and lose track of time.

Analysis

Jessica's distress went beyond the scope of the three classic symptoms of PTSD—avoidance, heightened arousal, and reexperiencing of trauma—because she experienced additional problems that affected all aspects of development. She was eventually diagnosed with PTSD and DDNOS (dissociative disorder not otherwise specified).

Jessica's dissociative symptoms included the reliving of traumatic events and amnesia for past trauma. In addition, at times she experienced herself and her surroundings as unreal. Jessica also had difficulty concentrating for more than a few minutes at a time. As she told her therapist early in therapy, "I tend to space out a lot."

Jessica also had developed two dissociated parts—"the little girl" who couldn't stop crying and "Revenge," who was always seething with anger. Though Jessica initially experienced these ego states as "people inside her," over time she saw that they simply contained some of the overwhelming feelings—such as shame, sadness, helplessness, and rage—generated by the traumatic events in her life.

Problems Regulating Emotion and Arousal

Children with complex PTSD are likely to oscillate between extreme arousal and numbed responsiveness. These "all or nothing states," as previously described, are biologically driven. Although chronically traumatized children may often appear detached, this can occur not because they don't have *any* feelings but because they have *too many*. They may no longer even be consciously registering their own emotions, but they are there, often stored in bodily sensations.

Furthermore, in contrast to children who have been exposed to a single traumatic event, chronically traumatized children often engage in self-destructive behaviors to regulate their emotional states. For maltreated children, van der Kolk and Fisler (1994) argue, the loss of capacity to regulate intense emotions is the most far-reaching effect of early trauma. Normally, through coregulation of internal states, infants and young children learn to calm and soothe themselves by internalizing the nurturing behaviors of their caregivers. Many maltreated children can't do this because they haven't had loving attachment figures. To survive, they must develop (and rely on) atypical methods to calm and soothe themselves. Some abused children discover a seemingly paradoxical way to handle anxiety. By doing something physically traumatizing (such as burning themselves, as was the case with Larry in Chapter 3) or by provoking interpersonal conflicts, they can precipitate an autonomic nervous system crisis. The escalating intensity of arousal eventually triggers the brain's natural calming mechanisms including a sudden release of cortisol and endogenous opioids, inducing a calm, sometimes hypnotic-like or numbed state.

This cycle of hyperarousal and numbing may be one of the reasons why traumatized children can have such intense negative reactions to seemingly positive events. As Beverly James (1994) notes,

> Veteran professional caregivers can predict with incredible accuracy the length of time before a child damages a new item of clothing or a gift he has received. They know that a child who has just had a good time on a family outing will be asking for punishment by the end of the day, or they await with dread the predictable aftermath when the youngsters played well on the soccer team. (p. 18)

In previous generations, therapists typically explained these self-destructive patterns of behavior in terms of low self-esteem. In other words, the child sabotages anything positive because he feels undeserving of anything good. Although this may be part of the dynamics, biology, most likely, plays a significant role. For instance, these children may be unable to differentiate a state of arousal that is based in pleasure, joy, and excitement from one rooted in fear; thus, any strong feelings at all can induce a state of panic. Some traumatized children have learned to control this escalating emotional state by upping the ante until it reaches a peak. The calming mechanisms associated with the stress response then take over and the child no longer is troubled by the uncomfortable emotions. Although this strategy appears to "work," it is a self-destructive solution that ends up jeopardizing the child's psychological health. As children get older, troubling symptoms such as substance abuse, thrill-seeking behavior, bingeing and purging, starvation, and obsessive-compulsive behaviors typically emerge.

Dissociation

To ward off the overwhelming feelings stemming from repeated trauma—feelings of anger, rage, fear, and despair—which are constantly being evoked, survivors of abuse typically resort to the coping mechanism known as dissociation. Whenever the intensity of feeling becomes too much, this defense takes over automatically. The child begins to send herself messages such as "This isn't real," or "This isn't happening to me." According to Bruce Perry (2000a), dissociative responses include "distraction, avoidance, numbing, daydreaming, fugue, fantasy, derealization, depersonalization, and, in the extreme, fainting or catatonia" (p. 8).

Defined as a disruption in the normal integrative functions of consciousness, memory, identity, and perception (American Psychiatric Association, 1994, p. 477), dissociation is a kind of mind-clearing trick that enables a child to escape an ongoing terrible experience and achieve a state of calm. The child learns how to induce this state through self-hypnosis. As Terr (1994) writes:

> The childhood gateway to pathological dissociation is self-hypnosis—counting, focusing on objects such as Venetian blinds or spots on the ceiling, visualizing another place, or repeating certain phrases over and over. Eventually the dissociation comes automatically, with no preliminary forays into autohypnosis. (pp. 70-71)

To use dissociation successfully—to achieve a true separation of self from the present situation—usually takes practice—such as learning how to play the piano. The neural mechanisms that mediate the behavior must be built step by step; one traumatic event is generally not enough to get them going. Some survivors of childhood abuse describe how they are able to dissociate and still keep an eye on themselves. They are able to maintain some self-awareness through a kind of divided consciousness. As Bessel van der Kolk (1997) notes, "Many traumatized children (and adults who were traumatized as children) have described how under stress, they can make themselves disappear, while watching what is going on from a distance. This gives them the sensation that what is happening is not really happening to them, but to someone else" (p. 93). These children watch their abuse from afar. Although dissociation can be a resourceful survival mechanism during trauma, it is pathological when it becomes the primary response to stress.

(continued)

(continued)

Scientists have been studying dissociation even before Freud's day. Though the research of a hundred years ago is still relevant, what is new in our contemporary understanding is the biological dimension of dissociation. It can become a "biological habit"—a neurological pattern of brain activity that automatically kicks in whenever an abused child experiences emotions he cannot handle. At that point, the mind and body start to fragment. As Perry (2000a) notes:

> In our experiences with young children and infants, the predominant adaptive responses during trauma are dissociative. Children exposed to chronic violence may report a variety of dissociative experiences. Children describe going to a "different place," assuming the persona of superheroes or animals, a sense of "watching a movie that I was in" or "just floating"—classic depersonalization and derealization responses. Observers will report these children as numb, robotic, nonreactive, "day dreaming," "acting like he was not there," staring off in a glazed look. Younger children are more likely to use dissociative adaptations. Immobilization, inescapability or pain will increase the dissociative components of the stress response patterns at any age. (pp. 8-9)

For most abused children, however, the typical response to stress is a combination of alternating states of arousal and dissociation.

Alterations in Consciousness and Memory

> Survivors of atrocities, whether they were at the hands of strangers, trusted clerics, or in the private sanctum of family do not speak easily of their experiences. . . . They forget because they were told to forget. Whether by threats ("if you tell, I'll kill you") or by edict ("this did not happen"), reality gets reshaped.
>
> Linda Katherine Cutting
> *Memory Slips*

For many abused children, *dissociation* (the primary mechanism underlying disturbances in consciousness and memory) becomes a way of life. Dissociation provides the abused child with a means of avoiding painful memories and the terror of ongoing abuse. Dissociation also provides a way out of the terrible interpersonal dilemma faced by child victims of abuse by a parent. They are subjected to the excruciating pain of the abuse, and since the perpetrator happens to be a parent, they remain dependent on her for their very existence. By allowing survivors to disconnect from their abuse memories, dissociation preserves their life-sustaining connections with their parents. As Judith Herman (1997) reminds us:

> All of the abused child's psychological adaptations serve the fundamental purpose of preserving her primary attachment to her parents in the face of daily evidence of their malice, helplessness, or indifference. To accomplish this purpose the child resorts to a wide array of psychological defenses. By virtue of these defenses, the abuse is either walled off from conscious awareness and memory, so that it did not really happen, or minimized, rationalized, and excused, so that whatever did happen was not really abuse. Unable to escape or alter the unbearable reality in fact, the child alters it in her mind. (p. 102)

A professor of psychology at the University of Oregon (and herself an abuse survivor), Jennifer Freyd (1996) uses the term *betrayal trauma,* to highlight that abuse is much more damaging when it is committed by parents—whose love and protection children urgently need.

Thus, dissociation creates a variety of memory problems including the abnormal reexperiencing of traumatic events (described in Chapter 3) and amnesia. Jeffery, a teenage death row inmate with a history of abuse and neglect, describes what it was like for him to remember. "See the way I look back on things, I look back on it and remember the feelings that I had. *I remember it like it's happening again when I remember it*" (Karr-Morse and Wiley, 1997, p. 128).

Sometimes a child begins to believe that the abuse didn't even happen, or that it didn't happen to him, but to some dissociated fragment. Whereas brief traumatization generally results in increased clarity (hypermnesia) and accurate recall of the event, severe and chronic early abuse is correlated with dissociation and amnesia (Chu et al., 1999). Numerous studies show that amnesia among abused children is very common, particularly when a child continues to live with the per-petrating parent. For instance, psychiatrist Dorothy Lewis and neurolo-gist Jonathan Pincas have studied some notorious killers on death row over the past quarter century, often finding evidence—in the form of medical records and eyewitness accounts by relatives—of horrific acts of abuse committed by parents early in childhood. Remarkably, most of the prisoners report no conscious memories of the heinous abuse (Lewis, 1998).

Studies documenting amnesia as a common by-product of abuse have been conducted on both clinical and nonclinical populations. In a landmark prospective study of 129 women with documented histo-ries of sexual abuse, Linda Meyer Williams (1994) found that 38 per-cent did not recall the abuse when interviewed seventeen years later. In addition, another 16 percent stated that there was a time in the past that they did not remember the abuse. "Forgetting" was associated with age and relationship to the offender. Very young children and those who were abused by someone they knew were more likely to forget.

In a study involving ninety patients admitted to an inpatient facility specializing in the treatment of trauma-related disorders, the researchers concluded that childhood abuse is associated with high levels of dis-sociative symptoms and amnesia for the abuse. Recall of the abuse gen-erally occurred at home, alone, or with family and friends, and inde-pendent corroboration was usually present (Chu et al., 1999).

Reviewing the entire literature on traumatic amnesia to date, Brown, Scheflin, and Hammond (1998) conclude: "The data on full or partial amnesia for trauma are robust across all of the studies on different types of trauma. . . . Traumatic amnesia is a common occurrence in a subsample of traumatized individuals for most types of trauma, includ-ing childhood sexual abuse" (p. 198). Today, this literature comprises about seventy-five studies.

Since dissociation often blocks the full perception and storage of events, traumatic memories are typically incomplete. These memo-ries tend to return in fragments—bits and pieces—and are apt to be condensed, with several episodes combined into one memory, partic-ularly if they date from early childhood. No matter whether traumatic memories have always been remembered or lost and then retrieved, the gist of the memory is generally accurate even if some of the de-tails are wrong (Brown, Cohen, et al., 1998).

If amnesia simply does away with a horrible event, isn't it to be encouraged? No, because though traumatic memories may get walled off, they can never really be forgotten. Although the conscious or explicit memory system may be temporarily turned off, the unconscious or implicit memory system continues to operate. Implicit memories, which may surface as specific phobias, sensations, and negative self-perceptions, affect behavior. One little boy who as an infant was put in the freezer by his abusive parents and later rescued by his sister, frequently complained of an icy spot or a cold spot in the middle of his back (Waters and Silberg, 1996). Behavioral problems (e.g., a sexual acting out) often represent a failed attempt to ward off the memory of a horrible event. According to Terr (1994), this makes sense because "if a person has endured horrible moments in life, these moments should leave a scar" (p. 33). The scar is there, whether or not the child is aware of it.

Tragically, the abused child typically not only forgets his own traumas, but ends up developing a distorted sense of interpersonal reality per se. Whereas healthy families encourage metacommunication, or talking about the way in which they communicate, abusive families preclude such dialogue. A child in a healthy family might feel safe enough to say, "Mom, you're not listening to me," "Dad, I don't understand why you are mad at me," or "Mom and Dad, what you said doesn't make sense." In abusive families, however, children are conditioned to disbelieve their own senses and to refrain from talking about what they see and hear. They are taught to ignore reality, or what psychologists call "the elephant in the living room." Because their parents often deny their perceptions, maltreated children generally have a poor level of self-awareness. As Liotti (1999) points out, "Lies, deceptions and other sources of seriously distorted family interactions force the growing child to exclude new and potentially meaningful information already stored in the implicit memory system or in the episodic memory system, from communication and therefore from semantic processing and from conscious thought" (p. 307).

Not only must abused children struggle with the overwhelming feelings caused by the abuse itself, but also, due to warped communication patterns in the family, they may experience feelings per se as dangerous. That's another reason why they so readily resort to dissociation. They have so much to feel, yet have trouble processing any feelings at all.

Abusive parents can be masters at what communication theorist Paul Watzlawick (1964) calls *disqualifications*. In his words, "a disqualification is a technique which enables one to say something without really saying it, to deny without really saying no, and to disagree without really disagreeing—and what is meant by 'really' is: to take a stand for which one is prepared to accept responsibility" (p. 18). Disconfirmation is one such disqualification and goes hand in hand with physical or emotional neglect. Thus, parents who fail to hold, touch, and cuddle with their baby, in effect, disconfirm or deny the child's existence. A second disqualification is distortion, which refers to confusing, inaccurate, often irrational communications that deviate from reality. For example, a parent might give a mixed message, one in which the nonverbal communication indicates that the verbal communication is false. A third form of disqualification is disparagement, whereby a parent degrades the child either by belittling her or by name-calling.

Damage to Self-Concept and Identity

Maltreatment directly attacks identity formation in other ways than blocking out memories. As psychiatrist Harry Stack Sullivan (1953) first recognized some seventy years ago, self-concept is rooted in *reflected appraisals*. In other words, our view of ourselves depends on how significant others treat us. If a child is treated as a person to be hated and despised, he will inevitably incorporate this attitude into his own self-perception. Sullivan considered identity, or as he called it the "self-system," to be organized into the "good me," "bad me," and "not me." Whereas positive experiences feed into the "good me," negative experiences feed into the "bad me." However, traumatic experiences, because they generate feelings of overwhelming fear, shame, and helplessness, become disconnected from personal identity—the "not me."

Research has since corroborated Sullivan's theoretical speculations. Typically, abused and neglected children see themselves as weak, ineffectual, helpless, and utterly alone. Their sense of shame and self-loathing is often profound as they mistakenly assume that they deserved the abuse. As Judith Herman (1997) states:

Inevitably the child concludes that her innate badness is the cause. The child seizes upon this explanation early and clings to it tenaciously, for it enables her to persevere a sense of meaning, hope, and power. If she is bad, then her parents are good. If she is bad, then she can try to be good. If, somehow, she has brought this fate upon herself, then somehow she has the power to change it. If she has driven her parents to mistreat her, then, if only she tries hard enough, she may someday earn their forgiveness and finally win the protection and care she so desperately needs. (p. 103)

By identifying with the perpetrator's pathological aggression, survivors gain an illusory sense of control over both their past and present.

To preserve their attachment to parents who are abusing them, some children end up with more than just a damaged self-concept; their psyches become so fragmented that they experience the "self" as "multiple selves." This is how Marilyn Van Derbur, the 1958 Miss America, walled off memories of incest that suddenly reemerged at the age of twenty-four. Previously, she had split into the "day child" and the "night child." Whereas the day child was happy, competent, athletic, and successful, the night child embodied helplessness, fear, and shame. The day child had no awareness of the night child. Marilyn later recalled that

> During the days, no embarrassed or angry glances ever passed between my father and me, because I, the "day child" had no conscious knowledge of the traumas and the terrors of the "night child." . . . I believed I was the happiest person who ever lived. I truly believed that. (Quoted in Terr, 1994, p.124)

Typically, the alters or parts contain various painful emotions such as the "angry one," the "sad one," the "helpless one," or the "shameful one." As time goes on, the abused child may create other parts of her mind that are protective and create feelings of safety and security. By creating separate domains of consciousness, she is able to ward off painful memories and resolve irreconcilable conflicts. As Putnam (1997) says, "By compartmentalizing overwhelming experiences and feelings, a child can both know that he or she is being terribly maltreated by a parent and can simultaneously idealize that parent"

(p. 71). He goes on to say that the failure to develop metacognitive thinking, coupled with experience that repeatedly triggers circumscribed emotional/behavioral states, results in brain circuits that become autonomous and hardwired; at the same time, identity becomes more and more fragmented.

Remarkably, unity of consciousness is a developmental achievement that does not happen automatically. Infants experience each emotional state as separate and distinct. They feel like a different self, depending on their emotional state. Around eighteen months to two years of age, as long as the attachment relationship is secure, more complex emotional states appear. For instance, the toddler can now hold a positive image of a loving parent in her mind and also feel outraged with that same parent from time to time. Thus, maturation of the prefrontal cortex allows for the development of a "metaself," an "observer self" that exists outside the present situation and current emotion and makes it possible to form an integrated identity. Tragically, because of the nature of the attachment relationship, some abused children fail to achieve these basic mental capacities.

By definition, dissociative identity disorder (DID), formerly known as multiple personality disorder (MPD), is said to be present when, as in the case of Marilyn Van Derbur, a patient has two or more such personality states that periodically assume control of behavior. Although this controversial disorder was identified over 150 years ago (Fine, 1988), few cases were diagnosed until the 1970s when the best-seller *Sybil* renewed interest in it. Since the 1980s, a vast empirical literature has sprouted up and studies suggest that as many as 3 percent of the general population and between 5 and 15 percent of psychiatric inpatients meet the diagnostic criteria for DID (Putnam, 1997).

Only in the last decade have clinicians also begun diagnosing and treating DID in children. Given the developmental origins of DID, it is not surprising that it affects children, too. However, as one psychologist acknowledges, few therapists have been trained to look for it: "Considering the old medical aphorism 'if you hear hoof beats, think of horses, not zebras', for those in child and adolescent psychiatry, psychology and social work, the horses are attention-deficit hyperactivity disorder, conduct disorder, and major depression—but decidedly *not* dissociative identity disorder" (Peterson, 1996, p. 6). As it turns out,

DID may be the primary diagnosis for some of the severely troubled children who suffer from any one of the "horses" previously listed.

Disruption of Cognitive Capacities

Beginning with the identification of battered child syndrome in the 1960s, a growing body of evidence continues to document cognitive deficits in abused and neglected children (Einbender and Friedrich, 1989; Kendall-Tackett, Williams, and Finkelhor, 1993). For instance, Carrey and colleagues (1995) found that an abused group of school-age children had significantly lower IQ scores than a control group. The verbal IQ performance showed the greatest disparity. Bruce Perry (2000a) and Martin Teicher and colleagues (1997) have also found poorer verbal abilities in children with a documented history of abuse or neglect. Likewise, Bremner and colleagues (1995) have found deficits in short-term verbal memory among abuse survivors that were significantly correlated with the severity of the abuse.

In 1987, Arnold Sameroff, a psychology professor at the University of Michigan, and his colleagues published data from the Rochester Longitudinal Study showing the relationship between IQ and risk factors such as dysfunctional parenting, family violence, maternal mental illness, absence of father, parental substance abuse, and poverty. According to their findings, one or two risk factors didn't typically affect cognitive development; however, three or four were associated with a sharp drop in IQ (Sameroff et al., 1987). Subsequent measures of cognitive, social, and emotional competence at ages thirteen and eighteen show poor outcomes when there were two or more risk factors (Sameroff et al., 1993; Sameroff, 1998). Michael and Marjorie Rutter (1993), citing evidence from longitudinal studies, note that in addition to the sheer number of risk factors, when the sources of stress were family problems such as a mother's psychiatric condition, a father's criminal behavior, or a child's placement in foster care, the cognitive and emotional impairments rose significantly.

Trauma also seems to create a rigid thinking style. It interferes with the two basic mental activities defined by Jean Piaget as *assimilation* (the integration of new experiences into existing concepts known as schemas) and *accommodation* (the creation of new frameworks and relationships). Sadly, traumatized children have difficulty with both types of thinking, so their thinking processes lag behind their peers. As Bessel van der Kolk (1987) notes in his study comparing six- to eleven-year-olds with and without a history of abuse or neglect:

> Thus far, our strongest finding in these abused children has been the inflexibility of organized schematas and structures in all domains [of intelligence]. . . . Accommodation was not operating efficiently, apparently because autonomic nervous system arousal and steady state anxiety caused by conditioned fear and anticipatory frustration inhibited the ability to make guiding plans, to play with alternative approaches, or to anticipate probabilities at age appropriate levels. (p. 101)

The constricted play of maltreated children also contributes to learning problems. When children play, they learn about themselves, their world, and how to adapt. When we watch young children during play, we witness the dynamic interplay of assimilation and accommodation. One moment a child will change the present situation to fit into his existing cognitive framework and current needs and desires. A second later, that same child will readjust his internal model of the world to adjust to the realities and demands of the environment. For example, Joey, the two-year-old brother of one of the students in a preschool classroom, was trying to join a group of four-year-old boys who were playing with trucks. In Joey's mind everything that had wheels was a "twuk." He came with a race car, a bus, and an ambulance, only to be told by the boys, "You need a truck." A puzzled Joey soon learned what a truck really was. Minutes later, he was proudly pointing out various "caws" and "twuks" in a picture book. Unlike Joey, maltreated children can't adjust their brittle internal mental structure so readily.

Hyperactivity and Attention Problems

Given that abused children often find themselves emotionally overwhelmed, it's not surprising that they have attention problems. Children who are hyperaroused tend to be restless and excessively active. A study by Glod and Teicher (1996), using belt-worn monitors to measure activity levels, found that children with PTSD were almost as active as children with ADHD. In the classroom, abused children may have a hard time focusing because they are constantly scanning the environment, looking for subtle nonverbal cues that may suggest hostile intent.

The DSM-IV (1994) states that the "essential feature of Attention-Deficit/Hyperactivity Disorder is a persistent pattern of inattention and/or hyperactivity-impulsiveness that is more frequent and severe than is typically observed in individuals at a comparable level of development" (p. 78). This description characterizes many children with complex PTSD (Haddad and Garralda, 1992). According to psychiatrist Frank Putnam (1997), the former head of the developmental psychobiology research unit at the National Institute of Mental Health, although ADHD symptoms are present in only 3 to 5 percent of the general population (Barkley, 1998), they are present in 25 to 45 percent of severely maltreated children (p. 41).

ADHD is not a tidy disorder. As of this writing, no specific biological marker accounts for it.[4] Though most researchers typically consider ADHD to result from a genetic defect, they rarely consider whether the genes in question may have been altered by the environment. In fact, research identifies both prenatal exposure to alcohol and nicotine (Barkley, 1998), as well as trauma, as etiological factors. Teicher (2000), who also found that 30 percent of children with a history of childhood maltreatment meet diagnostic criteria for ADHD, speculates that early childhood abuse may be directly related to the development of ADHD symptoms:

> Interestingly, one of the most reliable neuroanatomical findings in ADHD is reduced size of the cerebellar vermis. Some studies have also found an association between reduced size of the mid portions of the corpus callosum and emergence of ADHD-like symptoms of impulsivity. Hence, early abuse may produce brain changes that mimic key aspects of ADHD. (p. 63)

Likewise, neglect during infancy may also lead to ADHD. In Chapter 2, we described Schore's work, showing that the development of the dopamine system is dependent on the positive and reciprocal emotional relationship between infant and caregiver. As it turns out, a dysregulated dopamine system is one of the key biological findings in ADHD. This neurotransmitter regulates several brain areas that are implicated in ADHD (e.g., the frontal cortex, striatum, and the nucleus accumbens—the reward center in the brain) (Ernst and Zametkin, 1995; Ratey, Middeldorp-Crispijn, and Leveroni, 1995). Putting theoretical speculations aside, when a child has both complex PTSD and ADHD, the ADHD is best understood as a trauma-related disorder rather than a separate comorbid condition.

Relationship Problems

Survivors of childhood abuse generally have difficulty relating to others. This is not surprising, given that their relationships with their parents, which typically serve as a blueprint for peer relationships, have been so chaotic. Uncomfortable both expressing and receiving affection, maltreated children often find themselves in a sticky bind. On the one hand, they have a tremendous longing for intimacy and connection; on the other hand, getting their emotional needs met leads to intense fear because, in their experience, closeness means pain. In the words of author Beverly James (1994), "Intimacy is commonly avoided by adult and child trauma survivors because the inherent emotional closeness leads to feelings of vulnerability and feelings of loss of control. . . . Intimacy represents a threat, not safety" (p. 15). In young children, the approach-avoidance conflict is evident in behaviors such as wanting to be held, but then stiffening and turning away from the parent. Avoidance of eye contact, hypervigilance, withdrawal, hyperactivity, and oppositional behaviors are also common. When working with these children, therapists often notice the bungee cord effect (Waters, 1996). A child will move closer, become frightened, and then withdraw.

Perhaps most frustrating for the adults who care for troubled children is their obsessive need to be in control. Because of their history of helplessness with those who held power over them, abused children fight against any authority. To depend on someone makes them feel incredibly vulnerable. At a conference workshop in 1998, Joyanna Silberg observed that just being a child is a traumatic reminder for a traumatized child. Many become oppositional as a way to gain an illusory sense of control. When they irritate people and make people angry, they get a perverse sense of power. Often the need for control makes these children oblivious to the effect of their actions on others. As a rule, maltreated children are unable to identify the factors behind interpersonal problems. Instead they organize their lives around a belief that "None of it's my fault," which occasionally may oscillate with its polar opposite, "All of it's my fault."

Repeatedly abused children typically experience relationships in terms of dominance or submission. They are stuck in a *complementary* or codependent mode of relating where there is an exchange of opposite but interdependent behavior, such as parent-child, teacher-student, or perpetrator-victim. In many instances, relating in this way is an appropriate, healthy style of interacting. For abused children, however, this kind of hierarchical relationship is all they know. A healthy relationship, for example one between partners in a loving marriage, involves a fluid back-and-forth pattern between complementary communication and *symmetrical* communication where there is mutual give-and-take and the exchange of similar behavior. Abused children are often incapable of engaging in symmetrical communication because they have rarely felt the joys of reciprocal interaction that is based in respect and acceptance.

For these reasons, along with the unconscious urge to reenact past traumas, maltreated children are likely to become involved in relationships that bear a striking resemblance to abusive experiences in their past. In a study involving 169 maltreated and 98 nonmaltreated children, Shields and Cicchetti (2001) found that bullying was especially prevalent among children who were physically or sexually abused. Also, maltreated children were far more likely to be victimized by their peers. According to Judith Herman (1997), the risk of revictimization is about double for survivors of abuse:

> Almost inevitably, the survivor has great difficulty protecting herself in the context of intimate relationship. Her desperate longing for nurturance and care makes it difficult to establish safe and appropriate boundaries with others. Her tendency to denigrate herself and to idealize those to whom she becomes attached further clouds her judgment. Her empathic attachment to the wishes of others and her automatic, often-unconscious habits of obedience also make her vulnerable to anyone in a position of power or authority. Her dissociative defensive style makes it difficult for her to form conscious and accurate assessment of danger. And her wish to relive the dangerous situation

and make it come out right may lead her into reenactments of the abuse. (p. 111)

One of the big benefits of trauma therapy is that once survivors of abuse begin reconstructing their painful childhoods, they rarely feel the need to abuse others (e.g., their own children).

Although most children who have been abused do not become violent criminals, tragically, some do turn into murderers, rapists, and even serial killers. Over the past twenty years, psychiatrist Dorothy Lewis (who has examined over 150 murderers) and neurologist Jonathan Pincas, have published a series of studies that detail the medical and psychiatric histories of violent criminals. They concluded that the most heinous crimes are committed by people with some combination of childhood abuse, brain injuries, and psychotic symptoms, especially paranoia (Lewis, 1998). Given the neurobiological sequelae of maltreatment, further loss of cortical modulation due to brain injury is likely to increase an individual's impulsivity and capacity for violence.

Bipolar Disorder in Children: What's in a Name?

Though no one doubts that millions of children suffer from the seven core symptoms that we sketch in this chapter, considerable controversy rages about how to classify the underlying disorders. Some mental health professionals tend to zero in on the most dramatic presenting symptom. Thus, a very troubled child who engages in some aggressive behavior toward authority figures might simply be diagnosed with oppositional defiant disorder (ODD) and one who can't sit still with attention deficit hyperactivity disorder (ADHD). Treatment then focuses exclusively on reducing the specific difficulties of one disorder without exploring other symptoms or interpersonal dynamics.

One emerging view mirrors our own in that it also lumps the seven core psychological symptoms together under one diagnostic classification; however, in this case, the overriding problem is not complex post-traumatic stress disorder (PTSD), but rather early onset bipolar disorder. Though this hypothesis accounts for the same phenomena, it makes very different assumptions about what causes the child's distress and what to do about it.

(continued)

(continued)

In their recently published *The Bipolar Child,* Demitri and Janice Papolos (1999) claim that bipolar disorder—rather than PTSD—is "a seriously neglected public health problem" (p. 4). In their view, bipolarity (which originally was used to designate swings between depression and mania) can masquerade as numerous other disorders including ADHD, obsessive-compulsive disorder (OCD), depression, borderline personality disorder, and psychosis. They identify behaviors such as the following as common among bipolar children: oppositionality, impulsivity, risk taking, depression, low self-esteem, learning disabilities, poor short-term memory, lack of organization, hypersexuality, suicidal thoughts, and delusions. The Papoloses link these psychological symptoms to the very same biological abnormalities that we have just discussed—such as damage to the hippocampus and hypothalamus and an overactive stress response. However, from their standpoint, these biological abnormalities are inherited—a function of a faulty set of genes that are passed on from parents. Any role that experience may play in gene expression is never considered.

To illustrate their theoretical stance, the authors cite the case of William, a twelve-year-old boy who was distractible, moody, and often fought with peers. They observe his two personas, quoting the boy as follows:

> It's like I have two minds, one for living and one for fighting—like two different organisms with two different sets of logic, and they seem to have no connection to each other. When my fighting self, William Fight, takes over, he is unscarable, invulnerable. (p. 186)

The other persona is called "William Live," who is optimistic. "He even thinks I still may be able to go back to being normal," the boy says (p. 187). As previously explained, the fragmentation of identity is a common response to child abuse. In fact, as the Papoloses note, when he goes to bed, William fears both physical and sexual abuse. Curiously, in their interpretation of the case, William is seen as himself causing his own fears. It's assumed that his environment is safe and that he is simply overreacting. It doesn't appear to occur to the authors that his symptoms may reflect an attempt to cope with painful life events such as actual or threatened abuse.

In the final analysis, what's the difference between diagnosing a child with the seven core symptoms as suffering from bipolar disorder versus complex PTSD? It depends. At stake is the course of treatment. Though both models often rely on a combination of drugs and therapy

(continued)

(continued)

drugs are the primary form of treatment for bipolar disorder. In contrast, when drugs are used to treat PTSD, they play an adjunctive role. Long-term outcome studies are needed to solidify the scientific foundation for what works best.

Alteration in the System of Beliefs

Repeated trauma shatters a child's system of beliefs. Unable to envision a way out of their inner turmoil, traumatized children become hopeless about the future. For example, one fourteen-year-old boy whose American foster parents rescued him from the streets of Brazil at ten, didn't feel any relief about his change in circumstances because "I never expected to live" (personal communication). Likewise, another severely traumatized boy noted that he gave up using his imagination at age six because "imagination is hope and I couldn't have hope" (Silberg, 1998). Unfortunately, hopelessness may lead to antisocial attitudes. Without the support of a loving family, children may be incapable of developing basic moral values such as empathy, kindness, compassion, honesty, and responsibility.

Despair, hate, and the desire for revenge are an understandable response to abuse or neglect. Unfortunately, without appropriate support or mental health treatment, traumatized children are likely to understand these feelings—not as the residue of something uniquely horrible that has happened to them, but as a guide for action. If they latch on to a malignant belief system that promotes acting on these negative emotions, disaster may ensue. As Bruce Perry (1997) writes, distorted belief systems fuel violence:

> Belief systems, in the final analysis, are the major contributors to violence. Racism, sexism, misogyny, children as property, idealization of violent "heroes," cultural tolerance of child maltreatment, tribalism, jingoism, nationalism—all unleash, facilitate, encourage, and nurture violent individuals. Without these facilitating belief systems and modeling, neglected and abused children would carry their pain forward in less violent ways. (p. 139)

Once this vicious cycle gets started, it may be difficult to stop. Hateful feelings, which result in antisocial acts, simply produce more rage and alienation.

Although there is no substantiation that Eric Harris and Dylan Klebold, who led the killing spree at Columbine High School in the spring of 1999, suffered early childhood trauma, ample evidence suggests that a malignant belief system played a pivotal role in their murderous rampage. A hateful ideology justified the thirteen murders in the eyes of the killers. It was widely reported that when a girl told one of the boys that she believed in God, he responded by saying, "There is no God," and shot her in the head. As a journalist (Gibbs, 1999) reports:

> And it was also, as we now know too well, Adolf Hitler's birthday. In the handwritten diary of one of the suspects, the anniversary, say the police, was clearly marked as a time to "rock and roll." Some members of Harris' and Klebold's clique, tagged in derision a few years before as the Trenchcoat Mafia, had embraced enough Nazi mythology to spook their classmates. They reportedly wore swastikas on black shirts, spoke German in the halls, reenacted World War II battles, played the most vicious video games, talked about whom they hated, whom they would like to kill. (pp. 26-27)

The home videos Harris and Klebold made before their deaths, as reported by Gibbs and Roche (1999), also show evidence of their all-consuming hatred and desire for retaliation. They speak of all those they hate: "niggers, spics, Jews, gays, f—ing whites" (p. 42). The list includes names of specific people who humiliated them or who did not stand by them. "I hope we kill 250 of you," Klebold says. "It's going to be like f—ing Doom. Tick, tick, tick, tick . . . Haa! That f—ing shotgun is straight out of Doom" (Gibbs and Roche, 1999, p. 42).

Fortunately, connections with caring adults can be crucial in helping traumatized children develop constructive ways to channel aggressive impulses so that they don't succumb to the lure of malevolent beliefs and violent acting out.

CONCLUSION

A growing body of evidence links childhood abuse and neglect with significant brain changes that impede the maturation of the brain, disrupt memory and learning, and fragment brain functioning. These new findings help explain the cognitive, emotional, and behavioral problems typically seen in abused and neglected children. Thus, the common symptoms of troubled children—hyperarousal, impulsive aggressiveness, dissociative responses, memory disturbances, and learning problems can be seen from a new perspective. Both abuse and neglect overwhelm the stress response, leading to damage to key parts of the brain. In addition, neglect by itself can warp neurological development as it deprives the brain of the interpersonal experiences crucial for growth.

Safe attachments help children regulate stress-related emotions because nurturing actually builds the biological capacities that moderate the negative effects of stress and promote psychological health. Unfortunately, abused children often lack this needed buffer. Not only must they process overwhelming experiences, but they are also often stuck in attachment relationships rooted in fear. Dissociation is a self-preserving escape route from such a painful predicament. However, new, healthier relationships with others may be able to undo many of the devastating effects of abuse. Remarkably, research is now showing that areas of the hippocampus, a structure thought to be damaged by abuse, can also regenerate neurons. In the next chapter, we illustrate the recovery process.

Chapter 5

Healing the Brain: An Interactive Approach to Treating PTSD and Complex PTSD in Children

At present, only a tiny fraction of the millions of children suffering from PTSD and complex PTSD are receiving appropriate mental health treatment. Sadly, children such as the girls whom we introduced in the preceding chapters—Brittany, who was diagnosed with PTSD in the wake of a fire in her home, and Jessica, who developed complex PTSD as a result of family violence and sexual abuse by her uncle—often suffer in silence. Likewise, some abused children are labeled as "bad" or "difficult" and get caught in a vicious cycle whereby they manifest troublesome symptoms and caretakers respond by punishing them—thus exacerbating their mental health problems. Others get stuck in the child welfare system and repeatedly experience loss and abandonment. Furthermore, as mentioned earlier, those children who end up in a therapist's office are often misdiagnosed with disorders such as ADHD, depression, anxiety, or bipolar disorder—and may, as a result, not respond well to treatment. Another barrier to effective treatment is that therapy specifically designed for child victims of trauma remains in its infancy. Although mental health professionals have made great strides in developing treatment models for adults with PTSD, only recently have they directed their attention toward children. Though children with complex PTSD typically suffer from biological impairments, purely biological interventions (i.e., psychoactive drugs), often have only a limited effect. In fact, we believe that a new set of interpersonal experiences, which generate new ways of thinking, feeling, and behaving, is needed to put brain development back on track.

We begin this chapter by discussing the goals of treatment. Next, we map out the three phases of the therapy process: (1) safety and stabilization, (2) symptom reduction and memory work, and (3) developmental skills. We also include a section on adjuncts to therapy such as exercise/movement and healing touch. The treatment concepts presented in this chapter can be used not only by child and family therapists, but also by other adults who interact with traumatized children including school counselors, teachers, caseworkers, parents, and foster parents. We illustrate the course of treatment through the case studies of Brittany and Jessica.

THERAPEUTIC GOALS: AN OVERVIEW

In Chapters 3 and 4, we described how childhood trauma can impede the hierarchical maturation of the brain, and impair memory and learning. Trauma, research suggests, fragments brain functioning by uncoupling the emotional and cognitive systems from one another, lessening the capacity of the right and left hemispheres to work together, and interfering in the development of brain areas (e.g., hippocampus and prefrontal cortex) that have major integrative and inhibitory functions. From a biological perspective, treating traumatized children requires reorganizing brain functioning (strengthening the working relationship among the different parts of the brain) and creating a physiological state that promotes healthy brain development.

Scientists used to believe that we are given a finite number of cells at birth and are doomed to lose cells as we age. However, new research is showing that specific areas of the human hippocampus are capable of regenerating new nerve cells (Eriksson et al., 1998). In fact, evidence from animal studies shows that the hippocampus may be very responsive to experience (Kempermann, Kuhn, and Gage, 1997, 1998).[1] For example, adult rats housed in an enriched environment had increased neurogenesis in the hippocampus, which was associated with improved spatial memory (Nilsson et al., 1999). According to neuroscientist Bruce McEwen (2002), animal research has revealed that stress-induced damage to neurons is reversible. He (2001) explains that

> As far as neurogenesis is concerned, both glucocorticoids and NMDA receptor activation inhibit dentate granule neuron formation by a common process, whereas, serotonin appears to be an enhancer of neurogenesis via 5HT1A receptors. Moreover,

neurogenesis can be increased by such events as exercise and an enriched environment, and suppressed by acute and chronic stressors. (p. 83)

An intriguing study by Nijenhuis, Ehling, and Krikke (2002) found that recovery from dissociative identity disorder, a disorder invariably linked to a history of overwhelming childhood trauma, was associated with a 9 to 18 percent increase in hippocampal volume. Although this study suggests that experience may promote neurogenesis in the hippocampus, to date, no studies on humans have specifically documented that experience can increase neurogenesis. Multiple problems impede this type of research on humans. For example, MRI imaging studies are not capable of reaching to the cellular level. Also, many uncertainties remain regarding the factors leading to a smaller hippocampus in humans. One study by De Bellis, Keshavan, and colleagues (1999) showed that girls with a history of child abuse had a smaller overall cerebral volume with larger ventricles, but did not show a smaller hippocampus. McEwen (2001) suggests that one possible explanation could be that damage to the hippocampus seen in adult subjects with a childhood history of abuse comes from the accumulative effects of ongoing trauma.

Although we cannot directly apply animal research to humans, the animal data are intriguing and suggest that early intervention with maltreated children and positive life experiences (e.g., healthy relationships, symptom reduction, movement/exercise, cognitive stimulation) may be able to reverse some of the brain impairments now linked to chronic stress (Francis et al., 2002). Many more studies, including longitudinal ones, are needed to determine the precise effects of positive experience on the brain.

Treatment Goals

Psychobiological:

- Restore the natural hierarchy in the brain by decreasing the reactivity of the stress response and enhancing the inhibitory capacities of the cortex.
- Create a physiological state that promotes healthy brain development through the modulation of emotion.

(continued)

(continued)

- Enhance integrative functions by helping the child to process experience through the various modes of experience.
- Build, reorganize, and strengthen new brain circuitry through experiences that generate new ways of thinking, feeling, and behaving.

Psychological (Adapted from the ISSD Guidelines for Treatment, 2000):

- Help the child learn how to regulate her emotions.
- Promote acceptance of painful feelings.
- Promote the direct expression of feelings in healthy attachments and relationships.
- Help the child to reduce symptomatic behavior, e.g., withdrawing or acting out.
- Desensitize traumatic memories and correct the faulty beliefs about life caused by traumatic events.
- Promote a unified identity by helping the child achieve a sense of cohesiveness about her own thoughts, feelings, and behavior.
- Enhance motivation for growth and future success.

Family:

- Learn that the child's behavior is part of an interactional process (system).
- Change family patterns of communication that maintain and reinforce symptomatic behavior.
- Reinforce responsibility and accountability for *all* behavior.
- Accept responsibility for abuse, express repentance, apologize for lack of protection, and offer reparation. (This goal assumes that the child continues to live with his family of origin where maltreatment occurred.)
- Enhance attachment—closeness and connection—as well as autonomy.
- Stay in charge through the use of empathic limit setting.
- Use explicit communication that does not deny, distort, or disconfirm.
- Encourage the child/family to accept *all* emotions.
- Discourage emotional contagion by enhancing personal boundaries.

Ultimately, treatment must reduce the pathological effects of chronic stress by enhancing the inhibitory and integrative capacities of the brain, thus restoring the balance of power between the emotional and cognitive systems of the brain. As Joseph LeDoux (1996) points out, all forms of psychotherapy involve a process "through which our neocortex learns to exercise control over evolutionary old emotional systems" (p. 21). In PTSD, the stress response system becomes hyperreactive, and in complex PTSD, evidence suggests that the hierarchy of the brain is put in further jeopardy by the abnormal development and functioning of the cortex (e.g., left hemisphere, prefrontal cortex, anterior cingulate). An underdeveloped cortex is less able to modulate and inhibit the lower reactive parts of the brain. As we have learned, the cognitive and emotional systems are connected by complex feedback loops. Normally, our thinking helps us to process our emotions and our emotions help us clarify our thinking. In the case of many traumatized children, these systems aren't able to enhance each other. The prefrontal cortex cannot be fully activated because children are experiencing too much anxiety and arousal. Typically, treatment begins with techniques that are aimed at reducing stress and helping children find new ways to regulate their emotions and calm themselves. This step, in turn, enables children to develop their cognitive resources. Strengthening cognition further enhances the ability to regulate emotions.

Healing also involves improving the flow of information throughout the brain. Traumatic memories are more apt to create symptoms because the "memories" are often stuck in one mode of experience. For example, Brittany was locked into behaviorally reenacting elements of the fire in her play, and Jessica was overwhelmed by feelings of anxiety and hopelessness. Likewise, because traumatic memories are often firmly lodged in the right hemisphere, children tend to be controlled by negative emotions (e.g., fear, helplessness, or despair) and self-defeating behaviors (e.g., avoidance, immobility, or aggression). Thus, an important goal of treatment is to help children process experience through as many modalities as possible (e.g., images, thoughts, emotions, sensations, and movement), and to design experiences that can activate both hemispheres, especially the left (e.g., experiences that stimulate positive emotions and encourage initiative and action). The brain is functioning at its best when *all* parts are joining forces to meet life's challenges.

To rebuild brain circuitry, traumatized children need a new set of interpersonal experiences. They must first learn that people are not always a source of pain, but can actually provide comfort and support. By learning to reach out to others, they can begin to internalize healthy ways of processing their feelings. Abuse teaches children that feelings are shameful rather than a valid piece of information for guiding actions. Each time a child takes a step to bring his feelings into awareness (e.g., asks for and receives validation of painful feelings from a parent rather than banishing and/or acting out on those feelings), he is actually helping to rewire his brain. Thousands of these steps and experiences do add up, altering brain structure and functioning.

Drugs can also help alter brain chemistry. For instance, SSRIs (and some anticonvulsant medications) can dampen the reactivity of the limbic system and perhaps enhance activity in the cortex. Currently, SSRIs are considered the drugs of choice in the treatment of PTSD (Davidson, 2000). New types of drugs are being introduced in the treatment of PTSD, including CRF antagonists, neuropeptide Y enhancers, drugs to downregulate cortisol receptors, anticonvulsants, and anti-adrenergic agents (Friedman, 2000). Furthermore, drugs that block the effects of opioids can be effective in inhibiting dissociative symptoms. Bruce Perry tells the story about being summoned to the emergency room to treat a traumatized adolescent girl who was in a catatonic state. After an injection of naloxone, she woke up and was able to respond normally (Perry, 2000b). Although drugs can have some remarkable effects, they are generally not sufficient to change brain circuitry by themselves. Research shows that new experiences are the most effective way to change the pattern of connections between nerve cells, networks, and systems (Ratey, 2001).

Treatment Overview

According to Steinberg, Pynoos, and Goenjian (1996), the following treatment options are available to treat PTSD in children:

- Psychoeducational approaches
- Social skills training
- Psychodynamic therapy

(continued)

(continued)

- Cognitive-behavioral therapy
- Pharmacological therapies
- Educational assistance
- Remedial interventions to address developmental disturbance

Treatment that occurs in an individual, group, family, classroom, or community setting typically combines one or more of these options. (p. 355)

For treatment to be effective, therapy also needs to address family issues. Symptoms typically stem from not only past experience, but also current interactions with family members. In most cases, the therapist must design a three-pronged treatment plan. Although *cognitive/behavioral* interventions address problematic behaviors and help the child build new skills, *psychodynamic* interventions are needed to help integrate traumatic memories and emotions along with buried parts of the self. At the same time, the therapist must pay close attention to family interactions—sequences of action and reaction—to root out any that maintain and reinforce symptoms. The *family* component addresses issues revolving around family hierarchy, patterns of communication, parental conflict, covert alliances, and projection of conflict. Typically, the therapist assumes the role of a "coach" who helps the parents understand the child's unconscious dynamics, gives them directives (a plan of action) designed to alter unhealthy patterns of interaction, and teaches parents more effective ways to communicate. If the child remains in the home where the maltreatment occurred, the parents need to accept responsibility for the abuse, apologize to the child for the lack of protection, and offer reparation (Madanes, 1990).

DEMYSTIFYING THE THERAPY PROCESS

Based on her clinical work with adult survivors of child abuse, Judith Herman (1997) mapped out three essential phases of trauma therapy: (1) *safety*, (2) *remembrance and mourning*, and (3) *reconnection*. During the safety phase, the therapist works on regulating emotion, acknowledging the trauma, reducing symptomatic behavior, maintaining normal functioning, and enhancing social support systems. In the case of an adult who might engage in self-mutilating behavior such as cutting her wrists with a pen knife from time to time, safety might entail setting up a therapeutic contract whereby she would agree to substitute less self-destructive ways to regulate her disturbing emotions. Remembrance and mourning involves processing traumatic memories and correcting maladaptive patterns of behavior. Reconnection focuses on moving forward to tackle challenges in the present.

Herman's model does not carry over directly to children because unlike adults, treatment must also address the developmental needs of a child. We set forth three analogous stages for treating children: (1) *safety and stabilization,* (2) *symptom reduction and memory work,* and (3) *developmental skills.* Another contrast between child therapy and adult therapy is a greater fluidity between the stages. The therapeutic work associated with different stages may happen concurrently. For example, addressing a problem associated with school attendance may require a child to work on exploring painful emotions and memories that may be interfering with attention and concentration.

Although assessment marks the beginning of treatment, it is actually an ongoing process throughout therapy. Therapists are always incorporating new information, revising hypotheses, and evaluating the effectiveness of their interventions. At the outset of treatment, clinicians typically conduct assessment interviews with the child and his parents. To gather more information, they may also administer a number of assessment instruments, such as the Trauma Symptom Checklist for Children (Briere, 1996), Child Dissociative Checklist (Putnam, Helmers, and Trickett, 1993), and the Child Sexual Behavior Inventory (Friedrich et al., 1992). In young children, developmental testing should be part of the assessment. With older children and adolescents, an evaluation of academic skills is often necessary. Children are routinely given a medical exam to rule out health problems, including sexually transmitted diseases.

Ultimately, therapists must assess the impact of trauma on the child's overall personality development. They must understand the mechanisms the child uses to regulate his emotions. How does he find comfort? Who does he go to? What does he do when upset? What is his pattern of arousal? What trauma-related symptoms and processes are operating—flashbacks, intrusive thoughts, reenactments, fears? What about dissociative symptoms—trance states, forgetfulness and/or amnesia, imaginary friends,[2] and hallucinations? Are there somatic symptoms such as headaches, stomach pains, or a loss of sensation to pain? Does the child show signs and symptoms of other trauma-related conditions (e.g., attachment disorder, depression, obsessive-compulsive disorder, substance abuse)? How exactly are family members interacting? What family patterns of communication are reinforcing symptomatic behavior? What changes need to be made in the school environment? How can the community—church, neighborhood, extended family, and friends—help? Everyone needs to be on the treatment train pulling in the same direction—toward health. For children with complex PTSD, family therapy typically needs to be conducted concurrently. Besides individual sessions with the child, the therapist usually includes some family sessions and some sessions only with the parents.

STAGE ONE: SAFETY AND STABILIZATION

Creating a Safe, Predictable Environment

Before beginning the work of therapy, the child must be safe and protected from perpetrating adults. To ensure safety, limits and boundaries need to be established. In Jessica's case, her abusive father had to be removed from the family and his visits had to be supervised. Maintaining a predictable daily structure both reinforces a child's sense of control and counteracts the tendency to regress and become fully immersed in the traumatic past. For example, by going back to school, Jessica was also focusing on developmental tasks rather than just simply processing her abuse memories.

Stopping Self-Destructive Behaviors

Often the first task of therapy is to put an immediate halt to all self-destructive or violent behavior. We cannot stand by while a child puts himself or others in danger. Unfortunately, a traumatized child often sees dangerous behavior as normal. "Gouging and scratching, that's just what I do sometimes," said Jessica. We can explain to a child that abuse often leads to strange behavior. After discussing with the child exactly what the problematic behavior is and when it manifests itself, the therapist can help the child develop new coping strategies for whatever circumstances trigger the behavior. It is difficult for children to renounce symptomatic behavior if they don't know about any other options. Jessica, for instance, was asked to think of things she could say to herself and do whenever she felt self-destructive urges. Making a contract with a child can be useful (Waters and Silberg, 1996). For example, a child might sign a piece of paper requiring her to do the following:

- When I am upset, I will not cut myself (hurt my little brother, harm the hamsters, punch holes in the wall, etc.).
- I will take inner control by counting to ten (taking big deep breaths, closing my eyes, and saying to myself, "I am a good person," etc.).
- I will take external control by talking to someone (using the trampoline, punching bag, taking a walk, writing, drawing, etc.).

To enhance motivation, the therapist, child, and parent can work together to add incentives—such as privileges and rewards—as the child begins to abide by the contract.

Using Time-Outs to Provide Safety

With young children, therapists can teach parents to use time-outs, one of the most effective behavioral interventions for stopping dangerous behavior. Time-out can be used even in instances when a child is out of control (e.g., hurting himself or destroying property), if the adult follows these steps:

1. Contain/hold the child while calming and soothing him until he regains emotional control. (It is crucial that the adult remains calm. It is through the coregulation of states that the adult moves the child's emotional state from distraught to relaxed. This step takes time and patience.)

(continued)

(continued)

2. When the child is calm, have him sit for two to five minutes. (For very young children, using a sand timer that the child can watch, counting, say to twenty, etc., may promote a state of calm and bolster coping capacities.)
3. Review the situation that precipitated conflict, and discuss more adaptive behavior. If noncompliance was the cause, make sure the child follows through with the original request. If social conflict triggered the loss of control, the child should return to the situation and role-play socially appropriate alternatives.
4. Praise the child for following through with the request or practicing alternative solutions to the problem. Steps three and four ensure that *all* interactions end successfully and positively. Without the positive replay of the situation, negative behavior is likely to escalate. Typically, parents, teachers, or others in authority get so caught up in the temper tantrum or punishment that they forget to follow through on the original directive or to teach socially acceptable alternatives.

A time-out is enforced when redirection, loss of privileges, and/or social problem-solving strategies have failed to deter negative behavior. The following script contains prompts that are typically used during this procedure:

A. "It looks like you need some time to calm down before you can go back to the group."
B. "Tell me when you are ready to sit quietly so that I can start the sand timer."
C. "Watch the sand go down."
D. "You were able to sit quietly." (praise)
E. (If noncompliance was the issue) "Let's now clean up the toys." (If conflict triggered the loss of control) "Tell me what was going on. So you were (name feeling). What could you have done? What else?"
F. "Let's practice (pretend) . . . I'll be . . . and you say . . ."
G. "You did such a good job you were able to . . . (name some specific behavior that was adaptive)."
H. "Next time you will be able to . . . (repeat above statement) and maybe even . . . (suggestions that prime future behavior)."

Psychoeducation on Trauma and Its Effects

Education empowers and helps absolve the child of blame. Therapy begins by sharing with the child and her family some thoughts about the problems the child is experiencing. Therapists should emphasize that the child's problematic behavior constitutes an understandable response to overwhelming experiences. Metaphors can be particularly useful to explain the child's baffling symptoms. Silberg (1998) suggests that a therapist might say, "Kids who tell me about horrible things that have happened to them often experience the bad memories as if they are happening now. Like a broken jack-in-the-box, these scary thoughts just pop up without your having to turn the crank" (Silberg, 1998).

Abused children are prone to developing their own faulty explanations for dissociative symptoms such as flashbacks, amnesia, auditory hallucinations, and depersonalization. For instance, an abused child who relies on imaginary friends as a coping mechanism might think that he is besieged by "aliens." Psychologist Joy Silberg (1996a) stresses that such notions, no matter how bizarre, should always be "understood as the child's attempt at a logical theoretical framework to make sense of their own experiences" (p. 118). After all, dissociative symptoms are not always easy for adults to understand. Silberg recommends giving children user-friendly definitions. She gives the following examples of simplified explanations:

> [For flashbacks] Sometimes, if we try really hard to forget something, we stick it away far back in our brain too quickly without putting it away really neatly or carefully, just to get rid of it. Sometimes those memories can push themselves back out as if they're saying "Remember me." They come back so quick and fast that they almost seem real, not like memories at all. What we need to do is just put them away better so they don't pop out and scare you when you're not expecting them. We can work together so that I can help you to do that with your scary memories. (p. 120)

> [For experiencing themselves as distinct parts] People's minds are made in a wonderful way (or "God made people in a wonderful way," introducing the idea of God as a positive world

force that can have a healing effect over time). When things get really, really scary and hard to take, the brain has special ways of helping children. It can help children forget really bad things. Sometimes separate parts of the brain can take over so kids won't remember stuff that was really bad. It's important to stay friends with all parts of your mind so we can find out how they have helped you and how they can keep on helping you. (p. 120)

[For auditory hallucinations] Sometimes when children keep hearing something, like someone yelling at them "You're dumb," it can get stuck in their mind like a broken tape and then they just keep hearing it again and again. I can help you with some tricks for fixing that broken tape. (p. 119)

Therapists should also provide a brief sketch of the recovery process. Usually, the length of treatment depends on the severity of the presenting symptoms and the support the family can provide. With children such as Brittany who experience a single traumatic event and have a supportive family, progress is likely to be speedy and treatment relatively brief—perhaps ten sessions or fewer. In contrast, Jessica, who suffered repeated traumas in a chaotic household, needed more extensive individual and family therapy. She is also likely to need intermittent treatment as she moves from one developmental stage to another and her needs change. Often the length of treatment cannot be determined ahead of time. Even in the most severe cases, therapy may not take years, particularly with early identification and intervention. Experts in childhood trauma have suggested that "it is appropriate to maintain an open-minded and hopeful stance about the possibility of rapid treatment even for the most severe presentation which has occurred in many cases" (ISSD Task Force on Children and Adolescence, 2000, p. 118).

Treatment: Stage One

Brittany

In the wake of the fire, Brittany's parents increased their level of nurturing and were careful not to add new stresses to her life. In addition, they spent more time with her and made sure that she had ample time for unstructured play. Her teachers also planned some soothing sensory activities such as play with sand and water. Regarding Brittany's generalized anxieties, such as not wanting to leave her grandmother's house, her parents were advised to continue her normal routine. They expressed their sympathy, noting that this was a hard time, but also asked her to engage in her regular activities—even if they sometimes made her uncomfortable. Brittany was soon enjoying being back with her friends at school, shopping for groceries with her dad, and taking long trips to the park with her grandmother.

Jessica

Jessica and her therapist, "F.W.," began discussing situations that would trigger the urge to scratch her arms. Jessica soon noticed that her self-mutilating behavior had emerged as a way to express intense anger and rage. She made a list of things she could say to herself and do when she felt the tightening in her stomach—a list she taped to her mirror. Her favorite self-talk was "stay cool." She would also imagine herself as a fairy princess dressed in a flowing white gown with a magic wand that had the power to do anything. She made a list of people she could go to when she was having difficulty controlling her self-destructive impulses, and also decided to keep a journal in which she expressed these feelings of rage as they surfaced She signed a contract that also included rewards and privileges for following through with the plan.

Fear had paralyzed Jessica. She said she rarely attended school because it made her feel anxious. She had few friends and spent most of her time in her room. Thus, one of the initial goals of treatment was to normalize functioning. Oftentimes, the anxieties and conflicts of parents mirror those of the child, inadvertently contributing to the child's symptomatic behavior. Jessica's mother, for instance, said she had a hard time insisting Jessica attend school because she knew how anxious Jessica got. She too, had suffered through school-related fears. Also, she felt guilty about "all she had put her through." Both Jessica and her mother soon agreed that Jessica needed to return to school. She decided that she wanted to go with a friend and have her mother drive her to school rather than ride the bus. They also role-played situations at school that Jessica worried about, such as being teased or being called on by the teacher to answer a question. Incentives for attending school were built into the plan. Jessica was encouraged to socialize more with her family and friends. She also decided to join the youth group in her church.

STAGE TWO: SYMPTOM REDUCTION AND MEMORY WORK

Reducing Arousal and Regulating Emotion

In this stage of treatment, a critical challenge involves helping traumatized children learn healthy ways to reduce emotional arousal. Traumatized children need to learn how to calm down without the use of dissociation. One common strategy is progressive relaxation that reduces the harmful effects of stress and restores the natural rhythms of the body. The child can be taught to relax by concentrating on slowing his breathing and alternately tightening, holding, and eventually relaxing all the muscle groups in the body. Even young children can learn this technique. For example, they can have fun letting their entire body go limp and pretending to be a Raggedy Ann doll.

Dr. Herbert Benson (1996), founder of Harvard's Mind/Body Medical Institute, calls the state of calm, which counteracts the fight-or-flight response, the *relaxation response.* In this state, heart rate, breathing rate, metabolic rate, and blood pressure are lowered. When we relax the mind, the body also calms down. According to Benson, this response, which relies on the cortex's ability to regulate the limbic system, can be elicited by following two steps: "(1) Repeat a word, sound, prayer, phrase, or muscular activity. (2) Passively disregard everyday thoughts that come to mind, and return to your repetition" (p. 134). Autogenic training and meditation can also decrease arousal and restore the natural rhythms of the body, as can soothing activities such as warm baths, water and sand play, and singing. Trauma therapist Beverly James (1994) writes that, "children readily learn to employ self-soothing 'power' techniques when we characterize the techniques as being used by whoever might be heroic to the child—firefighters, Olympic champions, or teenagers" (p. 72).

When emotions spin out of control, adults need to convey the following message: "I am here to support you when you are upset and to help you find a better way to express the emotions and impulses you are feeling." Thus, adults can help the child recover from a dysphoric state. Considering how provocative these children can be, it can be a real challenge for teachers, parents, and even therapists to remain calm and empathic and not get caught up in the child's negative mood. Emotions, as we have noted, are contagious. Getting someone else to feel the same emotion we are experiencing is one of the most basic techniques that human beings use to feel understood. Rather than becoming enmeshed in the negative emotions of the traumatized child, adults must try to empathize, and simultaneously maintain a "meta-mood" of relative calmness. In some ways, it is a contest of moods. Whose mood will win—the child's negative mood or the adult's positive one?

Adults can use a wide range of strategies to transform a child's negative emotional state. With young children, nonverbal techniques such as gentle touch, a calm, low voice, and refocusing attention on pleasant stimuli often work. Pictures, stories, and other roundabout ways to access emotions can also be used. For instance, you might say to a preschooler, "You look kind of mad. Sometimes when I am feeling unhappy, a hug feels so good. . . . Other times I like reading about *Alexander and the Terrible, Horrible, No Good, Very Bad Day,* or drawing a mad, very crabby picture." Typically, these nonverbal approaches serve to encourage a child to talk about what happened to cause these feelings and how she might act next time the same source of frustration arises. With older children, parents can provide cues to convey to the child that her emotions are beginning to escalate and that she needs to do something to regain control, such as use "self-talk" or relaxation techniques. If the child's behavior continues to deteriorate, removing her from the situation, or instituting a time-out can be useful in breaking this negative cycle. As children mature and become healthier, they gradually learn to regulate their own emotional states. Eventually, they can spontaneously shift to more pleasant stimuli and channel their emotions in positive and creative ways.

Finding Comfort from Others

Another crucial step in managing the overwhelming emotions stemming from trauma involves teaching victims to reach out to others for support and comfort. Children who have experienced a single traumatizing event generally do not have difficulty seeking comfort from adults. In contrast, for maltreated children, abuse has shattered their ability to trust. These children must go against the grain of their prior experience to seek and expect nurturance. Usually, distraught people seek connections with others. This impulse is innate. Young children are naturally drawn to adults for protection and comfort when they feel frightened. Normally, a nurturing parent comforts a child by establishing eye contact, using soothing touch, and a calm, reassuring voice. For maltreated children, however, their cries for help were usually met with indifference or perhaps further abuse. Adults were the source of pain, not comfort.

Abuse "teaches" children that dependency is dangerous. To defend themselves against further hurt, they ward off their feelings of vulnerability and act as if they have no need for affection.

Tragically, some children can become more comfortable with hostility than affection. Harry Stack Sullivan (1953) called this phenomenon *malevolent transformation.* In his words:

> For a variety of reasons, many children have the experience that when they need tenderness, when they do that which once brought tender cooperation, they are not only denied tenderness, but they are treated in a fashion to provoke anxiety or even, in some cases, pain. A child may discover that manifesting the need for tenderness toward the potent figures around him leads frequently to his being disadvantaged, being made anxious, being made fun of, and so on, so that, according to the locution used, he is hurt, or in some cases he may be literally hurt. Under those circumstances, the developmental course changes to the point that the perceived need for tenderness brings a foresight of anxiety or pain. The child learns, you see, that it is highly disadvantageous to show any need for tender cooperation from the authoritative figures around him, in which case he shows something else; and that something else is the basic malevolent attitude, the attitude that one really lives among enemies. (p. 214)

Traumatized children will learn to accept comfort from others if they consistently experience empathy and acts of kindness. However, trust comes in small steps. Even for children such as Brittany, who had single-event PTSD, the "Play Baby" intervention (Wachtel, 1994) can help them accept the need for nurturing without jeopardizing their growing autonomy. Parents can begin by saying something similar to, "You've gotten so big and can do so many things by yourself, but sometimes I just miss my little baby. I remember how little you were when you came home from the hospital. Let's pretend. . . ." Depending on the age of the child and the preferences of the parents, they may wrap the child in a blanket, rock, sing to her, or perhaps pretend to give the "baby" a bottle. Making it a game allows for regression, and at the same time, supports age-appropriate behavior. To avoid unintentionally reinforcing immature behaviors, it is important that the parent initiates the Play Baby game when the child is behaving appropriately. For older children, parents can reminisce about their early childhood—looking at baby pictures, their favorite baby toys, blanket—to communicate that their vulnerable parts can be appropriately nurtured. For example, Jessica, who had walled off her feelings of helplessness, vulnerability, and her need for nurturing into a dissociated identity—"a little girl crying"—quickly warmed to her mother's reminders of the tender loving moments they had shared when she was a baby.

Tolerating Affect

Severely traumatized children are often described as affect-phobic. These children, who tend to believe that *all* emotions are both dangerous and a source of shame, often experience emotional arousal as a hodgepodge of visceral sensations or they feel nothing. For example, they may have difficulty distinguishing between the sensations related to happiness and those associated with fear or anger. Consequently, emotion is often quickly dissociated—disconnected or compartmentalized from awareness. Alternatively, they may try to whip up their emotions to force the body's calming mechanisms to come into play.

Learning to tolerate emotion depends on gaining emotional awareness. Many maltreated children need to go back to square one, that is, to learn to identify and label the emotion(s) they are experiencing. This step takes practice. Healthy affect boundaries—whereby families and caretakers avoid emotional contagion—are essential. Emotional awareness is only possible when those closest to the child do not become enmeshed in his emotional state. Talking about specific feelings helps, as does just sitting back and observing an emotion. For children who have been severely traumatized, even watching their own thoughts can be frightening. The mind, it can be explained, is similar to a television. Scary stuff comes on, but you don't have to do anything; you can just sit back and observe. Weather, Beverly James (1994) writes, can be a great metaphor for affect:

> Weather, like emotion, is always present. You can't make it go away, and you really wouldn't want to, because it makes life interesting. The child can understand that we can deal with any amount of weather if our house is good and strong but that even a small rainstorm can be uncomfortable if we are not used to it or are caught unaware. . . . They learn to notice not only the hurricane but also what happens before, during, an after the storm; they learn the elegant signals our feelings are designed to convey. (p. 71)

Integrating Disavowed Emotions and Accepting Ambivalence

Traumatized children need to learn that it is OK to feel their feelings, particularly distressing ones such as anger, sadness, and anxiety. Feelings, they can be told, will never kill you. Pushing feelings away, however, is what really causes trouble. (Damming up emotions can lead to a variety of health problems, such as body aches, colds, asthma, etc.). As Thich Nhat Hanh (1991), a Vietnamese monk nominated for the Nobel Peace Prize, writes: "If we face our unpleasant feelings with care, affection, and nonviolence, we can transform them into the kind of energy that is healthy and has the capacity to nourish us" (p. 52). The goal of therapy is not to get rid of uncomfortable emotions or thoughts, but to integrate them. As Jim Chu (1998) writes, "These parts of themselves need to be accepted and nurtured rather than hated and rejected. Acceptance and integration of past feelings and behaviors, as opposed to rejection and disavowal, lead to the resolution of these internal conflicts" (p. 88).

Guidelines for Parents and Foster Parents: Setting Limits and Boundaries

All animals that organize into groups develop hierarchies of power and status. Because most groups carry out a variety of functions, several hierarchies usually operate simultaneously. The most basic hierarchy involves the generational lines between parents and children. Parents nurture children who are, in turn, expected to nurture the next generation (Haley, 1987). Since families and individuals go through stages of development, hierarchies change. Over time, a remarkable, but natural, reversal in status and power occurs. Children go from being cared for by their parents, to gradually becoming peers of their parents as they reach adulthood, to taking care of their parents in their old age.

A hierarchy in which parents take charge is an absolute necessity. When parents are not in charge, behavior problems are bound to occur. Obviously, discipline and its flip side, nurturing, are not possible if parents treat children as peers or cede authority to them. Without nurturing, children feel unloved, vulnerable, and insecure. To cope with these troubling feelings, children typically try to gain more control, usually through some form of misbehavior. This acting out may, in turn, trigger anger, rejection, and even abuse in parents, causing a child to feel even more unlovable. Once set in motion, this vicious cycle can be difficult to stop.

Hierarchy can also become confused when family members form alliances to undermine the chain of authority. For example, if a grandmother supports a child's rebellious behavior toward his mother, the mother loses her power to discipline the child. Likewise, when one parent joins with a child against the other parent, parental authority is eroded. The same holds true when a professional joins with a child against a parent. A fundamental rule of organizations is that when coalitions—defined as a joint action against a third person—occur across levels of a hierarchy, they create instability (Haley, 1987). Because maltreated children feel so vulnerable, they may try to manipulate the family hierarchy in an attempt to gain power—often pitting one parent against the other, or a teacher or therapist against their parents. These efforts should be recognized and resisted.

Although rewards are the cornerstone of any behavior plan, children must also be held accountable for any unacceptable behavior. As discussed in Chapter 4, most abused children need external controls to fortify their internal controls. Limits, however, are frightening to

(continued)

(continued)

them because of fears about being out of control. In their minds, the exercise of parental power usually means abuse and humiliation. If parents are able to communicate empathy for the child's perspective, a traumatized child will be less likely to interpret the limits as simply a way to dominate and exploit. Thus, empathic limit setting requires a two-part statement. In the first part, convey an understanding of the child's feelings to show you are on her side. In the second part, make sure to state clearly the boundary that the child has crossed (Chu, 1998). For example, you might say: "I know it's hard for you when your sister says something that hurts your feelings. However, I cannot let you hurt her." Over time, children will internalize the message and start respecting the boundaries you set without any prompting from you.

Trauma therapist Fran Waters (1996) uses the metaphor of a child's favorite dessert to illustrate the principle that recovery involves experiencing all feelings, whatever they may be. For example, if the child likes chocolate chip cookies, he or she can be told that it takes all the ingredients—flour, sugar, butter, salt, baking soda, vanilla, besides the chocolate chips—to make the cookies taste good. Likewise, to develop into a complete person, the child must get in touch with all the parts of the mind. Many traumatized children lack a continuous sense of self when they experience emotions, such as anger, sadness, and joy. Therapy can help them learn to accept and embrace all parts of their mind, including the angry, hateful introjects of perpetrators (Waters and Silberg, 1996). For example, the child can come to understand that the angry part of her mind, which helped her survive by containing her rageful feelings, can continue to provide the strength needed to help her overcome obstacles in the future. By breaking down these internal barriers within the mind, the child builds a stronger, more cohesive sense of self. The traumatized child also needs to learn how to express and accept ambivalence—the simultaneous experiencing of contradictory emotions. As Silberg (1996a) suggests:

> As emotions are expressed, the therapist encourages toleration of the feeling of ambivalence. . . . If feelings can be expressed without guilt or shame and all types and ranges of affects tolerated equally, the child can move away from the rigid compartment-

alization of feelings to tolerance for ambivalence and ambiguity, a clear step towards growth. (p. 125)

Overcoming Avoidance

In acute trauma, avoidance is circumscribed, and treatment usually involves gradual exposure to the specific stimuli that serve as traumatic reminders. In chronic trauma, as in the case of Jessica, fear tends to contaminate all parts of a child's life. Traumatic reminders are everywhere. Joy Silberg (1998) notes that, just being a kid is a traumatic reminder, because being a child automatically puts you in a dependent, and potentially vulnerable position. Thus, avoidance becomes habitual—a way of life. Instead of withdrawing, which usually makes matters worse, children need to learn to initiate action—and operate from their left hemisphere rather than the right. Active coping—identifying challenges and carrying out a plan to meet them—builds self-esteem and a sense of control.

Though trauma survivors need to face situations that stir up painful emotions, they must be allowed to do this at a manageable rate—a process called *desensitization.* To get over her school phobia, Jessica, for example, had her mother accompany her for the first week. With young children, such as Brittany, the presence of a trusted attachment figure—a parent, therapist, or teacher—is crucial in reducing anxiety. Close physical contact with a relaxed, confident, and caring adult can help them learn to tolerate uncomfortable feelings, in part, because young children are particularly susceptible to taking on the emotions of those close to them.

Improving Attention and Chipping Away at Dissociation

Dissociation is a defensive strategy that traumatized children use to cope with overwhelming feelings. They often find themselves entering a trance state, where they do not think, feel, or remember. Eventually, dissociation becomes a neurobiological habit that gets triggered in response to even minor stressors. As one five-year-old girl said, "When I'm scared, even just a little bit scared, my mind walks away" (Waters, 2000). In a nonabusive environment, dissociation is maladaptive and prevents the child from coping with the problems at hand. Therapists use a variety of techniques to help children stay engaged. For example, when a child begins to drift away, he is asked to touch a necklace or other object that acts as a symbolic reminder to stay tuned in to the present situation (Waters, 2000). Other behavioral techniques (e.g., rewards for staying engaged), can be added.

Sometimes traumatized children are amnestic during a stressful interpersonal encounter, such as with a teacher or parent. In these instances, therapists must expect the child to eventually be able to access these memories that she has walled off. One way to encourage "remembering" disavowed behavior is to empathize with her painful feelings that led to the compartmentalization. For instance, "I can understand how someone would get really angry," "feel very sad," etc. The therapist can also have the child "imagine" the forgotten incident or role-play the situation as others have described it. This may lead her to access the memory. Accepting responsibility for all actions allows for greater conscious control over behavior (Silberg, 2000).

Many children are troubled by flashbacks. Some simple behavioral techniques can help him acknowledge the painful sensations and remain connected to his present reality. According to psychiatrist Jim Chu (1998), grounding techniques can be effective in controlling flashbacks:

> A well-lit environment can be helpful in grounding patients, particularly in the evening or at night; often, patients feel compelled to sit in half-darkened rooms, which increases their propensity to lose their bearings in current reality. Contact with other persons (particularly eye contact) is also enormously effective and conveys two critical therapeutic messages: Control of dissociative processes is possible, and other people can be helpful and safe. Finally, use of familiar and soothing objects can be helpful in reorienting patients who are having difficulty with reexperiencing phenomena or other dissociative symptoms. (p. 81)

Bedtime is often a trigger for traumatic memories, particularly if the child was sexually abused. Recurrent nightmares can be another problem. To help children feel less anxious, parents may need to establish a bedtime routine that is comforting, yet empowering, by promoting cognition. For example, a parent may want to play thought-provoking games, read books that metaphorically speak to overcoming adversity, or focus on the positive events of the day.

Underneath the child's dissociative defenses are the frightening memories of abuse. In child therapy, as opposed to adult therapy, clinicians tend to address the traumatic recollections as they relate to current experiences. So, a child who is talking about a humiliating experience in school may suddenly "remember" something from the past where he also felt shame. Therapeutic work would then oscillate between processing specific memories and coping with the present situation. By empathizing with the child's feelings, no matter what they are, therapists can make it easier for him to remember painful experiences.

Memory Work: Issues and Techniques

Though memory work is critical to helping traumatized children recover, therapists must proceed deliberately and cautiously. Traumatic events tend to be stored in bits and pieces—isolated images, sensations, thoughts, feelings, and behaviors—that become dissociated, walled off from the rest of their memory networks (see Figure 5.1). Blocking off painful emotions resulting from trauma often dampens the ability to experience any emotion, even pleasant ones. It is important to remember that although dissociative symptoms and processes can work quite effectively for awhile, such as bulimic eating can soothe, in the long run, these symptoms pose a threat to a child's mental and physical health.

Memory work addresses disturbing events (and the associated emotions) in order to help the child integrate them with other life experiences. Once these painful memories are transformed, they no longer produce feelings of terror and helplessness. As children speak of traumatic experiences within the context of the therapeutic relationship, fragmented perceptual and emotional memories are integrated into the explicit memory system. Eventually, the memories will cease triggering the implicit memory system and a child will be able to remember feeling scared without experiencing the full extent of the original physiological arousal. Also, as memories become part of the conscious memory system, they can be reframed. In other words, by reinterpreting past experiences, a child can restore his sense of efficacy. Furthermore, the positive emotions, feelings of safety and security that are

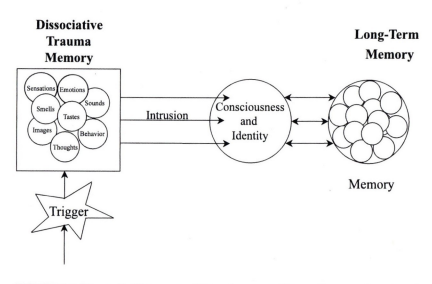

FIGURE 5.1. Traumatic Memory and Consciousness. Traumatic memories are not stored in the usual memory networks. Instead, they tend to be walled off from other long-term memories, stored as disconnected fragments and emotional (implicit/unconscious) memories that are highly unstable and not under voluntary control. Traumatic memories often intrude into awareness when the individual is exposed to reminders of the traumatizing event, or experiences the same emotions (e.g., fear and helplessness) as during the trauma. When trauma survivors experience flashbacks, they typically experience the memories as if they were happening in the present. Adapted from *The Post-Traumatic Stress Disorder Sourcebook* by G. Schiraldi. Copyright 2000 by G. Schiraldi. Used by permission of The McGraw-Hill Companies.

generated in the therapeutic interactions, begin to rest side by side with the painful feelings. Now, whenever the memories resurface, they are much less overwhelming. As a rule, treatment is more effective when the child uses several sensory modalities to process the memories.

Telling the Story

Memory work revolves around helping the child tell the story of the traumatic event(s). The therapist should give the message that he or she is " 'an expert on children who have had really bad things happen to them,' is not afraid of the material and is willing to listen empathetically without being horrified. The therapist also reassures the child that the office is a safe place to talk and together they will work on alleviating painful feelings" (Waters and Silberg, 1996, p. 155). Once in place, the trauma narrative helps alleviate feelings of shame and guilt, as it eliminates the fear and secrecy that keeps memories dissociated. Children understand that they are not to blame for being victimized. When they are telling about the bad things, the accompanying emotions can be intense. To help children manage these negative emotions, therapists can make suggestions, such as encouraging them to take the emotion to a safe place or asking them to turn down the imaginary "volume" dial for their intense feelings (Silberg, 1998).

Typically, the story comes out in bits and pieces over time. In cases where the traumatic event occurred recently, the therapist must walk the thin line of encouraging the child to talk about it, but remain sensitive and not push too hard. Therapists use the metaphor of *titration* to refer to the pacing of memory work. Whereas adults and adolescents can engage in dialogue about specific events, children usually require an indirect approach. Thus, they need to tell their story using dolls, puppets, a sand tray, or role-play. As Nancy Boyd Webb (1999) writes in her book, *Play Therapy with Children in Crisis:*

> Play therapy ingeniously undertakes the hard work of child psychotherapy in the appealing guise of play. Since children behave and think differently from adults, the approach to working with them must reflect this difference. Play therapy has adapted its methods to accommodate to the world of childhood, using the medium of play as the means for communicating symbolically with the child. (p. 29)

Moreover, since trauma seems to be lodged in the right hemisphere, metaphor, the language of the right hemisphere, is ideally suited to accessing and expressing trauma. As Lenore Terr (1990) puts it, metaphor "hits the child on two levels—on the 'story' level and on his own, more internal level. Highly visualized language, after all, is probably the real language of psychic trauma" (p. 302). Artwork, stories, and play all offer numerous opportunities to make use of metaphor.

Some play therapists use a nondirective approach—utilizing the innate healing power of play where mastery gradually comes through abreaction—along with careful interpretation by the therapist. Other play therapists take a more active role. For instance, they may encourage reenactment by providing toys that relate to the trauma and join in the child's play to change specific thoughts, behavior, and trauma-based emotions such as shame and fear. In the case of very young children who are not yet able to engage in complex symbolic play, therapists may have to replay the traumatic events using puppets, dolls, or other props (Hewett, 1999).

In either case, in order to restore the child's sense of control, therapists often add positive endings so that the child begins to feel as if he has "mastered" the trauma. For example, a therapist might symbolically bring a parent in to "rescue" the child or throw the "bad" guys in jail. (Discretion should be used if the child will be testifying in court.) Conducting play therapy is challenging as it involves engaging in a number of activities at the same time, such as observing and describing the child's play; asking the child to describe her play; joining in the play; setting limits when needed; or metaphorically commenting on motivations, feelings, and behavior. The therapist, as Nancy Boyd Webb (1999) sees it, "is simultaneously trying to understand the themes and underlying meaning of the child's play, in order to provide communication that validates the child's feelings while also sharing a new vision to help the child through his or her struggles" (p. 41).

Desensitizing and Transforming Traumatic Memories

Most of us are familiar with the compulsive need to talk about a distressing event. We tell the story again and again until our anxiety begins to abate. The memory can then be smoothly filed away. As with a scrapbook, we want to be able to take it out, look at it, and then put it back on the shelf. Unfortunately, traumatic memories, like a broken record, are involuntarily played over and over again. Therapists can use a variety of special techniques to transform traumatic memories, including cognitive restructuring, healing imagery, and counting and EMDR (eye-movement desensitization and reprocessing).

Cognitive Restructuring

Trauma, by definition, overwhelms the mind's coping capacities. To help control the pain of traumatic memories, the mind automatically churns out a series of distortions and misinterpretations. In his book on DID, psychiatrist Colin Ross (1997) lists several cognitive errors common in abuse survivors:

> I am responsible for the abuse.
> It is wrong to show anger.
> The past is present (i.e., the abuse is still happening to me now).
> I can't trust myself or others. (pp. 161-162)

Survivors believe such statements to be true because this helps them ward off feelings of sadness, rage, and loss. Unfortunately, these distorted thoughts can be destructive, reinforcing symptoms. For example, if a child is convinced that no one can be trusted at all, he cannot possibly begin to form healthy attachments with family members or peers. The goal of cognitive restructuring is to replace these faulty assumptions with more realistic ones about others and the world in general.[3]

To correct these cognitive errors, therapists may need to inform the child about parental mental illness, and/or history of maltreatment, or simply say that no child deserves to be abused. Child psychotherapist Constance Dalenberg (personal communication) has found that some children feel strongly that they deserve abuse, but are quite open to the idea that other children do not deserve abuse. An initial intervention, in these cases, might entail an agreement that a hypothetical "other child" should not be treated so.

Time lines and genograms can be used not only to create a cohesive autobiographical memory, but also to shift responsibility for the maltreatment from the child to the perpetrator. Sandra Wieland (1998), author of *Techniques and Issues in Abuse-Focused Therapy with Children and Adolescents: Addressing the Internal Trauma*, writes:

> For the child to be able to start shifting the internalization of being bad, the child needs to become aware of the role of the larger system in which the abuse and the reactions to the abuse oc-

curred. This larger system includes the family as it has developed through the generations as well as the society around the family, for example, the church. (p. 80)

Wieland mentions that a genogram, a diagram of a child's family tree, can help foster discussion about all of the abuse that occurred in the family. It offers an opportunity to recognize patterns of behavior that have evolved over the years and gather information about family history, culture, alliances, and coalitions.[4]

Healing Imagery

Although cognitive restructuring change thoughts as a way to neutralize painful memories, imaging techniques help children, especially adolescents, alter the disturbing pictures in their mind. According to Sandra Wieland (1998), imaging can help children process flashbacks, work through abuse-related self-perceptions, and explore emotions. In addition, it can help facilitate collaboration between different aspects of the mind. She notes:

> Imaging can be used to help a child, within a safe setting, process a flashback all the way through. The imaging allows the child to bring her present capabilities into the reexperiencing of the past. With this new experience, she realizes she can survive the flashback. In addition, imaging can help the child and therapist identify the distress symbolized by the flashback and the situations triggering flashbacks. When flashbacks are adequately worked through, they usually do not continue to occur. (p. 54)

Wieland cites transcripts from sessions to illustrate how to help children work through flashbacks. In the following excerpt, she shows how she helped a sixteen-year-old named Jenny process the sexual abuse by her father, which took place when Jenny was between the ages of twelve and fifteen (p. 55):

THERAPIST: Before we start to work on the flashback, let yourself go to a place that is peaceful and calm for you . . . and now, knowing that you can go back there, that that place is there for you, let your mind float back to the flashback you had yesterday. And when you are back there, nod your head to let me know. (Jenny tenses and nods.) Tell me what it is you see or what it is you sense.

JENNY: I'm back in the living room at home and my father is threatening me with a knife.

THERAPIST: What do you notice yourself doing or saying?

JENNY: I'm telling him to stop, I'll tell on him.

THERAPIST: And what is he doing?

JENNY: He is laughing. He is saying no one will believe me. Nobody will help me.

THERAPIST: What is happening now?

JENNY: He is chasing me.

THERAPIST: And what do you have now, that you didn't have then, that you can bring into the picture?

Wieland goes on to help Jenny envision a different outcome. After Jenny reports that she sees herself running away, Wieland encourages her to see that she doesn't have to be a victim anymore (p. 56):

THERAPIST: And let yourself feel that running, and feel the opening of the door, and feel the running. And that running is you and you are the one who created it, who did it. You are the one who helped you. (pause) And when you have felt the running and enjoyed the feeling of the running, let me know what is happening.

JENNY: I'm walking; it's great. I'm just walking.

THERAPIST: Tell me about that place where you are walking. (Jenny describes.) And, when you are ready, let your mind go back to that place that was peaceful and calm, that place that was for you. (pause) And when you are ready to come back to the room. . . . What did you notice about what was going on in the flashback?

JENNY: Well, no one could help me, just like he said.

THERAPIST: But someone did help you.

JENNY: I guess I did.

This new sense of mastery will eventually enable Jenny to cope whenever the memory is triggered by present circumstances.

Guided imagery is not the same as hypnosis. Nevertheless, imaging techniques must be used carefully. Wieland (1998) cautions that imaging is not recommended if a child is going to testify in court and needs to remember the exact details of the abuse. Memories of traumatic events (high-arousal experiences), especially those that are brief and limited, are usually more accurate and detailed (Cahill, 1997). These memories, however, can be altered through postevent experiences, such as therapy (Foa, Molnar, and Cashman, 1995; Brown, Scheflin, and Hammond, 1998). Imagery exercises are known to increase suggestion; therefore, they should be undertaken with great caution. When there is an active court case, other techniques should be used to help the child deal with intrusive memories.

Counting and EMDR

Techniques that involve counting and EMDR can also facilitate the processing of traumatic memories and emotions. In *The Psychobiology of Mind-Body Healing,* Ernest Rossi (1993) discusses *symptom scaling* as a way to coordinate the activity of the right and left hemispheres. He writes:

> The right hemisphere may encode a symptom or problem in the analogical-metaphorical processes typical of emotions, body language, and dreams. In this form the problem may not be available to the more linear, logical and rational resolution routines of the left hemisphere. These left hemispheric processes may be accessed and associated with the problem by scaling it, since the left hemisphere is more facile with both numbers and words such as more or less intense, better and worse. (p. 110)

He advocates a therapeutic approach that asks patients:

1. To experience the problem/emotion (presumably activating the right hemisphere).
2. To scale the problem from 1 to 100—with 100 being the worst (thus activating left-hemispheric skills).
3. To tune into the symptom and "notice what changes take place all by themselves." "Does it get stronger or weaker?" "Or change in quality?"

4. To rate their feelings once again from 1 to 100 (the therapeutic exercise ends when the client has made gains expressed by the lowering of the number). (p. 111)

According to Rossi, over time, this technique brings about psychobiological changes. By coordinating left- and right-hemispheric activities, patients can reframe and transform their traumatic experiences.

In a similar technique developed by Frank Ochberg (1996), the client recalls a traumatic memory as the therapist slowly counts to 100. Ochberg speculates that the emotional tone of the memory changes because of new associations to it—namely the therapist's soothing voice. In addition, the time-limited nature of the approach (i.e., it has a distinct beginning, middle, and end) helps the client gain a sense of control over these "involuntary" memories. The client determines when symptoms—intrusive memories—begin and end. In addition to these explanations, we might also presume that the counting exercise activates the left hemisphere and its unique resources.

EMDR, developed in the late 1980s by Dr. Francine Shapiro, can sometimes result in dramatic resolution of PTSD symptoms. EMDR is frequently used as a treatment for adults suffering from a single traumatic event—such as a car accident or earthquake. Amazingly, one or two sessions may eliminate symptoms. Its use as an adjunctive tool for children suffering from complex PTSD is relatively new. According to Tinker and Wilson (1999), authors of *Through the Eyes of a Child: EMDR with Children,* EMDR, which must be conducted by a mental health professional with specialized training as part of an overall treatment plan, can accelerate therapy by being "judiciously applied to traumas and emotional stuck points" (p. 56). In a typical EMDR session, the patient is asked to recall a traumatic memory, hold it in mind while moving her eyes from side to side, following the therapist's moving finger. With children, alternating left-right hemispheric stimulation may involve auditory, kinesthetic, and/or visual input—using, for example, hand taps or drums (Tinker and Wilson, 1999).

Although the precise mechanisms underlying the success of EMDR have not been determined, Shapiro suggests that one reason it works is that the safe therapeutic setting enables survivors to pair positive emotions with traumatic memories. She also believes that healing is a natural outcome of memory processing (Shapiro, 1995).

Tinker and Wilson (1999) trace the effectiveness of EMDR to the simultaneous activation of several sensory modes (e.g., visual, cognitive, emotional, and kinesthetic). As they note, EMDR "may activate processing in both hemispheres or many parts of the brain at the same time, thus facilitating a more complete resolution of the traumatic event than most therapies allow" (p. 19).

This conclusion is buttressed by the preliminary research of Bessel van der Kolk, showing that EMDR seems to promote the transfer of traumatic memories from the right to left hemisphere and enhance collaboration between the emotional and cognitive systems. In van der Kolk's study, PTSD patients underwent neuroimaging studies while listening to a narrative of their traumatic event. The results showed heightened activity in the right hemisphere and deactivation of areas in the left. Following successful treatment using EMDR, brain-imaging studies showed activation in both hemispheres—implying more movement of information from right to left hemisphere, as well as marked increases in the activity of the anterior cingulate—suggesting stronger collaboration between the emotional and cognitive systems of the brain (van der Kolk, Burbridge, and Suzuki, 1997).

It is also possible that the eye movements evoke neurological activation similar to that of REM sleep, which helps the brain process current experiences and also seems to be linked to new learning. High levels of arousal, as we know, freeze eye movements (the "1,000 yard stare" of traumatized soldiers) and block processing (the flow of information). Bruce Perry postulates that it is the patterned, repetitive, stimulation and its effect on the lower centers of the brain (i.e., the brain stem) that makes EMDR an effective therapy. He notes that all healing rituals include this type of input (Perry, 2000b). In the most likely scenario, multiple neurological mechanisms contribute to the success of EMDR.

Treatment: Stage Two

Brittany

When Brittany talked about the fire in a matter-of-fact way, her parents assumed she was coping well. In fact, however, Brittany was reenacting her frightening feelings in her play at school. Daily, she would build a house out of blocks, scream "Fire," and destroy the building. Then, with a dazed look in her eyes, she would wander aimlessly about the room for a few minutes. This repetitive play served to make her more anxious and keep at bay the trauma-related emotions. As part of Brittany's therapy, "P.S." encouraged her to experiment with new empowering scenarios, such as calling 911, or putting out the fire. Small doll figures representing mom, dad, and children were added to the scene. The firemen not only rescued the family from the fire, but also helped allay their fears. Over time, Brittany's play grew increasingly more complex and commanding as she donned a fireman's hat and coat, grabbed the fire engines, and walked about the room putting out fires.

Therapeutic storytelling was also used to help her integrate trauma-related emotions.[5] Her parents were assigned the task of telling her stories that incorporated the feelings that she had locked away. For example, one story discussed "a four-year-old named Jane whose house burned down. However, everyone got out safely, and no one was burned. Fortunately, her mommy and daddy were there to take care of her. They hugged her and whispered softly that everything would be OK, and they were not going to let her get hurt. However, it was not long before the little girl got real mad because she hated not living in her own house. She missed her toys, especially her teddy bear, and her favorite clothes. As time went on, she still wished she could be in her old house, but she was also growing attached to her new house."

Not surprisingly, fire drills, in fact, any loud, screeching noise, terrified Brittany. She would scream and cover her ears. In order to help desensitize her, the teacher carefully prepared her, telling her what to expect. On the days the class practiced fire drills, Brittany was designated "helper of the day," and was asked to ring the bell. At first, the teacher kept Brittany close to him, providing comfort when needed. He then instructed Brittany to hold the hand of her classmate as soon as the bell sounded. After a couple of fire drills, Brittany was able to walk calmly by herself into the courtyard.

Jessica

Given that Jessica, in contrast to Brittany, had endured a series of traumatic events, this part of treatment proved much more challenging.

In an early session, Jessica drew a picture of a container with all her feelings. In response to a question from her therapist, "F.W.," about what she could do to be in charge of her feelings, Jessica said, "Nothing, because there is a little girl inside me crying all the time." Jessica then identified another critical part of herself called "Revenge."

Jessica was frightened by these internal states. Although she knew they were parts of her mind, they felt as though they belonged to somebody else. She became increasingly fearful, withdrawn, and depressed. The more she pretended these parts didn't exist, the more vigorously they seemed to control her behavior. Sometimes for no reason at all, she found herself both crying uncontrollably and yelling.

Jessica's therapist began by helping her identify the feelings contained in these isolated states. Eventually, she recognized that the little girl represented her feelings of fear, shame, and helplessness as well as the need to be nurtured, and "revenge" represented her anger and rage toward her father and the uncle who had abused her. The therapist validated her feelings of helplessness and anger, and explained that her mind was trying to help her by walling off these uncomfortable emotions from the rest of her personality. However, she also noted that our emotions are important and that we have to make "friends" with them all, no matter how painful they may be at times. In this way, Jessica could begin to start integrating her feelings of overwhelming sadness, helplessness, and rage. She wrote thank-you notes to "Revenge" for giving her strength. She also thanked "the little girl" part, telling her she was safe and didn't have to hide anymore.

To help Jessica accept the baby part of herself and what it represented, her mother was given the task of reminiscing about Jessica's childhood. Together they looked at baby pictures and brought out some of her old toys. Jessica had also warded off her need to be nurtured by being overly responsible. She often took care of her younger brothers and sisters, making sure they had food, getting them ready for school, putting them to bed, etc. As part of her treatment, Jessica was to take less responsibility at home, even though her mother was often tempted to add more responsibility because "Jessica was so mature." Jessica was learning that "the little girl" part of her could be babied sometimes, and she would not fall apart.

Jessica found it especially difficult to express her anger directly. In her journal, she did express rage as well as a variety of other feelings toward her father and uncle. Only after several months of therapy could she allow herself to feel angry toward her mother. As Jessica described episodes when she would "blank out," she discovered that this happened when she felt irritated or angry with her mother. In a therapy session, Jessica was encouraged to tell her mother what she did that bugged her, and her mother was instructed, for the time being, to just sit and listen to these criticisms. Jessica was also asked to make a list of five things she liked about her mother and five things she did not like.

The therapist explained to Jessica and her mother that Jessica's excessive fear of anger was an attempt to ward off disturbing memories of violence and abuse that create feelings of vulnerability. Usually the family never spoke of the violence and abuse, but in a family session, Jessica recollected some of the scary events she had witnessed. She recalled how her father had thrown her younger brother against the wall and beat her mother, and how she used to lie in bed, listening to the screaming and fighting. She said the walls seemed to move and the house shook like there was an earthquake. She remembered nights that her uncle came into her room—which now all seemed to blur together—the sound of his footsteps and the rancid mixture of alcohol and aftershave lotion. Jessica's mother added some details to the specific memories. Tearfully she asked for forgiveness for not protecting Jessica from the abuse. She vowed that she would never let it happen again. In other individual sessions, EMDR and imaging techniques were used to neutralize particularly potent memories.

It is not surprising that Jessica's mother also had some unresolved issues. She too had disowned her angry feelings, and was urged to talk directly about her own reactions to frustrating situations. She was also encouraged to express her anger toward Jessica's father rather than disavow these feelings and make excuses for his brutal behavior.

STAGE THREE: DEVELOPMENTAL SKILLS

Trauma has a much greater impact on children than on adults because children are still developing a sense of self. The traumatized child must struggle to recover not only from the overwhelming event (or set of events), but also from the myriad ripple effects. In particular, trauma can prevent a child from mastering such critical developmental skills as problem solving, social skills, and self-awareness. So, in addition to addressing specific behavioral symptoms, therapy must also help children shore up their sense of self.

Enhancing Problem-Solving Capacities

Building cognitive capacities, such as problem solving, enhances the development of the cortex, especially the prefrontal area, forming new, more organized and stable networks of nerve cells. This, in turn, supports the hierarchical organization of the brain, making it easier for a child to give thoughtful rather than reactive responses. At the same time, a problem-solving style of thinking also fosters integration, especially between the emotional and cognitive systems. Reasoning and decision making depend on emotion as the guiding force. Important emotional information must be relayed to the frontal cortex in order to judge the meaning and significance of ideas, to differentiate the important from the unimportant, and to be sensitive to the needs of others. Remember the brain-damaged patient Eliot whose cognitive capacities were intact but whose decision making was impaired due to a lack of collaboration between the emotional and cognitive systems? Emotional awareness keeps information flowing from our emotional systems to the prefrontal lobes, which, by interpreting our emotions, can, in turn, help regulate them.

In his best-selling *The 7 Habits of Highly Effective People*, Steven Covey (1990) writes about the distinguishing feature of human beings—the freedom to choose. He writes:

> Because of our unique human endowments, we can write new programs for ourselves totally apart from our instincts and training. This is why an animal's capacity is relatively limited and man's is unlimited. . . . The extent to which we exercise and develop these endowments empowers us to fulfill our uniquely human potential. (p. 70)

Children who learn how to think about the problems they face can appreciate how other people feel, consider options, and plan a course of action. In contrast, if children restrict themselves to conditioned responses, they are doomed to experience more frustration and failure. Furthermore, just asking a child what he can do, what he can say to himself, or to consider various solutions to his problems shifts the locus of control onto the child rather than his parents, teachers, etc. A problem-solving approach can begin early, even with children as young as age three (Shure, 1995).

Although there are a number of ways to teach problem solving, most approaches use the following five steps:

1. *Define the problem.* It is much easier to think of alternative solutions when you know what the problem is. Some questions to ask: "What happened?" "What happened after you (grabbed)?" "Why did you (push) (hit)?" Different people may have different interpretations, so it is important to get everyone's ideas. When adults calmly ask these questions, children usually settle down and answer them.

2. *Think about feelings.* Children need to learn to tune in to their own feelings and to consider how their actions make others feel. "What were you feeling?" "What do you think Sara was feeling?" This helps them negotiate fair solutions with their peers. Thinking "win/win" means developing the habit of looking for solutions that mesh our own needs with the needs of others. Children need to be taught "feeling" words, such as happy, sad, angry, proud, and frustrated. They can learn about these words by discussing pictures and stories with an adult. Then, they can try to start "reading" others' feelings in their facial expression and tone of voice. Alternatively, they might just ask others how they feel.

3. *Consider alternative solutions.* For any given problem, children need to get in the habit of generating multiple solutions. This teaches flexibility of thought. "What else can you do?" "Can you think of a different approach that would leave nobody feeling angry?" At first, bringing *any* new option into play is useful, even if it is not particularly desirable—such as pushing "Johnny" off the bike in order to take a turn. For older children, making a list of solutions on a piece of paper or chalkboard is often effective. Research has shown that a child's capacity to generate multiple solutions is, perhaps, one of the most important factors in determining her social/emotional health (Spivak and Shure, 1974).

4. *Anticipate consequences.* The next step is to consider the consequences of particular actions. This might be difficult for young

children, but with practice, they, too, can become quite proficient. To encourage consequential thinking, ask questions such as, "What might happen if you do that?" "Do you think that is a good idea?" "Why?" "Why not?" "How might 'Joey' feel if you hit him?"

5. *Take action.* Once a child has thought of ideas and evaluated them, it's time for action. Before following through, the child might engage in role-play to test some alternative solutions to a conflict.

Teaching Problem Solving

To illustrate these concepts, consider how a teacher introduces problem solving to a three-year-old named Junior—with help from a four-year-old named Chad:

TEACHER: What happened?

CHAD: Junior hit me.

TEACHER: You mean, he just hit you? (gathering data and defining the problem)

CHAD: He was trying to take the truck.

TEACHER: Oh, so Junior wanted to play with the truck and you didn't want to give it to him. (teacher encourages the child to think of causes)

TEACHER: (to Junior) How do you think Chad feels when you hit him? (guides child to think of the feelings of others)

JUNIOR: (looks away)

TEACHER: Look at his face. He looks sad. Let's ask him. Are you sad?

CHAD: (lip down-turned) Mad!

TEACHER: You hit him and he is mad. I wonder if there is something different you can do and still get to play with the truck. (encourages child to think of other solutions)

JUNIOR: (shrugs) (in this early stage very young children will need prompting)

TEACHER: Chad, can you think of any ideas?

(continued)

(continued)

CHAD: He could ask me or wait till I'm done.

TEACHER: Good, that's two ideas. I wonder if we can think of more ideas. (introduces the idea there is more than one way to solve a problem as well as the concept of same/different)

CHAD: He could trade.

(At this point, the teacher would need to help Junior practice one of the alternatives. Most three-year-olds need experience with pre-problem-solving concepts and prompting.

TEACHER: Ask him—"When you are done, can I play with the truck?" (Praise — e.g., "You are really good at asking" is a crucial part because it reinforces the new behavior.)

Nurturing Self-Awareness

As previously noted, metacognition refers to the ability to think about our own thought processes and behavior. This allows us to stand apart from ourselves and think about our mood, feelings, behavior, and our sense of who we are. Without self-awareness we would not be able to understand the feelings and perspectives of others because we would be attributing our own feelings and urges to their behavior. The formation of a cohesive identity depends on the development of metacognitive capacities. This higher level of self-awareness also allows us to feel like the same person whether we are angry, happy, or sad or whether we are giving a lecture or just stepping out of the shower. When we teach problem-solving skills, when we ask children to reflect on their feelings, thoughts, and behavior, we are nurturing the self-monitoring capacities of the mind.

Our communication with children can confirm or negate their emotions, can build or block the development of self-understanding, or shore up or deflate their self-esteem. Maltreated children generally have poor self-monitoring capacities because they are raised in environments where communication denies, distorts, or disconfirms, and where metacommunication—communication about communication—is forbidden. At its core, self-awareness requires searching for the truth—examining the reality of both what we are experiencing internally and what we are perceiving externally. Adults who are able to successfully guide the emotional development of children understand the necessity of being honest both with themselves and with others.

Social Skills Training

As discussed previously, abused and neglected children often lack experience with mutuality. Instead, they have internalized a mental model of relationships that is based on dominance and submission. Thus, most will need to learn new ways of relating to their peers. Social skills training is a term used for methods designed to improve a child's interpersonal skills. The approach usually includes modeling, role-playing, positive reinforcement, and cognitive strategies. Research suggests that role-playing or behavioral rehearsal is the pivotal element that determines the success of the training program. For example, many young children do not know how to approach other children to ask if they want to play. Some will watch from afar, others may walk up to a group of children and just stare at the floor, still others decide on hit-and-run tactics. To teach a child this basic social skill, the teacher (trainer, therapist) may begin by modeling the behavior. Next, he or she may ask the child to role-play the situation. The child may get as far as walking up to a group of children, but not say anything. The teacher/trainer can then encourage the child to ask if he or she can play with them by providing the words. The trainer would then praise the child and provide concrete suggestions for the next time.

Social skills training can be used with inhibited children as well as those who are overly aggressive. Jessica needed social skills training to learn how to be more assertive. Such training helps children learn about how their behavior affects others and how they can influence others. Children can be asked to make a list of things they can do to make someone happy. Or, to make a list of the children they like and those they don't, as a way to access their feelings. They can be coached on new ways of interacting that will both please others and help them get what they want. Puppets can be used to illustrate how to handle teasing and to show the negative effects of annoying behavior.

Developing a Value System

Trauma forces us to take a moral position. Although proponents of specific belief systems can argue over what is "good" or "right," everyone can agree that violence against children is wrong. Traumatized children, who often grow up in families that deny them basic human rights, are at a high risk of developing antisocial attitudes. Recovery entails imparting to victims a new set of values. Most people try to adhere to some universal ethical principles: compassion, honesty, responsibility, and concern for family, friends, and society. Cloé Madanes (1990) identifies the following eight therapeutic goals and values that nearly all parents, professionals, and child advocates can readily endorse:

1. To control action: to change behavior.
2. To control mind: to change thoughts and feelings.
3. To control violence or anger.
4. To encourage empathy.
5. To encourage hope and humor.
6. To promote tolerance and compassion.
7. To encourage forgiveness and kindness.
8. To promote harmony and balance. (pp. 3-14)

These humanistic values, however, are not the same as organized religion, though there certainly is an overlap. Survivors often find it useful to conceive of recovery within the framework of their own specific religious beliefs.

Values affect every aspect of a child's life, from self-confidence and self-esteem to decision making. A moral center encourages children to think before acting, rather than merely rebounding off the will of others, either by letting them take control or by blindly opposing their wishes. If children do not value kindness, they will act in a mean-spirited way, leaving them with few friends. Accepting responsibility for their actions promotes learning from mistakes and developing alternative strategies in the future. If children value achievement, they will put forth extra effort to reach their goals. Finding a purpose in life builds a healthy mind and soul. Concentrated effort helps us focus our energy and brings our brain into balance. The passion, pleasure, excitement, and fulfillment, however, come from the actual doing. Active striving is usually more satisfying than success.

Treatment: Stage Three

Brittany

After a couple of months, Brittany was back to her old self again. The anxiety, fear, traumatic play, and nightmares had disappeared. Her play became complex and organized. She engaged in a wide variety of activities—blocks, puzzles, drawing, painting, and dramatic play. She was also interested in the sounds and meanings of new words. Other children were attracted to her; she had good problem-solving skills. She was comfortable both taking the lead in complementary exchanges (being in charge) and acceding to the requests of others (being a follower).

Jessica

Both mother and daughter were referred to the women's center for assertiveness training. Jessica began Tae Bo and loved how it made her feel so in touch with her body. Next she planned to learn karate. She continued to write, keeping a daily journal. Religion remained an important support system for the family.

After almost a year of treatment, Jessica began to develop some self-confidence. Separate emotional states no longer haunted her—dissociated aspects of herself were understood and integrated. Her depression, fears, and nightmares abated. Her schoolwork showed steady improvement. She developed a warm relationship with the school counselor who was tutoring her in math, made new friends at school, and related comfortably to adults.

ADJUNCTS TO THERAPY: RECONNECTING TO THE BODY

Abuse and neglect typically sever children not only from their feelings, but also from their bodies. Unsafe environments have taught them to ignore all sensory input—to become invulnerable to pain. Unfortunately, as van der Kolk (1994) notes, this attempt at self-protection is not adaptive because "the body keeps the score"

(p. 253). In fact, many maltreated children develop somatic symptoms, such as muscle aches and pains, especially in parts of the body that were actually or symbolically assaulted. Treatment should also help children experience their bodies in a different way, to take control over them. They need to learn to enjoy nonsexual body contact. In other words, *talking is not sufficient to combat the effects of abuse.* Children also need to build a repertoire of new body memories. When it comes to the body, the challenge involves building new implicit memories that are in direct contrast to the abuse experiences of the past. It requires reconditioning the senses through new sensory experiences that stimulate positive associations.

Touch can be especially frightening for these children. Soothing rituals are often a way to begin with young children—massage, playful wrestling, holding, and rocking. Magic lotions can be rubbed on arms, legs, and the back. Waters and Silberg (1996) describe a seven-year-old patient, Anita,

> who experienced intense pain at the site of a healed cigarette burn inflicted by her father. The therapist and child created a pretend magical secret lotion that the therapist and foster mother rubbed on the child's leg to alleviate the pain. During the course of the session, the foster mother was instructed to repeat, "I can love you enough to make all the pain go away." Symptoms diminished after this exercise. (p. 158)

Research is confirming what we have long known—that the "laying on of hands" has powerful effects on the brain/body system. Tiffany Field (1998) and other researchers at the University of Miami School of Medicine's Touch Research Institute (TRI) have found that massage therapy has measurable positive effects on infants including lower salivary cortisol levels (suggesting a lower level of stress), improved concentration, reduced hyperactivity, weight gain, and improved sociability and soothability.

Another way to develop a sense of mastery and control over the body is through music and movement—including sports, dance, karate, Outward Bound, musical instruments, and the performing arts. Abuse, as we have mentioned, impedes interhemispheric integration. Playing a musical instrument, which activates numerous areas of the brain and requires right- and left-hemisphere cooperation, can help heal the brain by facilitating the transfer of information. Exercise also improves brain functioning. A study involving high school students found that those students with a high level of exercise had better relationships with their parents, were less depressed, used less drugs, and had higher grade point averages (Field, Diego, and Sanders, 2001). Our brain, John Ratey (2001) points out, was designed for movement:

> Touch, movement, exercise—the physical aspects of our lives— are extremely important to our mental health. Our brains originally evolved to direct complex motions, such as succeeding in the constant competition for food and mates. Much of what the brain does is still quite similar; we should learn to view all brain functions as descendants of motion. Motion is involved in almost every aspect of human experience: thoughts move from one topic to another, emotions stir us deeply. Language is essentially a complex semantic dance by the tongue, a sophisticated form of motion that allows us to manipulate the contents of the world without laying a hand on them. To improve our brain we have to move our bodies, take action, get going. (p. 363)

Exercise increases the flow of blood to our brain, improves our mood, and helps us cope with stress. Increasing cerebral blood flow not only ensures the healthy flow of nutrients to nerve cells, but also increases the levels of neurotransmitters that promote growth and development of neurons. Beta endorphins, our brain's natural form of morphine, are released during and after exercise. Serotonin, which quiets the limbic system, making us feel less anxious, also increases with exercise. Exercise improves the metabolic efficiency of dopamine and regulates the amount of available norepinephrine. Movement also goes hand in hand with the development of cognitive capacities. The reason, Ratey (2001) suggests, is that

> The primary motor cortex, basal ganglia, and cerebellum, which coordinate physical movements, also coordinate the movement of thoughts. Just as they order the physical movements needed to move, they order the sequence of thoughts needed to think. Fundamental motions like walking and running trigger the most deeply ingrained neural firing patterns in these brain regions. It may be that as this happens, it helps the brain establish funda-

mental firing patterns among complex thoughts—helping us to find a solution or generate a creative idea. (p. 362)

Thus, physical activity can influence mental activity.

Bessel van der Kolk has recently been so captivated by body therapy, a new form of therapy that relies on movement to dislodge traumatic affect stored in the body, that he has begun questioning the value of traditional talk therapy. In a new paper, van der Kolk (2001) argues that narrative by itself is rarely sufficient to transform trauma. In his view, lengthy psychoanalytic treatments often lead to insight, but not necessarily to symptomatic improvement. Since the pernicious effects of trauma usually work their way into our viscera, words alone are often unable to achieve anything—particularly if, as often happens, patients use them to talk their way around feelings. As a result, van der Kolk now sees movement not so much as an adjunct to psychotherapy, but as a needed replacement to it. Recovery, according to this new paradigm, requires not thinking, but doing. Van der Kolk draws a distinction between top-down versus bottom-up emotional processing. Adults typically try to regulate their emotions from the top-down, meaning that they use their rational mind to guide their actions. In contrast, as van der Kolk (2001) notes:

> Bottom-up processing represents a different way of processing information. Young children and threatened adults cannot inhibit emotional states that have their origin in physical sensations. Top-down processing is based on cognition and is operated by the neocortex. . . . Traditional psychotherapy relies on top-down techniques to manage disruptive emotions and sensations. (p. 16)

According to van der Kolk, body therapy offers a bottom-up approach to processing the overwhelming affects generated by trauma. By immersing themselves in their physical sensations, patients can gain greater control over both their bodies and minds.

Current research by Teicher (2000) shows that abuse seems to damage the cerebellar vermis, which helps regulate emotion, and that "stimulation of the vermis through exercise, rocking, and movement may exert additional calming effects, helping to develop the vermis" (p. 57), strongly supports the approach advocated by van der Kolk.

A few years ago, Levine and Fredrick (1997) put body therapy on the map with the best-selling book, *Waking the Tiger: Healing Trauma*. Building on the research of van der Kolk, they note that trauma tends to cause the body to freeze. They write:

> The traumatized veteran, the rape survivor, the abused child, the impala, and the bird all have been confronted by overwhelming situations. If they are unable to orient and choose between fight or flight, they will freeze or collapse. Those who are able to discharge that energy will be restored. (p. 35)

EMDR for Children

EMDR treatment, which involves eight phases, was initially designed for adults. The following is a brief overview of the protocol that has been excerpted and adapted from *Through the Eyes of a Child: EMDR with Children* by Robert Tinker and Sandra Wilson (1999).

Client history and treatment planning. In the first session, parents provide information about the child's problems and developmental history; the child shares his ideas about the problem(s); and the therapist assesses family dynamics and patterns of communication that are maintaining and reinforcing symptomatic behavior. The therapist should also note developmental skills that will need to be learned.

Preparation. EMDR theory, procedures, and expectations are discussed with parents and the child. The therapist also introduces the idea of a "safe place." Tinker and Wilson suggest that the therapist might say something similar to: "'Let's try something. Can you think of a special place where you feel safe and happy? Can you get a picture of that in your mind? Describe what it looks (sounds/smells/feels) like. What does thinking of this place make you feel right now? Where are these feelings in your body?" (p. 58). The therapist then "installs" the "safe place" (i.e., pairs the image, sounds, smells, feelings, and sensations of this place with a set of eye movements, or hand taps). For children age eight and older, a short explanation of how EMDR can be used to process painful memories usually follows.

(continued)

(continued)

Assessment. As in adult therapy, after a target image(s) (related to the trauma) is identified, the child is asked to provide a negative and positive thought about it. For example, negative statements might be: "I'm bad"; "I'm stupid"; "Everybody hates me." And positive thoughts: "I had no choice then"; "I'm good"; "I'm safe now." The child is also asked to identify emotions and physical sensations associated with the event (tightness in the chest, nausea, and stomach pains) and to rate the degree of discomfort. Although children younger than eight years of age often have difficulty supplying negative and positive thoughts, they usually can identify feelings (e.g., sad, mad, scared, or frustrated).

Desensitization. During this phase, adults are usually asked to think about the targeted material including images, the negative thought, and disturbing feelings/sensations. While keeping this information in mind, the client engages in a set of eye movements by following the therapist's two fingers as they move rhythmically across the field of vision. More sets of eye movements are carried out as new aspects of a traumatic memory emerge, until the associations move from positive to negative. With children, this phase tends to be much shorter than with adults because the associative connections are not as elaborate as with adults. With children, the therapist uses theme development to encourage more associations. For instance, the therapist might ask questions such as: "What else was happening?" or "Can you think of another time when you felt scared or ashamed?"—to shift the emotional content from the negative to the positive. With very young children, the therapist simply "brings up the event in some way and has the child engage in alternating left-right stimulation while thinking or talking about the event" (p. 89). Tinker and Wilson caution that if the emotions evoked during these exercises cause the child to space out, the therapist needs to work on helping the child stay focused.

Installation. With adults and adolescents, installation, reinforced with a set of eye movements, occurs when the previously identified positive thought is paired with the target memory. Young children may need help coming up with positive thoughts, which can then be paired with the target material.

(continued)

(continued)

Body scan. The child is asked to notice any disturbing physical sensations as the target memory is again accessed. Tinker and Wilson suggest that for children who find this difficult, a simple question about feelings in the body may need to be asked.

Closure. To ensure that the child feels safe and protected at the end of the session, the therapist typically brings the child back to the "safe place," or initiates other soothing activities such as draw-ing, games, storytelling, or sand play. The therapist emphasizes that the therapeutic work should continue between sessions through draw-ing, writing, or any other medium that the child wishes to use.

Reevaluation. The therapist follows up by meeting with parents to determine if behavior, symptoms, and level of distress associated with the targeted traumatic material have improved. If there was improvement, another memory can be targeted for processing.

From *Through the Eyes of a Child: EMDR with Children* by Robert H. Tinker and Sandra A. Wilson. Copyright 1999 by Robert H. Tinker and Sandra A. Wilson. Used by permission of W. W. Norton and Company, Inc.

To access that energy, patients must first learn how to tune into their bodily sensations—to listen to what their bodies are saying. A central principle of body therapy is that since symptoms are stored in the body, it's the best site to address them. In a recent conference presentation, Levine (2001) explained how he used this technique to help a toddler recover from acute PTSD that resulted from the child's fall into a swimming pool. The boy had trouble sleeping and was generally fearful. Levine helped him to reexperience the accident in his office by allowing him gently to tumble off the office sofa. The boy suddenly felt like he was choking on water and had an upset stomach. As he processed various physical sensations associated with the accident, which he had been unable to process at the time, his PTSD symptoms dissipated. By tumbling several times, he began to achieve mastery over the trauma. Likewise, Ogden and Minton (2001) have also developed some innovative treatments using body therapy. For example, they help victims of violence reclaim their sense of bodily integrity and personal space. In one exercise, Ogden places her hands against a client's while encouraging the client to push against her. Most victims of interpersonal trauma are initially prone to back off because to fight her off directly would mean—on a symbolic level—standing up to the perpetrator. Over time, however, clients do learn to assert themselves in this exercise. This newfound ability to harness the full power of the body typically carries over into a variety of other settings.

CONCLUSION

Traumatic stress during childhood disrupts brain development. To treat PTSD and complex PTSD, therapists must restore integrated brain functioning. Surprisingly, psychoactive drugs alone are rarely able to bring about the needed changes in brain structure and functioning. Just as a stressful environment can overload the brain, a supportive environment can help it recover. To address their troubling symptoms, traumatized children ultimately need a new set of experiences that generate new ways of thinking, feeling, and behaving.

We have presented a new interactive treatment approach that is designed to improve the child's overall psychobiological functioning. The therapy is divided into three phases: (1) safety and stabilization; (2) symptom reduction and memory work; and (3) developmental skills. Whereas PTSD can often be treated rather quickly, complex PTSD is much more challenging. As we illustrated with Jessica, treatment for complex PTSD may also require addressing deeply rooted family dynamics. However, timely interventions are a sound investment, given that they can turn around a child's life and break a cycle of intrafamilial violence that may date back generations.

Chapter 6

Complex PTSD Compounded by Attachment Problems: Billy's Story

In Chapter 5, we mapped out a new, interpersonal treatment model designed to treat children similar to Jessica who suffer from complex PTSD. As noted, abused children need a strong therapeutic bond to complete the three stages of recovery—safety and stabilization, memory work, and developmental skills. However, for the many severely abused children—those who also have attachment problems in addition to complex PTSD—intensive psychotherapy by itself is not sufficient. Children born into poverty-stricken homes, who end up in the child welfare system, often fall into this category. To recover, they need both individual therapy and therapeutic foster parenting.

We begin this chapter by providing some background on children in the child welfare system. According to a 1999 U.S. Department of Housing and Urban Development (HUD) study, 27 percent of a national sample of homeless adults had lived in foster care—or some other form of out-of-home placement—as children. Unfortunately, the number of children in foster care jumped about 35 percent in the 1990s—reaching a record 547,000 by the end of the decade (Children's Defense Fund, 2000). Without adequate treatment, these children remain at high risk for antisocial behavior, chronic mental illness, as well as homelessness in adulthood. We illustrate the plight of abused children who go into foster care by telling Billy's story.

Born to a neglectful mother and violent father, Billy was shuttled between his parents, grandparents, and foster parents until his foster parents were finally able to adopt him at the age of seven. With large doses of love and patience, his foster mother was able to create attachment, and help him learn how to feel secure in relationships. By age eight, Billy had improved remarkably. However, he still needed individual therapy to address some of his deeply entrenched complex PTSD symptoms. Unfortunately, children such as Billy usually receive fragmented or partial treatment. This case study shows that children such as Billy are by no means "incorrigible," and that as a society we have much better options than simply "locking them up and throwing away the key."

CHILDREN IN THE CHILD WELFARE SYSTEM

Most public health experts agree that the nation's foster care system is in a state of crisis—defined by Patrick Curtis, the Director of Research at the Child Welfare League of America, as "the reality that too many children are staying in foster care for too long a time" (Curtis, Dale, and Kendall, 1999, p. 1). The number of children in foster care leveled off at about 300,000 for most of the 1980s, but then the crack cocaine epidemic began to permeate our inner cities, causing the figure to shoot back up to over a half a million (Curtis, Dale, and Kendall, 1999). Parental substance abuse, which tends to go hand in hand with child maltreatment, is the most commonly cited cause for out-of-home placement. Studies estimate that up to 80 percent of families in the child welfare system struggle with addiction to alcohol or illicit drugs. Furthermore, children with addicted parents are four times more likely to be neglected than children whose parents are drug free (Young and Gardner, 1998). Minority children are greatly over-represented in the foster care population; although African-American children comprised 16 percent of the U.S. child population in 1995, they accounted for 44 percent of the out-of-home care population (Curtis, Dale, and Kendall, 1999).

Abused and neglected children who are removed from their homes can go into four different types of foster care: family (nonrelative) foster care; kinship (relative) care; therapeutic foster care, which is what Billy received; and residential (group) care. Unfortunately, some children remain in the foster care system for many years, though the average stay is about three years. The three common ways to exit the system prior to age eighteen are: reunification with parents; moving in with relatives; or adoption. Family reunification, which is usually the preferred outcome, occurs in about 60 percent of cases, according to a 1999 survey conducted by the U.S. Department of Health and Human Services. Until recently, most judges sought to preserve the family at all costs, but the consensus has since shifted, with biological parents now regaining custody only if they are deemed to have remedied whatever problems (e.g., drug addiction) led to the initial placement. Thus, although the child is in foster care, social service agencies typically strive to offer parents supportive services (e.g., access to drug treatment), to help them achieve this goal.

Sadly, despite active outreach, some parents are unable to turn their lives around. Recognizing the plight of children mired in the foster care system, President Clinton achieved passage of The Adoption and Safe Families Act (ASFA) in 1997, which was designed to increase the number of adoptions each year. The law gives financial incentives to states to promote adoption and requires them to hold a permanency hearing once a child has been in care for a year. Furthermore, states can now terminate parental rights once a child has been in care for fifteen of the previous twenty-two months. The new policy appears to be having some effect as adoptions increased 29 percent from 1996 to 1998 (Children's Bureau, U.S. Department of Health and Human Services, 1999). However, for most children in foster care, the process that aims to terminate parental rights remains riddled with delays resulting from various bottlenecks such as high caseloads and lengthy appeals.

Research shows that the vast majority of children in the child welfare system experience mental health problems. This finding is to be expected, given that foster children suffer from the double whammy of abuse (and/or neglect) compounded by dislocation from their family of origin. In a study of about 200 foster children in Oakland, California, Halfon, Mendonca, and Berkowitz (1995) found that 80 percent had developmental, emotional, and behavioral problems. Researchers studying children entering foster care in Baltimore, Maryland, found that 51 percent of children ages two months to five years were identified as "suspect for delay" on the Denver Developmental Screening Test (Kendall, Dale, and Plakitsis, 1995). These emotional problems are typically accompanied by cognitive impairments. For example, the Baltimore study also found that from half to two-thirds of children ages eight to nineteen showed evidence of severe receptive-language difficulties (Kendall, Dale, and Plakitsis, 1995).

Historically, children in foster care rarely received any mental health services. However, this began changing in the early 1990s, when child welfare advocates filed a series of class action suits on behalf of abused children, and states typically began covering foster children under Medicaid. Though the use of mental health services in rural areas remains low, it is widespread in many urban areas. For example, according to a 1992 study, the roughly 50,000 foster children in California who comprised just 4 percent of the state's children eligible for Medicaid, made up over 40 percent of the users of mental health services (Halfon, Berkowitz, and Klee, 1992). However, improved access to mental health care does not necessarily mean that all foster children are receiving effective treatment. Social service agencies readily refer sexually abused children into treatment—in a San Diego study, for example, they were four and one-half times more likely to receive services than children placed into care for other reasons (e.g., neglect or physical abuse) (Garland et al., 1996). However, nationally, neglected children constitute over half of the maltreated children entering the system each year, whereas slightly more than 10 percent are sexually abused. Thus, many neglected children, who, as, research suggests, actually suffer from the most disabling symptoms, may be falling through the cracks.

INTRODUCING BILLY

Billy was just three, his sister Katie four, and his brother Joey seven, when his father hanged himself outside the door to their apartment. Devastated, his mother plunged deeply into depression and could not adequately care for the children. Eventually, the children were removed from the home and placed with a foster family. A month after moving in with the foster family, Billy entered a Head Start preschool program. That's when P.S. met Billy in her role as a consultant to the foster family and the Head Start program.

Even before their father's suicide, Billy and his siblings had endured a chaotic, violent life. Billy's father had possessed a volcanic temper and had been physically and emotionally abusive. His mother, who was unable to protect the children, was incapable of attending to their needs for nurturing. The family had moved from one run-down apartment to another every few months. Food, when available, mostly consisted of candy, chips, Kool-Aid, and chocolate milk. A series of random visitors would come to visit—often staying at the house for as long as a few weeks at a time. Joey, Billy's older brother, was sexually abused by one of these family "friends."

Billy was "hell-on-wheels" when P.S. first saw him. His play was often aggressive. For example, he would create gruesome accidents, bury small people and animal figures in the sand, and spank baby animals. At other times, his behavior was disorganized; he would dart around the room and randomly sweep toys off shelves onto the floor. He had a "tough-guy" attitude, acting as if he had no need for affection or approval. His delayed language abilities contributed to his poor social skills. Often misreading the behavior of his classmates as threatening, he was prone to lashing out and had frequent temper tantrums.

According to Billy's foster mother, he needed constant supervision because he couldn't sit still—even during mealtimes. "The only silent moments find him ripping, destroying, or taking apart anything he can get his hands on," she noted. Bedtime was particularly difficult because he was terrified of the dark and plagued by nightmares. Billy would sometimes scream to keep from falling asleep. One night his foster mother suggested his older brother, Joey, read him a story. Billy agreed, but added that he was "not going to have sex with him." This comment strongly suggests that Billy, too, had been molested—either, as in the case of Joey, by a family "friend," or perhaps by Joey himself. Another time, after losing a tooth, Billy refused to go to bed because he "did not want the tooth fairy to come in the night." In Billy's mind, "people" who came in the night, whether in dreams or in reality, did bad things to him. Billy was also haunted by other traumatic memories. His foster mother said that Billy would approach visitors to the home and tell them stories about his father, for example, that he had thrown his brother through a window and hanged himself. Apparently, Billy was the person who first discovered his father's body.

ANALYSIS

As a result of a long history of abuse and neglect, Billy suffered from the seven core symptoms of complex PTSD that we first explained in Chapter 4. For example, his ability to regulate his emotions was severely limited. When upset, he would usually cry in the manner of a protesting infant. Language delays contributed to his impulsive, immature behavior. His traumatic suffering manifested itself in his repetitive play, sleep disturbances, and intrusive thoughts of suicide. Furthermore, his hyperactivity made it impossible for him to stay focused for any significant length of time.

In addition to these symptoms, Billy also had an attachment disorder. His macho demeanor reflected not only his identification with a violent father, but also a rejection of his dependency needs. Renouncing the need to be loved and cared for is a common sequela of emotional deprivation early in life.

In the 1960s and 1970s, developmental psychologist Mary Ainsworth, PhD, expanded Bowlby's theory of attachment, which had been based on his clinical and empirical work with neglected and homeless children. Ainsworth created a standardized protocol called the *strange situation,* which enabled clinicians to assess the child's attachment style. During this twenty-minute procedure, which involves a series of two separations and reunions, the infant is alone with his mother, exposed to a stranger, separated from his mother, and finally reunited with his mother. Based on how infants behaved during the strange situation, Ainsworth identified three attachment styles—secure, avoidant, and ambivalent. It turns out that the reunion part of strange situation best exemplifies the nature of attachment relationship (Ainsworth et al., 1978). At the time of the reunion, researchers look at the way the infant seeks out his mother, how easily the infant can be comforted by his mother, and how quickly the infant returns to playing and exploring. Upon reunion, securely attached infants go to their mother for comfort, are easily soothed, and quickly return to playing. Insecurely attached infants may seek out their mother, but remain overanxious and distressed. These infants are generally unable to be comforted and do not resume playing. Avoidant infants do not cry upon separation and avoid or ignore their mother when she returns. Each style, based on the quality of the maternal bond, represents how the infant has learned to process interpersonal relationships and the environment in general.

Categories of Attachment

Secure (B)

Explores room and toys with interest in preseparation episodes. Shows signs of missing parent during separation, often crying by the second separation. Obvious preference for parent over stranger. Greets parent actively, usually initiating physical contact. Usually some contact maintaining by second reunion, but then settles and returns to play.

Avoidant (A)

Fails to cry on separation from parent. Actively avoids and ignores parent on reunion (i.e., by moving away, turning away, or leaning out of arms when picked up). Little or no proximity or contact seeking, no distress, and no anger. Response to parent appears unemotional. Focuses on toys or environment throughout procedure.

Resistant or Ambivalent (Insecure C)

May be wary or distressed even prior to separation, with little exploration. Preoccupied with parent throughout procedure, may seem angry or passive. Fails to settle and take comfort in parent upon reunion, and usually continues to focus on parent and cry. Fails to return to exploration after reunion.

Disorganized/Disoriented (D)

The infant displays disorganized and/or disoriented behaviors in the parent's presence suggesting a temporary collapse of behavioral strategies. For example, the infant may freeze with a trancelike expression, hands in air; may rise at parent's entrance, then fall prone and huddled on the floor; or may cling while crying hard and leaning away with gaze averted. Infant will ordinarily otherwise fit A, B, or C categories.

Classification of Infant Strange Situation Behavior. Adapted from Hesse (1999), *Handbook of Attachment*. Copyright 1999 by the Guilford Press. Reprinted in Siegel, 1999, p. 74. Descriptions of infant A, B, and C categories are summarized from Ainsworth, Blehar, Waters, and Wall (1978), and the description of the infant D category is summarized from Main and Solomon (1990).

Secure attachment occurs when the mother provides two things: predictable care and sensitive responsiveness to the infant's emotional needs. Predictability entails structuring a dependable and consistent routine. Responsiveness goes beyond feeding, washing, and entertaining the infant. A sensitive caregiver seeks to understand what the infant is experiencing and provides comfort even when she chooses not to respond to any given demand. Secure infants actively pursue new experiences without becoming overwhelmed by stress. By identifying with and imitating their caregivers, they also learn to soothe themselves. Unfortunately, infants who are not blessed with adequate attentive maternal care tend not to manifest such emotional wherewithal.

In recent years, psychologist Mary Main has identified a fourth attachment style, disorganized. Disorganized infants, predominantly those who have endured abuse and/or neglect (Carlson et al., 1989), relate to others and to the environment in a chaotic way. These children, whose mothers typically suffer from mental disorders or substance abuse, are likely to be significantly impaired in their functioning (Main and Hesse, 1990). As adults, they tend to have severe problems with emotional regulation and dissociative behaviors (van Ijzendoorn, Schuengel, and Bakermans-Kranenburg, 1999). Infants classified as disorganized show no organized response when the parent returns. For example, they may begin to turn in circles at random, freeze, develop a trancelike stare, and approach by walking backward or by turning away and not looking at the parent. These disorganized responses stem from the infant's double bind—the very attachment figure he needs for sustenance is a source of fear.

Given that the primary attachment figure provides basic sustenance and is also the source of fear and pain, disorganized children feel a deep sense of existential terror. They don't feel secure about their very survival. Tragically, because of the fear of abandonment, these children may cling to their abusive caretakers. Trauma therapist Beverly James (1994) has coined the term *trauma bonding,* to describe an attachment relationship based on terror. Abused children experience enormous turmoil because the source of harm and protection are the same. They don't learn how to protect themselves because to do so might mean further abuse or abandonment.

Informal observations of interactions between Billy and his birth mother suggested an insecure attachment relationship. As with many

insecurely attached children, Billy appeared anxious and preoccupied with his mother's reactions. Sometimes he looked distressed, at
other moments, angry. When his mother did try to connect with him,
her reactions seemed out of sync with what he seemed to be communicating. For example, when Billy was distressed, his mother did not
respond to his signals that he needed comforting. When he was beginning to play, she would suddenly approach him and lift him into
her arms. Insecurely attached children often experience this type of
inconsistent and insensitive parenting. They learn to closely monitor
their mother's emotional state because the response they get usually
depends on her mood. Billy's mother was not physically abusive.
However, her depressed state led her to be emotionally unavailable to
her children. We can surmise that for Billy, early interactions with his
mother left him in a constant state of uncertainty. In contrast, his father's violent behavior probably resulted in overwhelming fear. Un-
doubtedly, Billy's insecurities were magnified by his removal from
the home. It is no surprise that Billy responded to these painful experiences by rejecting his dependency needs.

Billy's case reminds us that the attachment relationship directly affects how the brain develops and organizes. In Chapter 2, we discussed
Schore's (1994) work, showing that the development of the cortex (especially the orbitofrontal cortex) and the pathways that join the cortical
and limbic systems, are directly influenced by the attachment relationship. The primary caregiver of the securely attached infant interactively regulates the infant's emotions by encouraging positive states
and modulating negative ones, thereby creating a biochemically growth-
producing environment for brain development. In contrast, according to
Allan Schore (2001):

> The abusive caregiver not only shows less play with her infant,
> she also . . . is inaccessible and reacts to her infant's expressions
> of emotions and stress inappropriately and/or rejectingly, and
> shows minimal or unpredictable participation in the various
> types of arousal regulating processes. Instead of modulating she
> induces extreme levels of stimulation and arousal, either too
> high in abuse or too low in neglect. . . . Such states are accompa-
> nied by severe alterations in the biochemistry of the immature
> brain. (p. 4)

Schore (2001) suggests that the chaotic biochemical environment created by abuse and neglect accelerates programmed cell death and results in overpruning of the connections between the orbitofrontal and limbic areas. He goes on to say that, "A severe experientially-driven pruning of these interconnections would allow for amygdala-driven states, such as fear-flight states to be later expressed without cortical inhibition" (p. 27).

Thus, children such as Billy, who have experienced trauma at an early age, are at risk for problems related to emotional regulation, impulse control, and social behavior. Fortunately, the human mind retains the capacity to grow and develop well into adulthood. Attachment relationships—emotion-regulating interactive relationships—at any age, can help children acquire self-regulation. As Daniel Siegel (1999) writes:

> A major theme of attachment research and effective treatment studies is that intervention via the medium of the attachment relationship is the most productive approach to creating lasting and meaningful results. Attachment research suggests a direction for how relationships can foster healthy brain function and growth: through contingent, collaborative communication that involves sensitivity to signals, reflection on the importance of mental states, and the nonverbal attunement of states of mind. (p. 86)

Thus, for children such as Billy, new attachments with foster parents, for example, can generate a healthy developmental pathway.

TREATMENT

P.S. worked with Billy's teachers and foster parents to help him through the three stages of recovery: (1) safety and stabilization; (2) symptom reduction and memory work; and (3) developmental skills. Attachment problems do not require a different treatment model, but simply must be addressed as they come up during each stage. Fortunately, Billy was placed with a very sympathetic foster mother who could offer him the secure attachment relationship he needed to begin to accept his need to be nurtured.

Stage One: Safety and Stabilization

We started by formulating a plan to cope with Billy's self-destructive and out-of-control behavior. Behavioral interventions involving clear limits and consequences, reward systems, and a predictable daily routine helped stabilize Billy. We first characterized Billy's troubling behaviors and then we developed specific interventions to address each category as follows:

1. Annoying and harmless behavior (e.g., making faces) was to be ignored.
2. Mildly disruptive behavior (e.g., poking or interrupting) was handled by redirecting or engaging Billy in problem solving.
3. Outright misbehavior (e.g., name calling or throwing toys), led to a warning and/or a problem-solving exercise.
4. Loss of control and/or noncompliance (e.g., failure to heed warning or follow directive), resulted in a time-out. (See the specialized time-out procedure described in Chapter 5.)

Since, as with many abused children, any schedule change or unexpected event triggered fears of abandonment and disorganized behavior, we came up with a structured daily routine. In addition, Billy's foster mother often gave him a step-by-step account of what to expect next. For example, if they were going to run some errands, she would forewarn Billy about each stop along the way, "First, we are going to the grocery store to pick up some bread, milk, and yogurt. Next, we will stop at the drycleaners to pick up clothes. Finally, we will swing by Dairy Queen for an ice cream cone." Without this detailed itinerary, Billy would scream and cry, or demand that they stop somewhere else, such as McDonald's or the toy store. According to his foster mother, sometimes Billy got so upset he would attempt to jump out of the car.

Billy's teachers also tried to make him feel safe in the preschool environment. They, too, carefully explained the day's activities in advance. For example, the teacher would say, "Today, during outside play time, we will be going for a walk to the park. We will be using the walking rope. When we get to the park, you can play on the swings and slide. When we return, it will be time for lunch." As with many verbally abused children, Billy was frightened by loud voices, so his teachers spoke to him calmly and quietly. They also designed a "quiet area"—replete with soft pillows, cuddly toys, books, and tapes—where he could go to calm down.

Stage Two: Symptom Reduction and Memory Work

During this phase of treatment, we aimed to help Billy feel cared about so that he might begin to learn how to be comforted by adults. This step was designed to help him learn healthier ways to regulate his emotions. Gentle touch proved useful. His teachers and foster parents would rub his back, tussle with his hair, and give him a hug from time to time. At first, Billy would withdraw, but little by little, he warmed to the affectionate gestures. Given that abused and neglected children are prone to block most sensory input, his teachers tried to create a preschool environment that would awaken his senses. They designed some multisensory experiences for him. At first, Billy watched as other children played in the sand and water, built blocks, painted pictures, and cut paper. He was fascinated with sand and water, and soon enjoyed pouring water from one container to another and mixing it with sand. He was learning that it was now safe to experience the world around him.

Billy was soon encouraged to start processing—rather than simply restaging—his traumatic memories in his play. During his visits to the classroom, P.S. would sit next to him and comment on what he was doing. When Billy said, "The baby dinosaur is buried under the sand," P.S. suggested, "The mommy dinosaur is helping to dig him out." Perhaps reflecting on his newfound safety in the classroom, Billy offered a correction, "It's not a mommy, it's a teacher." Billy incorporated other elements of trauma in his play by creating pretend "accidents" and then hauling the victims away in an ambulance. P.S. proposed driving the injured patients to the hospital, where they could be cared for. As Billy was fixing the broken legs of these "people," he was symbolically nurturing himself and integrating his own need for nurturing. Sometimes he pretended to be sick. Billy liked being wrapped in a blanket, rocked, told to rest in bed, and being given lots of good food to make him strong. Play offered Billy an opportunity to transform traumatic memories by building in scenes—images and ideas—that empower. Billy's teachers and his speech therapist also joined in his play in an attempt to help him build a sense of efficacy.

By the end of the school year, Billy had made considerable progress. Although he continued to have sleep disturbances, he was asking his foster mother to cuddle him when he awoke frightened. He had also begun learning how to communicate feeling states. Although he was quick to identify angry feelings, he still had trouble recognizing fear and sadness. However, he no longer simply tucked away all painful emotions and desires. The tough-guy stance was softening. From time to time, he would seek comfort from his foster parents and teachers. Unfortunately, just as he was starting to mourn his losses and rebuild his life, he had to cope with a series of new interpersonal traumas.

Temporary Setbacks on the Road to Recovery

Billy's placement with a foster family allowed him to experience adult protection and nurturing for the first time. However, as is the case for many children in the foster care system, Billy's first taste of security was all too fleeting. After about a year in foster care, Billy and his siblings were returned to their mother. During that time, Billy's mother had participated in a "wraparound" program, which provided her with a support network made up of social service personnel from various local agencies. A coordinator was assigned the task of helping her tackle logistical problems involving transportation, health care, and respite care for the children. Fortunately, the foster family was able to relate well to Billy's mother despite her missed visits with him and her poor parenting skills. They continued to have contact with Billy and his siblings and provided respite care once the mother regained custody.

Disaster struck just six weeks after the children had returned home. On the weekend of Billy's birthday, the foster mother agreed to have the children stay over at her house. During the visit, she was shocked to find sexually explicit words written all over Katie's (Billy's sister) body, including the vaginal area. After an investigation determined that the teenage son of her mother's new boyfriend had committed the abuse, the children were again removed from the home. Sadly, despite the extensive support services she had received, Billy's mother had been unable to break out of her pattern of relationships with abusive men.

Billy and his siblings were back on the emotional roller coaster. This time, the maternal grandparents took custody and the foster family continued to provide respite care for the children. The grandparents were ill prepared to cope with three severely troubled children. To attempt to prevent them from acting out, they resorted to frequent punishments—including spankings. (In the state where the children resided, family members—in contrast to foster parents—are allowed to spank children.) According to his foster mother, Billy once asked if he could stay with her, saying, "I can't be spanked every day for the rest of my life. However, I can sit in time-out for the rest of my life." This statement suggests that Billy appreciated his foster mother's more empathic approach to discipline. After about a year, his grandparents gave up custody of the children, and Billy was returned to his foster family. Billy's reentry into the foster care system is a common fate. According to the Multistate Foster Care State Archive, covering children in eleven states, about 30 percent of children who leave foster care after their first entry are back in the system within six months (Chapin Hall Center for Children at the University of Chicago, 1999).

Stage Three: Developmental Skills

Billy's recovery didn't get fully back on track until two years after he resumed living with his foster family. Until he was adopted by them at age seven, he had to live with constant fear of loss and abandonment. During this limbo period between five and seven, his behavioral problems increased. At times, he suffered from crippling anxiety and attention problems. A major crisis occurred when the family adopted two young teenage girls. The day the girls moved in, Billy "lost it" and "was screaming hysterically," according to his foster mother who also noted, "He was so anxious that if he was not attached with skin, he would have blown apart, disintegrated into bits." To help Billy cope, she stressed her continuing support. As she stated, "We [foster mom and dad] held him. He kept repeating, 'You're not going to love me. There is no room for me.' Over and over again we said to him, 'We love you and we will always be here for you.'"

At about five and a half, Billy was evaluated at a community mental health center. Diagnosed with ADHD, he was put on the stimulant Ritalin. In addition, the therapist gave his foster parents a behavior-modification program to follow. Although complex PTSD—rather than ADHD—appeared to be Billy's primary problem, the medication was helpful. A positive response to a medication, however, does not mean the problem or dysfunction is "genetically" based. Even though for abused children such as Billy, ADHD symptoms are often a direct result of an extensive trauma history, treatment with stimulant drugs can sometimes play a role in improving attention. Billy continues to be seen for medication checks.

Once the adoption was finalized, Billy's outbursts and anxiety decreased markedly. A year or so later, his outbursts became much less frequent, according to his adoptive mother who noted, "They can usually be tied to situations that bring out his insecurities about home and he is able to say why he is reacting and gain control on his own." He learned how to laugh, play, and even to love. The stable living situation with his adoptive family enabled him to internalize the nurturing he received. Through hundreds of interactions, he began to experience himself as competent, funny, and unique. He learned that he was special because of his dancing eyes, the shape of his ears, fingers, and toes. The bonds Billy formed with his adoptive mother and his teacher allowed him to feel valued for who he was and who he could be. These positive relationships with adults gave Billy a chance to build a sense of self.

Fortunately, Billy's sensitive adoptive parents did not shut the door on his relationship with his birth mother who continued to visit with him on occasion. Billy called his birth mother "Mom 1" and his adoptive mother "Mom 2." By maintaining contact with his birth mother, he could, in essence, let go by hanging on. As Billy shifted his dependency needs to his adoptive family, he has mourned the loss of having a mother who was incapable of caring for him. "Mom 1" actually helped Billy do this painful emotional work by saying that she wanted him to live with his adoptive parents, to love them, and call them Mom and Dad. She also told him that she regretted that she had not been able to take care of him.

Billy's adoptive mother shared some anecdotes that illustrate Billy's newfound capacity to cope with sadness and loss. Billy, she related, had just made out his Christmas list and had given it to her to mail to Santa. A few minutes later, he returned with tears in his eyes, imploring, "I wonder, what if I told Santa he could keep everything I asked for and instead he could bring Ashley back?" (Ashley was an eighteen-month-old foster child who had been living with them for the past year, but who had recently moved out.) Another time, he brought out a picture of twelve- and eighteen-month-old babies that the family had once cared for, and said, "Every time I look at these pictures, I feel so sad. I really respected those babies." (Respect is one of the family's words for love.) In both instances, Billy and his mother hugged and shared their sorrow. Billy's adoptive mother realizes that the coming and going of other foster children still makes Billy anxious. However, she continues to reassure him of her commitment: "The message we are giving to Billy is that people will come and go in our life—people we care about and can help—but, you will always be here, and we will always be here for you." The coming and going of other foster children also gives Billy emotional "practice" at expressing and processing pain and mourning in relationships. The pleasure Billy experiences in caring for others shows that he truly understands; he has grieved earlier losses and internalized his family's love for him.

Unresolved Issues

Remarkably, "home-remedy therapy" is beginning to heal several of Billy's key early wounds. After only a few years, the attachment relationship with his adoptive mother has helped him learn how to stay connected to others, recognize his feelings, and begin to regulate his emotions. However, issues and insights related to past attachment relationships with his birth mother and siblings are likely to reemerge at various stages of development. Work related to attachment disorders is best thought of as sequential. Typically, periodic consultation is necessary to rework attachment issues that may arise at later stages. Although a strong bond with his adoptive parents has gone a long way in resolving attachment problems and putting neurobiological development back on track, nevertheless, some trauma-based symptoms remain. Billy harbors many fears and phobias that creep into everyday life. As with many trauma survivors, he retains some degree of "affect phobia" (fear of his own fear). At present, when he feels he has lost control, he lapses into feelings of shame and helplessness, which in turn automatically trigger the thought, "I should just kill myself." As we have discussed, therapy can build new associations that will disrupt the circuitry that now links loss of control, anger, helplessness, and shame with thoughts of suicide.

A Foster Mother's Guidelines for Coping with Attachment Problems

Sadly, at present, foster parents rarely receive much support from teachers and social service workers. The process of helping an abused child learn to trust and feel safe is, out of necessity, drawn out. Paradoxically, to help a child feel attached, foster parents must help him process all the feelings of mistrust that are rooted in his prior experiences. There are no shortcuts. However, if foster parents can learn how to ride out the most stressful moments, they often find it tremendously satisfying to help a despairing child rebuild his life. In her book, *Handbook for Treatment of Attachment and Trauma Problems in Children* (pp. 197-198), Beverly James reprints a list of principles that one foster mother wrote as guidelines for this challenging work. The following is that list:

1. The social worker cannot always tell you the important things about your foster child, such as what might remind him of a frightening past experience, or how much or how little demonstrations of affection are needed or wanted.
2. You will need to speak out for the child, being his advocate at home, in school, everywhere.
3. Be prepared to accept the reality that court procedures rarely reflect what you believe should actually be happening.
4. Parents need to individualize. Everyone—school, court, social worker—seems to need to categorize and pigeonhole the child to fit.
5. Foster parents should not discuss the child's circumstances of background with anyone in the community.
6. Foster parents need to discuss their overwhelming feelings of confusion or frustration related to living with a disturbed child. Turning to those in the system may not be supportive. Commonly, foster parents are often judged or diagnosed, and given advice instead of just being heard and supported.

(continued)

(continued)

7. Foster parents should have a good reputation before the child enters the home because their reputation may be questioned repeatedly afterward. Police and neighbors may blame the family for children's acting-out behaviors.

8. Foster parent marriages must be solid and united before the child enters the home. The child may attempt to reenact a disruptive, violent past with behaviors that separate parents.

9. Foster parents should have had the opportunity to raise other children so that they can reaffirm their self-esteem with memories of their other children when their parenting skills do not work with the newcomer.

10. Do not bring a foster child into a new, fragile home with good furnishings. Slamming doors and destructive behavior are common. A safe time-out room is necessary—soundproofing would be ideal.

11. If your motive for being a foster parent is to be thanked and appreciated, try another profession. You cannot please biological parents, courts, lawyers, therapists, social workers, and/or the foster child.

12. Be prepared for a foster child's definition of love being fundamentally different from yours. He may think, for instance, that love means sharing a bed or giving pain.

13. Be prepared to experience feelings that you might never want to admit. You may never have even thought of hitting your own child but may be strongly tempted to hit a foster child.

14. Be able to forget. The foster child will do many things that you will need to let go of and start again. This is not a place to hold grudges.

15. Remember the one genuine laugh the foster child may produce. It reminds us there is still hope.

16. Be flexible. The foster child comes with a lot of anger and needs permission to get it out. Outlets might include sports, cleaning, weeding, kneading, or even shredding paper. As with anger, the child probably comes with a lot of sadness that also needs permissible outlets—journal writing, singing, drawing, and crying provide appropriate avenues.

17. Be with the child. Pick him up. Take him wherever he needs to go. Listen to his hopes, dreams, and desires while providing transportation and when he's not talking. Or play children's music that is fun and uplifting.

(continued)

(continued)

18. Whatever has happened to the foster child before coming to your home may not have helped him grow emotionally and socially. A five-year-old, for instance, needs to be seen as a negative five because it will take five years to get him to zero. When he is biologically twelve, he is emotionally only seven.
19. Appreciate that the foster child has a warrior personality. He has survival techniques that allowed him to persevere through severe abuse. Accept and respect his techniques while helping to give him healthier defense mechanisms.
20. When all else fails, laugh! Bring up the ridiculous or make something weird—anything—but help him laugh.

Reprinted and adapted with the permission of The Free Press, a Division of Simon and Schuster, Inc., from *Handbook for Treatment of Attachment and Trauma Problems in Children* by Beverly James. Copyright 1994 by Lexington Books.

Now that Billy feels secure and connected, he is strong enough to explore trauma-related feelings and experiences with a trained mental health professional. As previously discussed, to free themselves from their painful past, children such as Billy need to achieve mastery over their traumatic memories. Billy needs to tell his story, and imagine new endings that can make him feel empowered. Although he is no longer compartmentalizing troublesome emotions such as anger and sadness, he still needs to learn to be more accepting of these vulnerable parts of himself. Besides helping Billy with the memory work of stage two, therapy can help Billy improve critical skills—that is, engage in more extensive stage three work. For example, Billy could benefit from training in problem-solving and social skills. He might be asked to make a list of times that he acts impulsively and then to think of something to say to himself that would help him slow down, such as "take it slow and easy." Children usually like a system, and a number of programs offer a step-by-step process to check impulsive responses. Because Billy tends to get into power struggles with other children, social skills training for Billy might also include ways to enlist cooperation. For instance, instead of insisting that other children do what he wants, he would practice following another child's lead for awhile before offering his suggestions. In addition, he will probably need a reward system for stick-to-itiveness, i.e., for continuing to stay on task despite moments of frustration.

CONCLUSION

Over half a million children remain mired in the child welfare system each year. The abused and neglected children who enter foster care are at extremely high risk for developing long-lasting mental health problems and ending up in jail or on the streets by the time they reach adulthood. Foster children are particularly vulnerable because their psychobiological development has been derailed by a "double whammy"—maltreatment plus the unavailability of a stable attachment figure.

As noted throughout this book, attachment is critical in helping the brain to integrate experience and process emotion. Unable to process the series of overwhelming events that have disrupted their lives, foster children such as Billy often suffer from complex PTSD compounded by attachment problems. Fortunately, Billy was placed with a supportive foster family that was able to stabilize his functioning and provide him with the foundation for healing and growth. Billy has made remarkable progress in learning how to regulate his emotions. Nevertheless, it appears that he is still troubled by several trauma-related issues and emotions. Now that he is in a stable family, he will be able to address some of these problems with the support of a trained psychotherapist.

Billy's turnaround suggests that timely interventions can, in fact, help these acutely troubled children rebuild their lives—and in so doing, save society the costs it might otherwise have had to pay to "warehouse" them (e.g., in a prison cell or mental institution). In Chapter 7, we turn to the policy implications of our new interactive treatment model for all of America's children.

Chapter 7

Early Experience and Psychobiology: Translating Scientific Advances into Policy Prescriptions

Our brains are sculpted by our early experiences. Maltreatment is a chisel that shapes a brain to contend with strife, but at the cost of deep, enduring wounds. Childhood abuse isn't something you "get over." It is an evil that we must acknowledge and confront if we aim to do anything about the unchecked cycle of violence in this country.

Martin Teicher, MD, PhD

Myth: Child abuse and neglect inevitably lead to violent behavior later in life.

Youth Violence: A Report of the Surgeon General

In the preceding chapters, we have fleshed out a new psychobiological theory of child development that is leading to more effective treatments for children suffering from a wide range of mental health disorders. According to this perspective, since early interpersonal experiences with parents or caregivers shape brain growth, interpersonal stressors (e.g., neglect or parental mental illness), play a significant role in the onset of many psychiatric symptoms. Fortunately, a child's brain is remarkably plastic, so timely interventions can often produce dramatic results. Although the window of opportunity never quite slams shut, if we wait to intervene until children such as Bradley (Chapter 2) or Jessica (Chapter 4) reach adulthood, recovery would invariably proceed much more slowly.

Surprisingly, our new interactive treatment model has not yet captured the attention of most mental health professionals, even though most public health experts agree that our nation's children are in crisis. According to Surgeon General David Satcher's mammoth (1999) report on the nation's mental health, about one in five children suffer from a diagnosable mental health disorder. Anxiety disorders, which afflict 13 percent of children, are most common, followed by depression (5 percent), ADHD (4 percent), and conduct disorder (2.5 percent). (Note: Some children have more than one disorder.) Even more unsettling is the prevalence of violent behavior among children. The recent spate of school shootings represents merely the tip of the iceberg. According to the surgeon general, 30 to 40 percent of males and 15 to 30 percent of females commit a serious violent offense—such as assault or rape—by the age of seventeen.

As policy analysts weigh how to address these disturbing trends, the pendulum has once again swung away from the developmental psychobiological framework of this book toward one based purely in genetics. We do not believe that genes are unimportant since development is clearly the result of an interactive dance between nature and nurture. However, we are wary of any theory that downplays the role of environmental factors in general and abuse and neglect in particular on brain development. In our view, America's children are in distress largely because we, as a society, are failing them. In addition to the one million children who are confirmed victims of abuse each year, millions more have witnessed violence—a staggering 40 percent of adolescents (Kilpatrick and Saunders, 1997). Furthermore, many parents are unable to provide adequate love and support for children because of their own untreated psychiatric disorders. For example, about 10 percent of women of childbearing age (twenty-five to forty-four) suffer from clinical depression (Kessler et al., 1996), and research shows that the interactional style of depressed mothers represents a risk to an infant's cognitive and emotional development (Hart et al., 1999). For example, Jones, Field, and Davalos (2000) found that depressed mothers praised children less, and helped them less on a task, and that these children had greater relative right frontal EEG asymmetry (a pattern associated with negative affect) and poorer capacity for empathy. Persuaded by these sociological data, child advocacy groups such as the Children's Defense Fund urge investments in programs and services that respond to children's unmet mental health and medical needs. In contrast, for those wedded to the old model of biological psychiatry, which sees faulty brain chemistry as a direct result of defective genes, appropriate interventions involve identifying at-risk children and funneling them into psychiatric treatment—typically understood as psychoactive drugs designed to fix "biochemical imbalances."

In this chapter, we make the case for the policy prescriptions that flow from the developmental psychobiological approach. We begin by briefly contrasting the two policy tacks via an examination of two White House mental health conferences held two years apart—the 1997 conference sponsored by child advocates and the 1999 conference chaired by Tipper Gore, the wife of former Vice President Al Gore. We proceed to examine the underlying societal problems afflicting children. Sadly, our de facto national policy of neglecting the developmental needs of millions of children who are growing up in unsafe homes and communities exacts an enormous economic toll on our society—at least 100 billion dollars a year, according to one conservative estimate (Prevent Child Abuse America, 2001). After highlighting some model programs, we move on to offer some general recommendations on prevention and intervention strategies.

THE TWO APPROACHES: WHITE HOUSE CONFERENCES I AND II

Psychobiological Roots: The 1997 Early Childhood Development and Learning Conference

The early 1990s saw a flowering of pioneering research stressing the importance of early experience on child development. As we noted in the introduction to the book, that's when leading traumatologists—namely, Martin Teicher, Bessel van der Kolk, Bruce Perry, and Frank Putnam along with the developmental neuropsychologist Allan Schore, began publishing their first studies on how the environment shapes brain development. At the same time, researchers studying language and cognitive development were also discovering that childhood experiences had a much greater impact than previously thought. The concept of "a critical period," the window during which children must master critical developmental skills, was also reemerging after being out of fashion for a generation. What's more, policymakers had begun to take notice. In 1994, in its reauthorization package for Head Start, Congress created Early Head Start, an intervention program geared to children from birth to age three.

Newsweek reporter Sharon Begley captured many of these new scientific developments in her landmark (1996) cover story titled, "Your Child's Brain." This piece, in turn, was enormously influential, eliciting more reprint requests than any article *Newsweek* had ever published (Bruer, 1999). Begley concluded her review of the new research by stressing the need for policy interventions targeted at young children. Referring to an innovative training program developed by Paula Tallal of Rutgers University and Michael Merzenich of UC-San Francisco, which curtailed reading problems in learning-disabled children ages five to ten, Begley (1996) writes:

> Such neural rehab may be the ultimate payoff of the discovery that the experiences of life are etched in the bumps and squiggles of the brain. For now, it is enough to know that we are born with a world of potential—potential that will be realized only if it is tapped. And that is challenge enough. (p. 62)

Later that year, movie director Rob Reiner launched a nonprofit foundation called I Am Your Child to educate the public about the importance of the first three years of life. Reiner soon managed to get the attention of former President Bill Clinton and former First Lady Hillary Rodham Clinton, herself the author of the (1996) bestseller *It Takes a Village,* which had advocated investing more heavily in early intervention programs for children. At the urging of Reiner, the White House held a conference called Early Childhood Development and Learning: What New Research Tells Us About Our Youngest Children in April 1997. The speakers included several of the cutting-edge researchers mentioned in Begley's article. For example, Carla Shatz, a neuroscientist at the University of California at Berkeley, and Patricia Kuhl, a language researcher at the University of Washington, discussed critical periods. Rob Reiner drew the policy implications:

> If we want to have a significant impact, not only on children's success in school and later on in life, healthy relationships, but also an impact on reduction in crime, teen pregnancy, drug abuse, child abuse, welfare, homelessness, and a variety of other social

ills, we are going to have to address the first three years of life. There is no getting around it. All roads lead to Rome. (quoted in Bruer, 1999, p. 8)

Thus, in White House Conference I, national policymakers got the message that early experience shapes brain growth, which in turn determines behavior. It seemed as if we would soon be trying to intervene in the lives of millions of young children to eliminate the stressors that can derail brain development.

The Backlash Against Developmental Psychobiology

Rather than leading to a spate of new child-friendly policies, the 1997 White House Conference turned out to mark the end of broad public acceptance for the developmental perspective. A backlash quickly ensued. Two books downplaying the need for social programs to support young children and their caregivers soon captured the national imagination. *The Nurture Assumption: Why Children Turn Out the Way They Do* by Judith Rich Harris, a writer of psychology textbooks, appeared on bestseller lists in 1998 and was endorsed by a number of well-known psychologists. *The Myth of the First Three Years* by John T. Bruer, president of the James S. McDonnell Foundation, a policy research think tank in St. Louis, came out to rave reviews a year later. Harris' book stemmed from a celebrated article she wrote in 1995 for *Psychological Review,* in which she concluded that parents have no effect on the development of a child's personality. Two years later, she received a prize from the American Psychological Association for this controversial review article, which attempted to upend the consensus in the field of child development.

Harris challenges the *nurture assumption* defined as "what influences children's development, apart from their genes, is the way their parents bring them up" (Harris, 1998, p. 2). She does not argue that genes tell the whole story. Rather, she believes that a crucial environmental factor has been left out of the equation: peer influence. In *The Nurture Assumption,* Harris lashes out at developmental psychology in general and attachment theory in particular. In his foreword to Harris' book, MIT psychology professor Steven Pinker summarizes her critique:

Equally unlikely is the idea that a baby's attachment to its mother sets the pattern for its later commerce with the world— another dogma dissolved in these pages. . . . The attachment hypothesis owes its popularity to a tired notion bequeathed to us by Freud and the behaviorists: the baby's mind as a small blank slate that will retain forever the first few inscriptions written on it. (p. xiii)

Harris uses a variety of general arguments to make her case against parental influence. For example, the small amount of variance accounted for in parental influence studies is used to suggest that parents are unimportant. However, when peer studies are reviewed, no mention is made about the variance accounted for (typically also small). Furthermore, she claims that socialization research is inherently flawed because it ignores the effects that children have on parents. "Do beatings make children unpleasant, or are parents more likely to lose their temper with unpleasant children?" she asks (p. 27). Such dangerous reasoning is troubling, as it seems to both normalize beatings—which are a crime in many states—and to suggest that some child victims may be getting what they deserve. Equally unsettling is the claim that beatings are usually inconsequential—a conclusion that defies common sense. In fact, as we discussed in Chapter 5, research shows myriad effects of physical, sexual, and psychological abuse on the developing brain—including dysregulation of the stress response, limbic irritability, underdevelopment of the left hemisphere, poor integration between the hemispheres, and possibly, damage to key structures such as the hippocampus. In general, the research listed in the back of Harris' book is not clearly tied to the conclusions and statements she makes. Sharon Begley's (1998) *Newsweek* story quoted Jerome Kagan as saying that the book made him "embarrassed for psychology" and Wendy Williams, a Cornell University psychologist who studies the effects of environment on IQ, argued that "there are many, many good studies that show parents can affect how children turn out in both cognitive abilities and behavior. By taking such an extreme position, Harris does a tremendous disservice" (pp. 2-3).

John Bruer also subjects the effects of early interpersonal experience to a harsh scrutiny. However, as does Harris, he selectively ignores new psychobiological findings, claiming, "currently there is no research linking early childhood attachment with brain development"

(Bruer, 1999, p. 53). According to Bruer, psychobiology lacks a scientific foundation. As he argues, the "myth of the first three years" is based on three false assumptions:

1. The brain goes through a period of exuberant growth between zero and three.
2. Many key skills must be learned during critical periods.
3. Enriched environments enhance synaptic connections. (pp. 11-12)

Whereas Harris stresses peer influence, Bruer turns primarily to genes to attack the developmental position. He argues, for example, that environmental input has little to do with synapse formation after birth, stating that neither deprivation nor overstimulation necessarily has any long-term effects. Paradoxically, although he minimizes environmental factors, Bruer claims that the brain is much more plastic than commonly assumed. He notes, for example, that children can learn a variety of new skills (e.g., music, dance, or a second language), at any age. It seems odd that Bruer would try to make these two claims simultaneously, because if plasticity is the rule, then genes do not necessarily function independently of the environment. Despite such inconsistencies, Bruer's critique of developmental psychobiology won the plaudits of influential critics, including social psychologist Carol Tavris, writing in the *New York Times Book Review,* and Malcolm Gladwell of *The New Yorker.*

Though both Harris and Bruer make many valid points, a major impetus behind their work appears to be a desire to please parents and appease guilt feelings (rather than to tease out the key factors behind why children develop the way they do). Harris expresses this sentiment directly in the coda to her book, "As for what's wrong with you: don't blame it on your parents" (p. 362). Likewise, in commenting on Bruer's book, Harris notes, "Every parent of a young child should read it, rejoice and relax." Some commentators have suggested that the vast majority of Americans would simply prefer not to know about the traumatic experiences endured by a significant minority of our children. Given that this knowledge is emotionally disturbing, books that use academic arguments to support the backlash may prove influential because they provide a false sense of comfort. Judith Herman (1992) has used the term "cultural dissociation" to refer to the defense mechanism whereby our nation as a whole wards off the public health problem of child maltreatment. Although child maltreatment is not ubiquitous, the vast majority of Americans have endured some misfortunes in childhood (e.g., divorce or parental alcoholism). Thus, to recognize the acute suffering of severely abused children may trigger our own painful experiences, which we may prefer to keep at bay. As Robin Karr-Morse and Meredith Wiley (1997), authors of *Ghosts in the Nursery: Tracing the Roots of Violence,* observe:

> It may be hard to put ourselves in a position where we open old wounds and pain of early trauma. Many of us will immediately recoil at mention of the topic; others of us, upon further exploration, may choose to distance ourselves or insulate ourselves because it hurts too much to continue. (p. 278)

Although this need for emotional insulation may explain the widespread appeal of Harris' attack on developmental psychology, she is quite right to emphasize that peers do play an important role. The school shootings highlight just how intimidating bullies can be. In a recent study of sixteen school shooters, all subjects complained about being teased at school (McGee and DeBernardo, 1999). However, it seems a stretch to assume that peer influence nearly always dwarfs parental influence. For example, Martin Teicher (personal communication) is currently investigating the effect of bullying on the brain along with other critical parental variables such as verbal abuse.

Bruer does allude to some irresponsible policies generated by some overenthusiastic proponents of the developmental perspective. For example, in the late 1990s, in the wake of research on the so-called "Mozart effect," Georgia and Missouri began distributing classical music CDs to new parents. As Bruer aptly notes, this program was based on a misreading of the data. In fact, the studies demonstrating the cognitive benefits of listening to classical music were performed not on infants, but on college students. Bruer, however, overstates his case when he uses this error as a means to debunk all developmental research.

Such exaggerated rhetoric did not prevent Bruer and Harris from achieving a major victory in the court of public opinion. Unfortunately, scientific evidence does not necessarily translate into popular sentiment. As child psychiatrist Frank Putnam (1998) suggests, developmental psychobiology is complex:

[The problem of child abuse and neglect] is even difficult for many of us to understand. We have so many different disciplines involved. Pediatrics, nursing, psychiatry, psychology, social work, law enforcement, family systems, substance abuse. . . . All of us can only communicate some part of it. (pp. 9-10)

Skeptics such as Harris and Bruer no doubt have an easier time of it because they don't have to make the case for a series of subtle connections (i.e., traumatic experience and brain changes and the onset of psychological symptoms). What they did was to describe a watered-down version of developmental psychobiology and then poke holes in this "straw man." The simplicity of their message perhaps also contributed to its widespread acceptance. Rather than seeking to chart new theoretical waters, they focused primarily on casting doubt on the assumption that child-rearing practices matter at all.

Back to Genetic Determinism: The 1999 White House Conference on Mental Health

Within a couple of years, the first wave of enthusiasm for developmental psychobiology had faded. However, the backlash spearheaded by Harris and Bruer did not promote any alternative policies per se. Thus, when the rampages in America's high schools broke out again in the spring of 1999—in Littleton, Colorado, in April and in Conyers, Georgia, in May —and our nation's leaders felt compelled to act, they turned to old policy ideas based on a purely genetic understanding of human behavior. At the White House Conference on Mental Health hosted by Tipper Gore that June, the pressing mental health needs of America's children were on everyone's mind. Unfortunately, as opposed to White House Conference I, the prominent speakers never mentioned the importance of early childhood experiences. It was as if the 1997 conference had never happened. Hillary Clinton, who had been a key figure in the early childhood conference, introduced the two psychiatrists who, in the opening session, provided a very different assessment of the crisis affecting America's youngsters: Steven Hyman and Harold Koplewicz. After mentioning that two million children suffer from depression, Hyman, director of the National Institute of Mental Health, stressed that most psychiatric disorders are "incredibly genetic." Likewise, Koplewicz, author of *It's*

Nobody's Fault: New Hope and Help for Difficult Children (1996), characterized the distress of children as "no-fault brain diseases." He notes:

> . . . People who wouldn't dream of blaming parents for other types of diseases, like their child's diabetes or asthma, still embrace the notion that somehow absent fathers, working mothers, over-permissive parents are the cause of psychiatric illness. . . . And as Dr. Hyman pointed out, these diseases are physiological, they respond to medicine. (quoted in Breggin, 2000, p. 23)

However, the fact that a particular drug can reduce certain symptoms does not necessarily say anything about their causes. Physiological diseases may well also have psychosocial roots.

To the extent that America now has a national policy in place to address the mental health problems of children, it is largely driven by this purely genetic approach. At the 1999 conference, then-President Clinton unveiled a new program aimed to help schools identify and treat children with mental illnesses. The goal, it appears, is to funnel troubled children into treatment that typically centers around psychoactive drugs. Intervention efforts to ensure that young children grow up in healthy environments (via, for example, support programs for parents at high risk of child maltreatment) are left out of the equation. U.S. surgeon general David Satcher seems to have jumped on this genetic bandwagon. As he notes in his report on youth violence, the surgeon general maintains that abuse and neglect rarely contribute to violent behavior (U.S. Public Health Service, 1999, p. 17). Although we acknowledge that many abused children do not become violent, we are wary of policy statements that downplay the etiological role that maltreatment can play.

THE UNDERLYING SOCIOLOGICAL ILLS

The new science of psychobiology offers hope that even very troubled children can recover and lead productive lives. However, from a policy standpoint, prevention is even more cost-effective than treatment. For those wedded to a purely genetic view, prevention entails developing the potential to manipulate genes sometime in the not too distant future. Nancy Andreasen, editor of the prestigious *American*

Journal of Psychiatry, extends this vision in her book *Brave New Brain: Conquering Mental Illness in the Era of the Genome,* as quoted in *Cerebrum:*

> During the next several decades, we can expect to identify the abnormalities in brain geography and topography that define the various types of mental illnesses. Once this is accomplished, we will know where the enemy is. The techniques of molecular biology will give us the targets at which to aim. (Andreasen, 2001, p. 102)

In this futuristic scenario, scientists will be able to inject molecules directly into people's brains to fix the malfunctioning genes responsible for the troubling symptoms. In the wake of the recent advances in genetics, we must be careful not to be enticed by the promises of quick fixes that rely solely on the manipulation of genes. Instead of dreaming about simple solutions to complex problems, we should be examining the factors that put children at risk and protecting them from common sources of harm—such as neglect, abuse, poverty, and exposure to violence.

In his recent book, *Reclaiming Our Children: A Healing Plan for a Nation in Crisis,* psychiatrist Peter Breggin (2000) identifies a series of environmental stressors that block the healthy development of America's children. Critiquing the "genes and drugs" approach, he notes, "Instead of finding better ways of meeting the needs of all of our children, we label and drug those who most openly express the distress and anger that so many others suffer in relative silence" (p. 43). According to Breggin, all children are at risk—not just those presumed to be carrying psychiatric illnesses around in their DNA. Breggin lists five primary sources of environmental stress:

1. Stressors in the family (e.g., sexual and physical abuse or parental conflict)
2. Stressors outside the family (e.g., abuse by peers or poverty)
3. Lack of meaning/values
4. Legal and illegal drugs
5. Availability of guns (pp. 47-63).

We concur with Breggin's sociological analysis of what lurks behind the epidemic of troubled children. However, given that the focus of our book is on stress and trauma and the developing brain, we will zero in on the huge ripple effects of abuse and neglect and parental mental illness. This is not to minimize the significance of broad social problems such as child poverty, which remains alarmingly high—affecting one of every five children in 1998, up a couple of percentage points from where it was in the 1970s. Fortunately, not all children who grow up in poor families end up lagging behind in their psychobiological development. What most policymakers—even some in liberal think tanks—often fail to grasp is the full extent of the disruption—both to the child and society at large—of poor attachment relationships early in life.

A Snapshot of the Havoc Created by Child Maltreatment: Direct and Indirect Costs

> If we could eliminate child abuse and neglect tomorrow, the DSM would shrink to the size of a pamphlet.
>
> John Briere, PhD
> President of the International Society
> of Traumatic Stress Studies

Long-term investments in improving the conditions of young children remain a tough sell to legislators and taxpayers. At present, for every dollar invested in treatment, only one penny is spent on prevention. Nevertheless, the economic data in support of early intervention programs are overwhelming. Child maltreatment continues to exact an exceedingly high toll—about a quarter of a billion dollars a day or ninety-four billion dollars a year in direct and indirect costs, according to a recent study by Prevent Child Abuse America (2001), a Chicago-based advocacy group. The study's authors define direct costs as those associated with the immediate needs of abuse or neglected children. Examples include medical, legal, and mental health services that abused children currently are receiving. Indirect costs refer to the secondary effects or long-term effects of abuse including juvenile delinquency, lost productivity, and criminality (see Figures 7.1 and 7.2). From our perspective, since abuse is already draining our health care and criminal justice systems, we might look to get a bigger bang out of our tax dollars by supporting programs that address the roots of the problem.

Direct Costs   Estimated Annual Cost

Hospitalization
Rationale: 565,000 children were reported as suffering serious harm from abuse in 1993.[1] One of the less severe injuries is a broken or fractured bone. Cost of treating a fracture or dislocation of the radius or ulna per incident is $10,983.[2] Calculation: 565,000 × $10,983.   **$6,205,395,000**

Chronic Health Problems
Rationale: 30 percent of maltreated children suffer chronic medical problems.[3] The cost of treating a child with asthma per incident in the hospital is $6,410. Calculations: .30 × 1,553,800 = 446,140; 446,140 × $6,410.   **$2,987,957,400**

Mental Health Care System
Rationale: 743,200 children were abused in 1993.[4] For purposes of obtaining a conservative estimate, neglected children are not included. One of the costs to the mental health care system is counseling. Estimated cost per family for counseling is $2,860.[5] One in five abused children is estimated to receive these services. Calculations: 743,200/5 = 148,640; 148,640 × $2,860.
    $425,110,400

Child Welfare System
Rationale: The Urban Institute published a paper in 1999 reporting on the results of a study it conducted estimating child welfare costs associated with child abuse and neglect to be $14.4 billion.[6]
    $14,400,000,000

Law Enforcement
Rationale: The National Institute of Justice estimates the following costs of police services for each of the following interventions: child sexual abuse ($56); physical abuse ($20); emotional abuse ($20); and child educational neglect ($2).[7] Cross referenced against DHHS statistics on number of each incidents occurring annually.[8] Calculations: Physical Abuse – 381,700 × $20 = $7,634,000; Sexual Abuse – 217,700 × $56 = $12,191,200; Emotional Abuse – 204,500 × $20 = $4,090,000; and Educational Neglect – 397,300 × $2 = $794,600.   **$24,709,800**

Judicial System
Rationale: The Dallas Commission on Children and Youth determined the cost per initiated court action for each case of child maltreatment was $1,372.34.[9] Approximately 16 percent of child abuse victims have court action taken on their behalf. Calculations: 1,553,800 cases nationwide[10] × .16 = 248,608 victims with court action; 248,608 × $1,372.34.   **$341,174,702**

                               Total Direct Costs $24,384,347,302

[1] Sedlak, A. and Broadhurst, D. (1996). The Third National Incidence Study of Child Abuse and Neglect: NIS 3. U.S. Department of Health and Human Services.
[2] HCUPnet (2000). Available online at <http://www.ahrq.gov/data/hcup/hcupnet.htm>.
[3] Hammerle (1992) as cited in Myles, K.T. (2001). Disabilities Caused by Child Maltreatment: Incidence, Prevalence and Financial Data.
[4] Sedlak, A. and Broadhurst, D. (1996). The Third National Incidence Study of Child Abuse and Neglect: NIS 3. U.S. Department of Health and Human Services.

(continued)

FIGURE 7.1 *(continued)*

5 Daro, D. (1988). Confronting Child Abuse. New York: The Free Press.
6 Geen, R., Waters-Boots, S., and Tumlin, K. (March 1999). The Cost of Protecting Vulnerable Children: Understanding Federal, State, and Local Child Welfare Spending. The Urban Institute.
7 Miller, T., Cohen, M., and Wiersema, B. (1996). Victims' Cost and Consequences: A New Look. The National Institute of Justice. Available online at <www.nij.com>.
8 Sedlak, A. and Broadhurst, D. (1996). The Third National Incidence Study of Child Abuse and Neglect: NIS 3. U.S. Department of Health and Human Services.
9 Dallas Commission on Children and Youth (1988). A Step Towards a Business Plan for Children in Dallas County: Technical Report Child Abuse and Neglect. Available online at <www.ccgd.org>.
10 Sedlak, A. and Broadhurst, D. (1996). The Third National Incidence Study of Child Abuse and Neglect: NIS 3. U.S. Department of Health and Human Services.

FIGURE 7.1. Total Annual Cost of Child Abuse and Neglect in the United States: Direct Costs (*Source:* Prevent Child Abuse America, 2001). Reprinted courtesy of Prevent Child Abuse America 2002.

Indirect Costs	*Estimated Annual Cost*

Special Education
Rationale: More than 22 percent of abused children have a learning disorder requiring special education.[11] Total cost per child for learning disorders is $655 per year. Calculations: 1,553,800[12] x .22 = 341,386; 341,386 x $655.   **$223,607,830**

Mental Health and Health Care
Rationale: The health care cost per woman related to child abuse and neglect is $8,175,816/163,844 = $50.[13] If the costs were similar for men, we could estimate that $50 x 185,105,441[14] adults in the United States cost the nation $9,255,272,050. However, the costs for men are likely to be very different and a more conservative estimate would be half of that amount.   **$4,627,636,025**

Juvenile Delinquency
Rationale: 26 percent of children who are abused or neglected become delinquents, compared to 17 percent of children as a whole,[15] for a difference of 9 percent. Cost per year per child for incarceration is $62,966. Average length of incarceration in Michigan is fifteen months.[16] Calculations: 0.09 x 1,553,800[17] = 139,842; 139,842 x $62,966 = $8,805,291,372.   **$8,805,291,372**

Lost Productivity to Society
Rationale: Abused and neglected children grow up to be disproportionately affected by unemployment and underemployment. Lost productivity has been estimated at $656 million to $1.3 billion.[18] Conservative estimate is used.   **$656,000,000**

Adult Criminality
Rationale: Violent crime in the United States costs $426 billion per year.[19] According to the National Institute of Justice, 13 percent of all violence can be linked to earlier child maltreatment.[20] Calculation: $426 billion x .13.   **$55,380,000,000**

Total Indirect Costs **$69,692,535,227**
TOTAL COST **$94,076,882,52**

[11]Hammerle, N. (1992) as cited in Daro, D. (1988). Confronting Child Abuse. New York: The Free Press.
[12] Sedlak, A. and Broadhurst, D. (1996). The Third National Incidence Study of Child Abuse and Neglect: NIS 3. U.S. Department of Health and Human Services.
[13] Walker, E., Unutzer, J., Rutter, C., Gelfand, A., Saunders, K., VonKorff, M., Koss, M., and Katon, W. (1997). Cost of Health Care Use by Women HMO Members with a History of Childhood Abuse and Neglect. Arc General Psychiatry, Vol 56, 609-613.
[14] U.S. Census. Available online at <www.census.gov>.
[15] Widom, C. (2000). The Cycle of Violence. Available online at <U.S. Department of Justice, National Institute of Justice.
[16] Caldwell, R.A. (1992). The Costs of Child Abuse vs. Child Abuse Prevention: Michigan's Experience. Michigan Children's Trust Fund and Michigan State University.
[17] Sedlak, A. and Broadhurst, D. (1996). The Third National Incidence Study of Child Abuse and Neglect: NIS 3. U.S. Department of Health and Human Services.
[18] Widom, C. (2000). The Cycle of Violence. Available online at <U.S. Department of Justice, National Institute of Justice. Available online at <www.ojp.usdoj.gov/nij/victdocs.2001.HTM>.
[19] Trends to Watch: 1998 and Beyond: Readers Digest. Ministry Development Division: Washington DC, 1998.
[20] Miller, T., Cohen, M., and Wiersema, B. (1996). Victims Cost and Consequences: A New Look. The National Institute of Justice. Available online at <www.nij.com>.

FIGURE 7.2. Total Annual Cost of Child Abuse and Neglect in the United States: Indirect Costs (*Source:* Prevent Child Abuse America, 2001.) Reprinted courtesy of Prevent Child Abuse America 2002.

The Prevent Child Abuse America study actually downplays the full extent of the public health problems caused by child maltreatment. First, the economic projections are quite low. As one of us (J.K.) has noted in a *Business Week* feature story, the most common psychiatric disorders—namely, depression, anxiety, and substance abuse—cost the economy nearly a third of a trillion dollars a year. As experts in traumatology assert, an overwhelming majority of patients with these disorders have a history of child maltreatment. Second, this study underestimates the extent of the scourge of child maltreatment. Not only is the estimate of 733,000 abused children (based on 1993 data) low, but some categories of at-risk children are excluded entirely. According to the most recent statistics compiled by the United States Department of Health and Human Services (HHS), about one million children were victims of maltreatment in 1998 (with the major categories consisting of physical abuse, sexual abuse, psychological abuse, or neglect) (U.S. Department of Health and Human Services, 2000). Furthermore, as David Finkelhor, the director of the Family Research Laboratory at the University of New Hampshire and a leading expert on the epidemiology of child maltreatment emphasizes (personal communication), this figure reflects only those cases reported to state child protective service agencies. These victims come mostly from the urban underclass, and about half fall into the neglect category. Many more cases go unreported as abuse also occurs in all social strata, even among the very wealthy.

In addition, the HHS statistics fail to cover the plight of children whose parents may not be overtly abusive, but who themselves suffer from mental illness. Maternal depression is a much more widespread problem than commonly assumed—according to one recent study, up to 16 percent of women with infants and toddlers report high levels of depressive symptoms (Carter et al., 2001). Other at-risk children include those who have suffered the loss of a parent and those who witness violence, a staggering nine million teenagers, according to recent estimates (Kilpatrick and Saunders, 1997).

Child maltreatment does not always translate into mental health and behavioral problems, but it greatly increases the odds. About a quarter of the children who are exposed to such traumatic events— namely, abuse, neglect, parental mental illness, parental death, and witnessing violence—go on to develop PTSD. In a recent study of 337 children ages six to twelve, who were exposed to either single-event trauma or chronic abuse, McLosky and Walker (2000) report that the same percentage—25 percent—developed PTSD and complex PTSD. For these children, the level of distress is profound. As McLosky and Walker note, numerous other comorbid disorders are often associated with PTSD, such as phobias and separation anxiety. Childhood PTSD, in turn, increases the risk for all kinds of difficulties later in life. As Ronald Kessler (2000), the nation's foremost authority on the epidemiology of psychiatric disorders and a professor at Harvard Medical School, has shown, early onset PTSD is associated with a 40 percent greater risk of high school and college failure, a 30 percent greater risk of teenage motherhood, a 60 percent greater risk of marital instability, and a 150 percent greater risk of unemployment. Though the Prevent Child Abuse America does capture the link between abuse and the need for special education, it fails to take into account other associations between abuse and educational difficulties. As Frank Putnam (1998) observes, about 30 percent of abused children have cognitive impairments, and about 50 percent have serious school problems such as truancy and misconduct.

Based on the accounts given in books such as *The Myth of the First Three Years* and *The Nurture Assumption,* and in the popular press, we might conclude that researchers have given up even studying the relationship between childhood trauma and adult mental health. Nothing could be further from the truth. For example, psychologist Jeffrey G. Johnson and his colleagues at the New York State Psychiatric Institute have been tracking a community sample of 593 families and their offspring since the mid-1970s. In a series of groundbreaking studies based on their periodic assessments of parent and child psychopathology, they have highlighted the critical impact of parental behavior on child development (see, for example, Brown et al., 1998; Johnson et al., 1999, 2001). Children with parents who were unduly punitive have a three times higher risk of developing mental illnesses. Furthermore, 63 percent of the children whose parents exhibited poor parenting skills developed disorders such as depression, anxiety, and substance abuse.

Even some researchers who used to think solely in terms of genetic causes are beginning to appreciate the impact of adverse experiences. For example, Kenneth Kendler, a professor at Virginia Commonwealth University previously known mostly for his studies in behavioral genetics, recently published a study of 1,411 female twins in which he reported that sexual abuse had a profound effect on adult mental health problems (Kendler et al., 2000). Sexual abuse increased the risk of major depression, generalized anxiety disorder, panic disorder, alcohol dependence, and drug dependence, with the more severe the abuse (intercourse versus fondling) relating to the more severe the psychiatric distress. In particular, abused women who had endured intercourse had about a three times greater chance of developing a psychiatric disorder and about a four times greater chance of becoming a substance abuser.

The Prevent Child Abuse America study also glosses over the costs of mental and physical health problems in adults. Citing one study from 1997, it makes the conservative estimate that abuse raises an adult's health care costs fifty dollars per year. Would that this were the case! In fact, abuse in childhood greatly increases the risk for numerous adult health problems. Take chronic pain, for example. In a recent study of ninety-two chronic pain patients ages twenty to sixty-two, 55 percent reported a history of abuse—as opposed to 21 percent in a control group (Goldberg and Goldstein, 2000). Likewise, in a study of about 200 women in roughly the same age range, those who were distressed by child sexual abuse had significantly more visits to hospital emergency rooms in general and for chronic pain in particular than controls (Arnow et al., 1999).

Even more troubling is that abuse is associated with major medical illnesses. According to the pioneering Adverse Childhood Experiences (ACE) study by Vincent Felitti (1998) and his colleagues, which we referred to in Chapter 5, adults with a serious abuse history (who have experienced four or more adverse childhood experiences, such as physical abuse, sexual abuse, psychological abuse, and parental mental illness), are about one and one-half times more likely to develop diabetes and twice as likely to develop heart disease and cancer than nonabused controls. One hypothesis for this link—raised by Felitti and other prominent researchers such as Ed Walker of the University of Washington (see, for example, Walker et al., 1995)—is that abuse leads to self-destructive behavior, which, in turn, increases the risk of disease. As Felitti also reports in the ACE study, adults with four or more ACEs are 2.2 times more likely to be smokers, 1.6 times more likely to be obese, and 10.3 times more likely to have injected drugs. Research also suggests that stress, especially early in life, changes the expression of genes in brain regions that regulate the stress response, putting individuals at risk for multiple illnesses (Meaney, 2002). Bruce McEwen (2002), a neuroendocrinologist at Rockefeller University, states that hormones account for, and directly contribute to, atherosclerosis, atrophy of brain areas, bone loss, abdominal fat and obesity, hyperglycemia and diabetes, and sleep disturbances.

When the ACE study was originally published in *The American Journal of Preventive Medicine* in 1998, three commentaries appeared in the same issue, hailing it as a landmark in preventive medicine research. One commentator, William Foege (1998), of the Carter Center in Atlanta, noted that Felitti's work on ACEs brought up the need for further studies that asked the following questions:

> What should be done in the way of primary prevention, such as identifying persons of high risk who could receive help before they become parents or hurt other children? How could children

be identified early when primary prevention has failed and what should be done to minimize adverse effects? How could children and adults bearing such scars be helped in combating alcohol, tobacco and sexual problems that may not be amenable to the usual public health approaches? (p. 355)

These are crucial policy questions, and no one has yet produced any definitive answers.

WHAT'S BEEN WORKING SO FAR: INTERVENTIONS TO BUILD ON

The brain is never so malleable as during the first few years of development. This is both a curse and a blessing. It is during this sensitive period that much of the damages of birth and negative experience are the most reversible. Yet funding for research and intervention programs for young children as a percentage of federal and state support is far less than for any other period of life. It is tragic that during the period of development where we can do so much, we do so little; and during the period of development where the interventions of society can have the least long-term effect, we spend so much.

Michael Weiss, PhD
and Sheldon Wagner, PhD

The first wave of attachment research conducted a half century ago provided the impetus for social programs for children. During World War II, Anna Freud and Dorothy Burlingham studied the rescue efforts to attend to children who were abandoned by their parents in London during the German invasion (Burlingham and Freud, 1950). After the war, Bowlby (1951) published a monograph on the plight of children throughout the world suffering from maternal deprivation at the behest of the World Health Organization. These empirical studies helped make the case for a variety of policies on behalf of needy children.

In the United States, the first major intervention was Head Start, designed by developmental psychologists Julius Richmond and Edward Zigler, and launched as part of the Johnson administration's "War on Poverty" on May 18, 1965. Though initially designed as an eight-week program, Head Start has evolved into a nine-month program serving preschoolers ages three to five. According to the Government Accounting Office (1997), in its first thirty years, Head Start served fifteen million children and cost thirty-one billion dollars. Numerous studies point to how Head Start has increased the chance of school success for poor children—as defined by lower rates of enrollment in special education and higher rates of graduation from high school (e.g., Barnett, 1995). However, some research has shown that IQ gains—particularly for black children—are often transitory (e.g., Yoshikawa, 1995). These results have given opponents fuel to argue for dismantling the entire program. Considering what we know about brain development in the first three years of life, the lack of services in the first three years of life no doubt affects outcomes. In other words, perhaps it's not that early interventions don't work, but that they must begin earlier and provide more comprehensive services to the child's caregivers to be most effective.

Though not implemented across the nation as with Head Start, the second generation of early intervention programs, most of which first cropped up in the 1970s, include some of the missing ingredients. In 1998, the RAND Corporation (1998) published a study called *Investing in Our Children: What We Know and Don't Know About the Costs and Benefits of Early Childhood Interventions,* which documents that many of these citywide and regional programs are working (Karoly et al., 1998). The researchers found that program participants (children and parents) typically showed gains in the following areas: (1) cognitive and emotional development; (2) school achievement; (3) higher income—first for the parent and then for the child; (4) reduced delinquency; and (5) health improvements—namely, less child abuse and maternal substance abuse and better maternal reproductive health. Two of the most successful programs were the Elmira Prenatal/Early Infancy Project (PEIP) in Elmira, New York, and the Perry Preschool program in Ypsilanti, Michigan. In Elmira PEIP, 400 mothers in poor families received about thirty home visits by nurses trained in child development over a two-and-one-half-year period. By age four, the children ended up going to the emergency room one-third less than controls. In addition, the mothers spent one-third as much time on welfare. This demonstration project lasted from 1978 to 1982. By 1997, for the highest-risk families, savings to the government exceed cost by a factor of four (twenty-five thousand to sixty thousand dollars for each participating family).

In the Perry Preschool program, about 100 black children went to a preschool and received weekly home visits by a teacher for a period of one or two years. Twenty-seven years later, the children who had participated in the program were earning 60 percent more per year than controls. Developmental psychobiology suggests that these early intervention programs may succeed because they keep brain development on track. In any event, we support efforts to implement these experimental programs. Some steps in this direction have occurred. For example, under the Justice Department's "Weed and Seed" program, six cities in California, Florida, Missouri, and Oklahoma have begun replicating Elmira PEIP. Also, on the national level, Early Head Start has been serving children from birth to age three since 1994—though unfortunately, it has been reaching only 2 percent of the eligible population (National Institute of Mental Health, 2000).

PRINCIPLES FOR THE FUTURE

We concur with the authors of the RAND report who suggest that investments of hundreds of millions or even billions of dollars in intervention programs may well be warranted. As they note, although this expense may sound astronomical, over the long haul, it may not be so great because "the federal government still stands to benefit greatly from early intervention through increases in income and Social Security tax revenues and decreases in federal public assistance and criminal justice system spending" (Karoly et al., 1998, p. 120). In other words, the programs may eventually pay for themselves. Obviously, state and community programs should supplement federal efforts as needed. Further evaluation research along the lines of the RAND report can help determine the optimal design for specific programs. Our view is consistent with that of Marian Wright Edelman, the president of the Children's Defense Fund, who has been actively lobbying for an ambitious piece of federal legislation called The Act to Leave No Child Behind since May of 2001. This bill, sponsored by Senator Christopher Dodd of Connecticut and Congressman George Miller of

California, has the following key goals: (1) eliminate child poverty by 2010; (2) expand funding for Head Start and child care and preschool programs; and (3) protect all children from abuse and neglect.

With regard to policy directions in general, we recommend that policymakers adhere to four key principles: (1) zero tolerance for abuse; (2) the earlier, the better; (3) emotional intelligence over IQ; and (4) access to state-of-the-art mental health care. The following is a description of each principle, followed by a few innovative programs that are putting each principle into practice:

Zero Tolerance for Abuse

As previously noted, trauma therapy is not effective unless the child remains free of the threat of any further abuse. A child should have no further contact with any adults who are at risk of harming the child. Likewise, as a society, we must abandon all policies that tolerate—in any form—the abuse of children. In the 1990s, a vigorous debate occurred over the policy of "family preservation," which attempted to keep families mired in the child welfare system together at all costs. Most child welfare advocates have since come to the conclusion that some children are better off living away from their biological parents, given that they may never be up to the task of attending to their needs. In fact, in a recent study of about 150 foster children in San Diego, children who reunified with their parents were much more likely to exhibit mental health problems than those who didn't (Taussig, Clyman, and Landsverk, 2001). For example, children who reunified dropped out of school at more than twice the rate of those who didn't and were more than one and one-half times as likely to have been arrested. Likewise, policymakers should also have zero tolerance for domestic violence. In 30 to 60 percent of families in which women are battered, children are also abused (National Clearinghouse on Child Abuse and Neglect Information, 1999).

Innovative Programs

The Office of Juvenile Justice and Delinquency Prevention (OJJDP) has recently begun a five-year/five million-dollar initiative called Safe Start, designed to prevent and reduce family violence by improving the delivery of health and mental health services.

The National Council of Juvenile and Family Court Judges has (1999) published *Effective Intervention in Domestic Violence and Child Maltreatment Cases: Guidelines for Policy and Practice*. In the fall of 2000, the U.S. Departments of Justice and Health and Human Services combined to launch a demonstration project in five communities using these guidelines.

The Earlier, The Better

Prevention and intervention are always more cost-effective than treatment. Likewise, the earlier we intervene, the more bang we can get for our buck. Thus, as previously noted, Head Start could be more effective if it reached children earlier than three. Though we should never write off children of any age as "incorrigible," it does make sense to try to target as many programs as possible to the youngest and most vulnerable children.

Carolina Abecedarian Project

This project, which took place between 1972 and 1985 under the auspices of the Frank Porter Child Development Center of the University of North Carolina, targeted African-American children who were at high risk for poor academic achievement. It consisted of two components: (1) an eight-hour per day preschool program for children ages birth to five; and (2) an academic enrichment program consisting of fifteen home visits a year from a teacher for children ages five to eight. The preschool intervention proved to be highly effective, accounting for a seven-point differential in IQ (Ramey and Ramey, 1994; Campbell and Ramey, 1995).

Infant Health and Development Program

Modeled after the Carolina Abecedarian Project, this program focused on premature infants with low birth weight. The study, conducted at eight sites between 1985 and 1988, provided educational services to the infants (until age three) and support to their parents via home visits. At age three, the IQ of children in the program was, on average, ten points higher than controls (McCarton et al., 1997).

Emotional Intelligence Over IQ

For most of the twentieth century, IQ was the benchmark by which psychologists and other mental health professionals evaluated children's development. As previously mentioned, first-generation programs such as Head Start were designed specifically to raise the IQ of disadvantaged children. However, as noted in the (2000) report from the National Institute of Mental Health, *A Good Beginning: Sending America's Children to School with the Social and Emotional Competence They Need to Succeed,* IQ doesn't necessarily translate into school readiness and competence. IQ actually measures a child's intellectual ability at a given moment in time. Unless the child also develops his emotional intelligence (or the mental capacities associated with each stage of development), any intellectual gains are likely to be transitory because he will have difficulty adapting to the school environment. Simply put, emotional intelligence, which depends on early interpersonal experiences, is as crucial—if not more so—than IQ for success in school. As stated in the report:

> Children who do not achieve these age-appropriate social and emotional milestones face a far greater risk for early school failure. For example, children who have not formed secure attachments to a parent(s) or primary caregiver during their first year of life are less likely to be socially and emotionally competent during their second year of life. Children who master these social and emotional milestones during the infancy, toddler and preschool years are more likely to make a successful transition to school. (p. vii)

In other words, parents and educators would do well to focus less on what or how much a preschooler learns and more on what emotional capacities he is mastering. Surprisingly, simply by interacting with the child and making him feel secure and cared about, parents can help boost intelligence.

Innovative Programs

Healthy Families America (HFA) now offers home visits to new parents in more than 400 communities. This program helps "parent" parents so that they can, in turn, be attentive to their children's needs.

The U.S. Departments of Health and Human Services and Education have started Starting Early Starting Smart (SESS), which seeks to help at-risk children from birth to age seven. SESS includes a wide variety of interventions, from mental health and substance abuse treatment to parents and parent education to home visits. According to this treatment model, the more parents are able to improve their parenting skills and develop support networks, the more able they will be to promote their children's emotional development.[1]

Access to State-of-the-Art Mental Health Care

Abused and neglected children such as Billy—the boy thrown into the child welfare system whom we discussed in Chapter 6—urgently need mental health treatment from clinicians who understand the long-term effects of abuse. Otherwise, recovery may be stalemated because treatment is likely to focus exclusively on one symptom without taking into account the full dimensions of the child's distress. For example, in Billy's case, his ADHD symptoms represented the tip of the iceberg. Therapists need to learn how, for example, to ask a child about possible abuse without asking leading questions. Screening instruments such as the Trauma Symptom Checklist for Children, authored by psychologist John Briere (1996) of the University of Southern California, can be particularly helpful in allowing clinicians to get a quick overview of a child's trauma-based distress. Policymakers need to help promote organizations that provide training for mental health professionals in such advances in traumatology. Unfortunately, even today, most psychologists, psychiatrists, and social workers do not receive adequate instruction in this area during their graduate education. We hope that before too long traumatology will be fully integrated into the curriculum in all these disciplines.

Innovative Programs

The following organizations provide a wealth of valuable information and resources for mental health professionals who provide clinical services for child and adult survivors of abuse: the American Professional Society on the Abuse of Children, the International Society for Traumatic Stress Studies, the International Society for the Study of Dissociation, and the Family Violence and Sexual Assault Institute.

CONCLUSION

At the present time, our nation's policy toward the plight of children with mental health problems remains out of sync with the latest scientific advances. Although brain researchers continue to document how early interpersonal experiences provide a blueprint for a child's emotional development, this body of scientific knowledge has been slow to gain a footing in the culture at large. For a brief period in the mid-1990s, policymakers did appear to be warming up to developmental psychobiology. Unfortunately, the pendulum has swung back toward approaches that locate the distress of our children largely in faulty genes rather than in deficient environments. Despite this recent setback, we believe that in the long run, more and more public health experts will see the wisdom in investing in prevention and intervention programs that specifically address the scourge of child maltreatment.

Notes

Introduction

1. Gene expression begins when chemical substances such as neurotransmitters bind to specific receptors embedded on the surface of the neuron. When the right combination and concentration of these substances bind to the appropriate receptors, a cascade of biological reactions take place within the cell, eventually leading to the activation of a protein known as a transcription factor. This specialized protein molecule moves inside the nucleus of the cell, binds to the appropriate gene sequence, and triggers a process that ultimately affects the number of copies of the gene. These copies (RNA) function like blueprints, and are sent to a specialized part of the cell that manufactures new proteins. Depending on the protein manufacturered, the cell may grow new dendrites, create more synapses, alter production of neurotransmitters, change the number or type of receptors, etc. (Hedaya, 1996; Mack, 1996).

2. We alternate the use of the masculine and feminine possessive pronouns throughout this book.

Chapter 1

1. Current research shows that neurogenesis continues in certain areas of the hippocampus.

Chapter 2

1. The organization of neurons in the cortex facilitates pattern recognition. Neurons in the cortex are organized into six layers, each of which responds differently to incoming information. For example, the nerve cells in layer IV respond to highly specific features of a stimulus. In the visual cortex, these nerve cells in layer IV respond to discrete aspects of a stimulus, such as the angle of a line or the shade of a color. Similarly, in the auditory cortex, nerve cells in layer IV respond to discrete sounds. In contrast, neurons that reside in layers II and III respond to several features of a stimulus. The neurons in these layers are able to organize and combine random bits of information into patterns (Lyon, 1996).

Chapter 3

1. In recent years, traumatologists have rediscovered the "early" Freud before he shifted his focus toward the drive theory. See, for example, Bessel van der Kolk's (2000) article "Trauma, Neuroscience and the Etiology of Hysteria: An Exploration

of the Relevance of Breuer and Freud's 1893 Article in the Light of Modern Science."

2. The HPA axis and the autonomic nervous/norepinephrine system are also functionally interrelated. For example, norepinephrine stimulates ACTH secretion and CRF increases activity in the locus coeruleus/norepinephrine network.

3. CRF also seems to have a direct effect on the brain that increases arousal and attention.

Chapter 4

1. Categories of symptoms adapted from the work of Judy Herman, Frank Putnam, and Bessel van der Kolk.

2. Evidence also suggests that early relational trauma impedes the development of the orbitofrontal cortex (especially in the early developing right hemisphere) (Schore, 2001), which is central to regulating stress, processing emotion, and appraising body states. Studies indicate that atypical functioning in this area of the cortex is associated with PTSD (hyperarousal and dissociation), sociopathy, and a predisposition for violence (Davidson, Putnam, and Larson, 2000; Raine et al., 1998). As discussed in Chapter 3, data from imaging studies (Bremner, 1999b; Bremner et al., 1999) found that individuals with PTSD showed dysfunction in this area when compared with those who did not have PTSD. In dissociative states, the individual disengages from the internal and external environment. This clearly suggests a dysfunction of the orbitofrontal cortex—the area responsible for processing information about the external environment and integrating it with internal emotional and visceral information (Schore, 2001).

3. We are indebted to trauma therapist Francis Waters for allowing us to use a case study that she has presented in workshops and training sessions. Aspects of the case study have been changed to protect the privacy of the client.

4. Atypical functioning of the striatum, as demonstrated in a recent study, may be moving closer to identifying a marker (Vaidya et al., 1998).

Chapter 5

1. Researchers in London have found that the hippocampus of London cab drivers is larger than average ("Finding Their Way," 2001). Thus, navigating the streets of London may stimulate growth of the area of the hippocampus that is associated with spatial memory. However, it is also theoretically possible that those with superior spatial skills tend to seek jobs as cab drivers.

2. Imaginary processes should be assessed on the child's level of control (intrusiveness), whether imaginary friends are perceived as real, if the child feels the imaginary friends are in conflict with one another, affective quality, and general adaptability. For further information, see J. L. Silberg (1996a). Interviewing strategies for assessing dissociative disorders in children and adolescents. In J. L. Silberg (Ed.) (1996), *The dissociative child: Diagnosis, treatment, and management* (pp. 47-68). Lutherville, MD: The Sidran Press.

3. For an overview of cognitive therapy, which was initially developed to treat anxiety and depression, see Beck et al., 1979; Burns, 1980; and Beck and Emery, 1985.

4. The format described by Wieland is based on the system developed by McGoldrick and Gerson, 1985.

5. For more information on therapeutic storytelling, see *Annie Stories: A Special Kind of Storytelling* (1986), and *More Annie Stories* (1992), both by Doris Brett.

Chapter 7

1. In an editorial published on July 23, 2001, *The New York Times* (p. A20) criticized President Bush for his proposal to cut funding for Head Start by 2 percent in 2002. Sadly, Bush seeks to change the emphasis of the program away from emotional intelligence and the overall improvement of children and their families toward an exclusive focus on testing, specifically in the area of literacy. The limited focus on this type of testing will not measure the effectiveness of the Head Start program, whose mission includes providing physical and mental health services to families, linking families to community resources, and encouraging social and emotional competence in children. "Readiness for school" is equally dependent on a child's ability to successfully regulate her emotions and interact with adults and peers. Instead of focusing exclusively on whether a child can recognize letters and numbers, we need to broaden the measures used to evaluate programs. We need to assess the services that Head Start offers, e.g., ensuring that teachers are well trained and supervised, making sure the curriculum is developmentally appropriate and addresses individual differences in children, and showing families that these services improve the quality of their lives. Instead of narrowing our scope of assessment in regard to early childhood education, we need to be thinking about how the standards now applied to Head Start can be expanded to all day care settings, nurturing the cognitive, emotional, and social development of our children and ensuring that they have a "safety net" that can launch them into a pattern of successful lifelong learning.

References

Ainsworth, M., Blehar, M., Waters, E., and Wall, S. (1978). *Patterns of attachment: A study of the strange situation.* Hillsdale, NJ: Erlbaum.

American Psychiatric Association. (1994). *Diagnostic and statistical manual of mental disorders* (Fourth edition). Washington, DC: Author.

Ames, L. and Ilg, F. (1976a). *Your two-year-old.* New York: Dell.

Ames, L. and Ilg, F. (1976b). *Your three-year-old.* New York: Dell.

Ames, L. and Ilg, F. (1976c). *Your four-year-old.* New York: Dell.

Andreasen, N. (2001). *Brave new brain: Conquering mental illness in the era of the genome.* New York: Oxford University Press.

Andreasen, N. (2001). Genome map + brain map = brave new world. *Cerebrum, 3,* 100-118.

Aram, D. and Healy, J. (1988). Hyperlexia: A review of extraordinary word recognition. In L.S. Obler and D. Fein (Eds.), *The exceptional brain: Neuropsychology of talent and special abilities* (pp. 70-103). New York: Guilford Press.

Armony, J. and LeDoux, J. (1997). How the brain processes emotional information. In R. Yehuda and A. McFarlane (Eds.), *Psychobiology of posttraumatic stress disorder* (pp. 259-271). New York: New York Academy of Sciences.

Arnow, B.A., Hart, S., Scott, C., Dea, R., O'Connell, L., and Taylor, C.B. (1999). Childhood sexual abuse, psychological distress and medical use among women. *Psychosomatic Medicine, 61,* 762-770.

Arnsten, A.F. (1998). The biology of being frazzled. *Science, 280,* 1711-1712.

Barkley, R. (1998). *Attention-deficit hyperactivity disorder.* New York: Guilford Press.

Barnett, W. (1995). Long-term effects of early childhood programs on cognitive and school outcomes. *The Future of Children, 5,* 25-50.

Beck, A.T. and Emery, G. (1985). *Anxiety disorders and phobias: A cognitive perspective.* New York: Basic Books.

Beck, A.T., Rush, A.J., Shaw, B.F., and Emery, G. (1979). *Cognitive therapy of depression.* New York: Guilford Press.

Begley, S. (1996). Your child's brain. *Newsweek, 8,* February 19, 55-62.

Begley, S. (1998). The Parent Trap. *Newsweek.* Retrieved November, 7, 2001, from <http://www.washingtonpost.com/wp-srv/newsweek/parent090798a.htm>.

Benes, F. (1994). Development of the corticolimbic system. In G. Dawson and K. Fischer (Eds.), *Human behavior and the developing brain* (pp. 176-206). New York: Guilford Press.

Benson, H. (1996). *Timeless healing: The power and biology of belief.* New York: Scribner.

234   *PSYCHOLOGICAL TRAUMA AND THE DEVELOPING BRAIN*

Bonne, O., Brandes, D., Gilboa, A., Gomori, J.M., Shenton, M.E., Pitman, R.K., and Shalev, A.Y. (2001). Longitudinal MRI study of hippocampal volume in trauma survivors with PTSD. *American Journal of Psychiatry, 158,* 1248-1251.

Bowlby, J. (1951). *Maternal care and mental health.* World Health Organization Monograph (Serial No. 2).

Bowlby, J. (1965). *Child care and the growth of love* (Revised edition of *Maternal care and mental health: A report prepared on behalf of the World Health Organization as a contribution to the United Nations program for the welfare of homeless children.*). New York: Penguin.

Bowlby, J. (1969). *Attachment, Vol. 1 of Attachment and loss.* New York: Basic Books.

Breggin, P. (2000). *Reclaiming our children: A healing plan for a nation in crisis.* Cambridge, MA: Perseus.

Bremner, J.D. (1999a). Does stress damage the brain? *Biological Psychiatry, 45,* 797-805.

Bremner, J.D. (1999b). Alterations in brain structure and functioning associated with post-traumatic stress disorder. *Seminars in Clinical Neuropsychiatry, 4,* 249-255.

Bremner, J.D. (2001). Hypotheses and controversies related to effects of stress on the hippocampus: An argument for stress-induced damage to the hippocampus in patients with posttraumatic stress disorder. *Hippocampus, 11,* 75-81.

Bremner, J.D. (2002). *Neurobiology and treatment of PTSD.* A workshop presented at the 18th annual meeting of the International Society for Traumatic Stress Studies. Baltimore, MD.

Bremner, J.D. and Narayan, M. (1998). The effects of stress on memory and the hippocampus throughout the life cycle: Implications for childhood development and aging. *Developmental Psychopathology, 10,* 871-885.

Bremner, J.D., Randall, P., Scott, T.M., Capelli, S., Delaney, R., McCarthy, G., and Charney, D.S. (1995). Deficits in short-term memory in adult survivors of childhood abuse. *Psychiatry Research, 59,* 97-107.

Bremner, J.D., Randall, P., Vermetten, E., Staib, L., Bronen, R.A., Mazure, C., Capelli, S., McCarthy, G., Innis, R.B., and Charney, D.S. (1997). MRI-based measurement of hippocampal volume in posttraumatic stress disorder related to childhood physical and sexual abuse: A preliminary report. *Biological Psychiatry, 41,* 23-32.

Bremner, J.D., Staib, L.H., Kaloupek, D., Southwick, S.M., Soufer, R., and Charney, D.S. (1999). Neural correlates of exposure to traumatic pictures and sound in Vietnam combat veterans with and without posttraumatic stress disorder: A positron emission tomography study. *Biological Psychiatry, 45,* 806-816.

Brett, D. (1986). *Annie stories: A special kind of storytelling.* New York: Workman Publishing.

Brett, D. (1992). *More Annie stories: Therapeutic storytelling techniques.* New York: Magination Press.

Briere, J. (1996). *Trauma symptom checklist for children.* Odessa, FL: Psychological Assessment Resources.

Brown, D., Scheflin, A.W., and Hammond, D.C. (1998). *Memory, trauma, treatment, and the law*. New York: Norton.

Brown, J., Cohen, P., Johnson, J., and Salzinger, S. (1998). A longitudinal analysis of risk factors for child maltreatment: Findings of a 17-year prospective study of official recorded and self-reported child abuse and neglect. *Child Abuse and Neglect, 22*, 1065-1078.

Bruer, J.T. (1999). *The myth of the first three years: A new understanding of early brain development and lifelong learning*. New York: Free Press.

Burlingham, D. and Freud, A. (1950). *Children in institutions: Arguments for and against the education of small children in institutions*. London: Imago.

Burns, D.D. (1980). *Feeling good: The new mood therapy*. New York: New American Library.

Cahill, L. (1997). The neurobiology of emotionally influenced memory: Implications for understanding traumatic memory. In R. Yehuda and A. McFarlane (Eds.), *Psychobiology of posttraumatic stress disorder* (pp. 238-247). New York: New York Academy of Sciences.

Caldji, C., Tannenbaum, B., Sharma, S., Francis, D., Plotsky, P., and Meaney, M.J. (1998). Maternal care during infancy regulates the development of neural systems mediating the expression of fearfulness in the rat. *Proceedings of the National Academy of Science, USA, 95*, 5335-5340.

Camel, J.E., Withers, G.S., and Greenough, W.T. (1986). Persistence of visual cortex dendritic alterations induced by postweaning exposure to a "superenriched" environment in rats. *Behavioral Neuroscience, 100*, 810-823.

Campbell, F. and Ramey, C. (1995). Cognitive and school outcomes for high-risk African-American students at middle adolescence: Positive effects of early intervention. *American Educational Research Journal, 32*, 743-772.

Carlson, V., Cicchetti, D., Barnett, D., and Braunwald, K. (1989). Disorganized/disoriented attachment relationships in maltreated infants. *Developmental Psychology, 25*, 525-531.

Carrey, N.J., Butter, H.J., Persinger, M.A., and Bialik, R.J. (1995). Physiological and cognitive correlates of child abuse. *Journal of the American Academy of Child and Adolescent Psychiatry, 34*, 1067-1075.

Carson, B. (2003). *Hemispherectomy fact sheet of the Johns Hopkins Children's Center*. Retrieved February 26, 2003, from <http://www.drbencarson.com/hem-facts.html>.

Carter, A., Garrity-Rokous, E., Chazan-Cohen, R., Little, C., and Briggs-Gowan, M. (2001). Maternal depression and comorbidity: Predicting early parenting, attachment security, and toddler social-emotional problems and competencies. *Journal of the American Academy of Child and Adolescent Psychiatry, 40*, 18-26.

Carter, R. (1998). *Mapping the mind*. Los Angeles: University of California Press.

Chapin Hall Center for Children at the University of Chicago. (1999). *Foster care dynamics: An update from the multistate foster care data archive, 1983-1997*. Chicago: Author.

Chess, S. and Thomas, A. (1989). *Know your child: An authoritative guide for today's parents*. New York: Basic Books.

Children's Bureau, Administration for Children and Families, U.S. Department of Health and Human Services. (1999). *The AFCARS report, current estimates as of January, 1999.* Washington, DC: Author.

Children's Defense Fund. (2000). *Yearbook 2000: The state of America's children.* Washington, DC: Author.

Chu, J.A. (1998). *Rebuilding shattered lives: The responsible treatment of complex post-traumatic and dissociative disorders.* New York: John Wiley and Sons.

Chu, J.A. and Bowman, L.S. (2000). Trauma and dissociation: 20 years of study and lessons learned along the way. *Journal of Trauma and Dissociation, 1,* 5-20.

Chu, J.A., Frey, L.M., Ganzel, B.L., and Matthews, J.A. (1999). Memories of childhood abuse: Dissociation, amnesia, and corroboration. *American Journal of Psychiatry, 156,* 749-755.

Chugani, H. (1997). *Adaptability of the developing human brain.* Workshop presented at the annual meeting of the Michigan Council of Foundations. Detroit, MI, November.

Chugani, H. (1998). A critical period of brain development: Studies of cerebral glucose utilization with PET. *Preventive Medicine, 27,* 184-188.

Chugani, H., Phelps, M., and Mazziotta, J. (1987). Positron emission tomography study of human brain functional development. *Annals of Neurology, 22,* 487-497.

Clarke, A.S. and Schneider, M.L. (1997). Effects of prenatal stress on behavior in adolescent rhesus monkeys. *Annals of the New York Academy of Sciences, 807,* 490-491.

Clarke, A.S., Wittwer, D.J., Abbott, D.H., and Schneider, M.L. (1994). Long-term effects of prenatal stress on HPA axis activity in juvenile rhesus monkeys. *Developmental Psychobiology, 27,* 257-269.

Claverie, J. (2001). What if there are only 30,000 human genes? *Science, 291,* 1255-1257.

Clinton, H. (1996). *It takes a village.* New York: Touchstone Books.

Covey, S.R. (1990). *The 7 habits of highly effective people: Powerful lessons in personal change.* New York: Simon and Schuster.

Csikszentmihalyi, M. (1990). *Flow: The psychology of optimal experience.* New York: Harper and Row.

Curtis, P., Dale, G., and Kendall, J. (1999). *The foster care crisis: Translating research into practice and policy.* Lincoln, NE: University of Nebraska.

Dale, G., Kendall, J., Humber, K., and Sheehan, L. (1999). Screening young foster children for posttraumatic stress disorder and responding to their needs for treatment. *APSAC Advisor, 12,* 6-9.

Damasio, A. (1994). *Descartes' error: Emotion, reason, and the human brain.* New York: Norton.

Damasio, A. (1999). *The feeling of what happens: Body and emotion in the making of consciousness.* New York: Harcourt Brace.

Davidson, R. (1994). Temperament, affective style, and frontal lobe asymmetry. In G. Dawson and K. Fisher (Eds.), *Human behavior and the developing brain* (pp. 518-554). New York: Guilford Press.

Davidson, R.J. (2000). Pharmacotherapy of posttraumatic stress disorder: Treatment options, long-term follow-up, and predictors of outcome. *Journal of Clinical Psychiatry, 61,* 52-56.

Davidson, R.J., Abercrombie, H., Nitschke, J.B., and Putnam, K. (1999). Regional brain function, emotion, and disorders of emotion. *Current Opinion in Neurobiology, 9,* 228-234.

Davidson, R., Ekman, P., Saron, C., Senujlis, J., and Friesen, W. (1990). Approach-withdrawal and cerebral asymmetry: Emotion expression and brain physiology I. *Journal of Personality and Social Psychology, 58,* 330-341.

Davidson, R.J., Putnam, K.M., and Larson, C.L. (2000). Dysfunction in the neural circuitry of emotion regulation—a possible prelude to violence. *Science, 289,* 591-594.

Dawson, G., Frey, K., Panagiotides, H., Osterlikng, J., and Hessel, D. (1997). Infants of depressed mothers exhibit atypical frontal brain activity: A replication of previous findings. *Journal of Child Psychology and Psychiatry, 38,* 179-186.

De Bellis, M.D., Baum, A.S., Birmaher, D., Keshavan, M.S., Eccard, C.H., Boring, A.M., Jenkins, F.J., and Ryan, N.D. (1999). Developmental traumatology. Part I: Biological stress systems. *Biological Psychiatry, 45,* 1259-1270.

De Bellis, M.D., Burke, L., Trickett, P.K., and Putnam, F.W. (1996). Antinuclear antibodies and thyroid function in sexually abused girls. *Journal of Traumatic Stress, 9,* 369-378.

De Bellis, M.D., Chrousos, G.P., Dorn, L.D., Burke, L., Helmers, K., Kling, M.A., Trickett, P.K., and Putnam, F.W. (1994). Hypothalamic-pituitary-adrenal axis disregulation in sexually abused girls. *Journal of Clinical Endocrinology and Metabolism, 7,* 249-255.

De Bellis, M.D., Keshavan, M.S., Clark, D.B., Casey, B.J., Giedd, J.N., Boring, A.M., Frustaci, K., and Ryan, N.D. (1999). Developmental traumatology. Part II: Brain development. *Biological Psychiatry, 45,* 1271-1284.

Diamond, M.C. (1988). *Enriching heredity: The impact of the environment on the anatomy of the brain.* New York: Free Press.

Einbender, A.J. and Friedrich, W.N. (1989). Psychological functioning and behavior of sexually abused girls. *Journal of Consulting and Clinical Psychology, 57,* 155-157.

Einstein, A. (1956). *Ideas and opinions.* New York: Crown Publishers.

Elders, J. (1999). *The call to action.* A plenary presented at the San Diego Conference on Responding to Maltreatment, sponsored by the San Diego Center for Child Protection, San Diego, CA, January.

Eliot, L. (1999). *What's going on in there?: How the brain and mind develop in the first five years of life.* New York: Bantam Books.

Eriksson, P.S., Perfilieva, E., Bjork-Eriksson, T., Alborn, A.M., Nordborg, C., Pe, D.A., and Gage, F.H. (1998). Neurogenesis in the adult human hippocampus. *Nature Medicine, 4,* 1313-1317.

Ernst, M. and Zametkin, J. (1995). The interface of genetics, neuroimaging, and neurochemistry in attention-deficit hyperactivity disorder. In F. Bloom and

D. Kupfer (Eds.), *Psychopharmacology: The fourth generation of progress* (pp. 1643-1652). New York: Raven Press.

Fagot, B. and Kavanagh, K. (1993). Parenting during the second year: Effects of children's age, sex, and attachment classification. *Child Development, 64,* 258-271.

Felitti, V.J., Anda, R.F., Nordenberg, D., Williamson, D.F., Spitz, A. M., Edwards, V., Koss, M.P., and Marks, J.S. (1998). Relationship of childhood abuse and household dysfunction to many of the leading causes of death in adults: The adverse childhood experiences study. *American Journal of Preventive Medicine, 14,* 245-258.

Field, T. (1994). The effects of mother's physical and emotional unavailability on emotional regulation. *Monographs of the Society for Research in Child Development, 59,* 208-227.

Field, T.M. (1998). Massage therapy effects. *American Psychologist, 53,* 1270-1281.

Field, T., Diego, M., and Sanders, C. (2001). Exercise is positively related to adolescents' relationships and academics. *Adolescence, 36,* 105-110.

"Finding their way." (2001). *National Geographic, 199,* May.

Fine, C.G. (1988). The work of Antoine Despine: The first scientific report on the diagnosis and treatment of a child with multiple personality disorder. *American Journal of Clinical Hypnosis, 31,* 33-39.

Finkelhor, D. and Dziuba-Leatherman, J. (1994). Children as victims of violence: A national survey. *Pediatrics, 94,* 413-420.

Foa, E.B., Molnar, C., and Cashman, L. (1995). Change in rape narratives during exposure therapy for posttraumatic stress disorder. *Journal of Traumatic Stress, 8,* 673-690.

Foege, W. (1998). Adverse childhood experiences: A public health perspective. *American Journal of Preventive Medicine, 14,* 354-355.

Francis, D.D., Diorio, J., Plotsky, P.M., and Meaney, M.J. (2002). Environmental enrichment reverses the effects of maternal separation on stress reactivity. *Journal of Neuroscience, 22,* 7840-7843.

Freud, S. and Breuer, J. (1966). *Studies on hysteria* (Strachey, J. trans.). New York: Avon Books.

Freyd, J. (1996). *Betrayal trauma.* Cambridge: Harvard University Press.

Fride, E. and Weinstock, M. (1988). Prenatal stress increases anxiety related behavior and alters cerebral lateralization of dopamine activity. *Life Sciences, 42,* 1059-1065.

Friedman, M.J. (2002). What might the psychobiology of posttraumatic stress disorder teach us about future approaches to pharmacotherapy? *Journal of Clinical Psychiatry, 61,* 44-51.

Friedrich, W.N. (1990). *Psychotherapy of sexually abused children and their families.* New York: Norton.

Friedrich, W.N., Grambsch, P., Damon, L., Koverola, C., Wolfe, V., Hewitt, S., et al. (1992). Child sexual behavior inventory: Normative and clinical comparisons. *Psychological Assessment, 4,* 303-311.

Galvin, M.R., Stilwell, B.M., Shekhar, A., Kopta, S.M., and Goldfarb, S.M. (1997). Maltreatment, conscience functioning, and dopamine *B* hydroxylase in emotionally disturbed boys. *Child Abuse and Neglect, 21,* 83-92.

Garbarino, J., Dubrow, K., Kostelny, K., and Pardo, C. (1992). *Children in danger.* San Francisco: Jossey-Bass.

Garland, A., Landsverk, J., Hough, R., and Ellis-Macleod, E. (1996). Type of maltreatment as a predictor of mental health service use in foster care. *Child Abuse and Neglect, 20,* 675-688.

Gazzaniga, M. (1985). *The social brain: Discovering the networks of the mind.* New York: Basic Books.

Gibbs, N. (1999). The Littleton massacre. *Time, 153,* May 3, 25-36.

Gibbs, N. and Roche, T. (1999). The Columbine tapes. *Time, 154,* December 20, 40-57.

Gilman, S. and Newman, S. (1992). *Essentials of clinical neuroanatomy and neurophysiology* (Eighth edition). Philadelphia: F.A. Davis.

Gladwell, M. (1997). Damaged. *The New Yorker, 2,* February 24, 130-147. Retrieved February 27, 2003, from <http://www.gladwell.com/1997/1997-02-24-a-damaged.htm>.

Glod, C.A. and Teicher, M.H. (1996), Relationship between early abuse, post-traumatic stress disorder, and activity levels in prepubertal children. *Journal of the American Academy of Child and Adolescent Psychiatry, 34,* 1384-1393.

Glynn, L.M., Wadhwa, P.D., and Sandman, C.A. (2000). The influence of corticotropin-releasing hormone on human fetal development and parturition. *Journal of Prenatal and Perinatal Psychology and Health, 14,* 243-256.

Goldberg, R. and Goldstein, R. (2000). A comparison of chronic pain patients and controls on traumatic events in childhood. *Disability Rehabilitation, 22,* 756-763.

Goldberg, S., Muir, R., and Kerr, J. (Eds.). (1995). *Attachment theory: Social, developmental and clinical perspectives.* Hillsdale, NJ: The Analytic Press.

Goleman, D. (1995). *Emotional intelligence: Why it can matter more that IQ.* New York: Bantam Books.

Government Accounting Office. (1997). *Head Start: Research provides little information on impact of current program* (GAO/HEHS-97-59). Washington, DC: U.S. Government Printing Office.

Graham, Y.P., Heim, C., Goodman, S.H., Miller, A.H., and Nemeroff, C.B. (1999). The effects of neonatal stress on brain development: Implications for psychopathology. *Development and Psychopathology, 11,* 545-565.

Greenough, W.T., Black, J.E., and Wallace, C.S. (1987). Experience and brain development. *Child Development, 58,* 539-559.

Greenspan, S. (1997). *Growth of the mind: And the endangered origins of intelligence.* New York: Merloyd Lawrence.

Greenspan, S. and Greenspan, N. (1985). *First feelings: Milestones in the emotional development of your baby and child.* New York: Penguin Books.

Greenspan, S. and Paulson, A. (1998). *Assessment, diagnosis, and intervention for developmental and emotional disorders in early childhood.* Training session presented in Indianapolis, IN, August.

Gunnar, M.R., Brodersen, L., Nachmias, M., Buss, K., and Rigatuso, J. (1996). Stress reactivity and attachment. *Developmental Psychobiology, 29,* 191-204.

Haddad, P. and Garralda, M. (1992). Hyperkinetic syndrome and disruptive early experiences. *British Journal of Psychiatry, 161,* 700-703.

Haley, J. (1987). *Problem-solving therapy.* San Francisco: Jossey-Bass.

Halfon, N., Berkowitz, G., and Klee, L. (1992). Mental health service utilization by children in foster care in California. *Pediatrics, 89,* 1238-1244.

Halfon, N., Mendonca, A., and Berkowitz, G. (1995). Health status of children in foster care: The experience for the Center for the Vulnerable Child. *Archives of Pediatric and Adolescent Medicine, 149,* 386-392.

Hanh, T.N. (1991). *Peace is every step: The path of mindfulness in everyday life.* New York: Bantam Books.

Harris, J. (1995). Where is the child's environment? A group socialization theory of development. *Psychological Review, 102,* 458-489.

Harris, J. (1998). *The nurture assumption: Why children turn out the way they do.* New York: Free Press.

Hart, S., Jones, N.A., Field, T., and Lundy, B. (1999). One-year-old infants of intrusive and withdrawn and depressed mothers. *Child Psychiatry and Human Development, 30,* 111-120.

Hedaya, R.J. (1996). *Understanding biological psychiatry.* New York: Norton.

Heim, C., Newport, J., Heit, S., Graham, Y.P., Wilcox, M., Bonsall, R., Miller, A.H., and Nemeroff, M.D. (2000). Pituitary-adrenal and autonomic responses to stress in women after sexual and physical abuse in childhood. *Journal of the American Medical Association, 284,* 592-597.

Herman, J. (1997). *Trauma and recovery* (Second edition). New York: Basic Books.

Hewett, S. (1999). *Assessing allegations of sexual abuse in preschool children: Understanding small children.* Thousand Oaks, CA: Sage Publications.

Hofer, M.A. (1995). Hidden regulators: Implications for a new understanding of attachment, separation, and loss. In S. Goldberg, R. Muir, and J. Kerr (Eds.), *Attachment theory: Social, developmental, and clinical perspectives* (pp. 203-230). Hillsdale, NJ: Analytic Press.

Hoptman, M.F. and Davidson, R.J. (1994). How and why do the two cerebral hemispheres interact? *Psychological Bulletin, 116,* 194-219.

Hubel, D.H. and Wiesel, T.N. (1979). Brain mechanisms of vision. *Scientific American, 241,* 150-162.

Huttenlocher, P.R. (1994). Synaptogenesis, synapse elimination, and neural plasticity in human cerebral cortex. In C.A. Nelson (Ed.), *Minnesota symposia on child psychology: Threats to optimal development: Integrating biological, psychological, and social risk factor* (pp. 35-53). Hillsdale, NJ: Erlbaum.

International Society for the Study of Dissociation Task Force on Children and Adolescence. (2000). Guidelines for the evaluation and treatment of dissociative symptoms in children and adolescents. *Journal of Trauma and Dissociation, 3,* 109-134.

Ito, Y., Teicher, M.H., Glod, C.A., and Ackerman, E. (1998). Preliminary evidence for aberrant cortical development in abused children: A quantitative EEG study. *Journal of Neuropsychiatry and Clinical Neuroscience, 10,* 298-307.

Ito, Y., Teicher, M.H., Glod, C.A., Harper, D., Magnus, E., and Gelbard, H.A. (1993). Increased prevalence of electrophysiological abnormalities in children with psychological, physical, and sexual abuse. *Journal Neuropsychiatry Clinical Neuroscience, 5,* 401-408.

James, B. (1994). *Handbook for treatment of attachment and trauma problems in children.* New York: Free Press.

James, B. (1997). *Assessing and treating childhood trauma and attachment issues.* Harvard Medical School Summer Seminars, Brewster, MA, July.

Johnson, J., Cohen, P., Brown, J., Smailes, E., and Bernstein, D. (1999). Childhood maltreatment increases risk for personality disorders during early adulthood. *Archives of General Psychiatry, 56,* 600-606.

Johnson, J., Cohen, P., Kasen, S., Smailes, E., and Brook, J. (2001). Association of maladaptive parental behavior with psychiatric disorder among parents and their offspring. *Archives of General Psychiatry, 58,* 453-460.

Jones, N.A., Field, T., and Davalos, M. (2000). Right frontal EEG asymmetry and lack of empathy in preschool children of depressed mothers. *Child Psychiatry and Human Development, 30,* 189-204.

Kagan, J. (1986). Presuppositions in developmental inquiry. In L. Cirilla and S. Wapner (Eds.), *Value presuppositions in theories of human development* (pp. 63-78). Hillsdale, NJ: Erlbaum.

Kagan, J. (1994). *Galen's prophecy.* New York: Basic Books.

Kardiner, A. and Spiegel, H. (1947). *War, stress, and neurotic illness: The traumatic neurosis of war* (Revised edition). New York: Hoeber.

Karoly, L., Greenwood, P., Everington, S., Hoube, J., Kilburn, M., Rydell, C., Sanders, M., and Chiesa, J. (1998). *Investing in our children: What we know and don't know about the costs and benefits of early childhood interventions.* Santa Monica, CA: RAND.

Karr-Morse, R. and Wiley, M.S. (1997). *Ghosts from the nursery: Tracing the roots of violence.* New York: Atlantic Monthly Press.

Kempermann, G., Kuhn, H.G., and Gage, F.H. (1997). More hippocampal neurons in adult mice living in an enriched environment. *Nature, 386,* 493-495.

Kempermann, G., Kuhn, H.G., and Gage, F.H. (1998). Experience induced neurogenesis in the senescent denate gyrus. *Journal of Neuroscience, 18,* 3206-3212.

Kendall, J., Dale, G., and Plakitsis, S. (1995). The mental health needs of children entering the child welfare system: A guide for caseworkers. *APSAC Advisor, 8,* 10-13.

Kendall-Tackett, K.A., Williams, L.M., and Finkelhor, D. (1993). Impact of sexual abuse on children: A review and syntheses of recent empirical studies. *Psychological Bulletin, 113,* 164-180.

Kendler, K. S., Bulik, C.M., Silberg, J., Hettema, J.M., Myers, J., and Prescott, C.A. (2000). Childhood sexual abuse and adult psychiatric and substance abuse disorders in women. *Archives of General Psychiatry, 57,* 953-959.

Kessler, R. (2000). Posttraumatic stress disorder: The burden to the individual and society. *Journal of Clinical Psychiatry, 61*(Supplement 5), 4-12.

Kessler, R., Nelson, C., McGonagle, K., Liu, J., Swartz, M., and Blazer, D. (1996). Comorbidity of DSM-III-R major depressive disorder in the general population: Results from the US National Comorbidity Study. *British Journal of Psychiatry, 168,* 17-30.

Kessler, R., Sonnega, A., Bromet, E., and Nelson, C. (1995). Post-traumatic stress disorder in the National Comorbidity Survey. *Archives of General Psychiatry, 52,* 1048-1060.

Kilpatrick, D. and Saunders, B. (1997). *Prevalence and consequences of child victimization: Results from the national survey of adolescents, final report* (NCJ 181028). Washington, DC: U.S. Department of Justice.

Kluft, R.P. (1993). The treatment of dissociative disorder patients: An overview of discoveries, successes and failures. *Dissociation, 6,* 87-101.

Kolb, B. and Whishaw, I.Q. (1998). Brain plasticity and behavior. *Annual Review of Psychology, 49,* 43-64.

Koplewicz, H. (1996). *It's nobody's fault: New hope and help for difficult children.* New York: Random House.

Kotulak, R. (1993). Unraveling hidden mysteries of the brain. *Chicago Tribune,* April 11, p. 11.

Ladd, C.O., Owens, M.J., and Nemeroff, C.B. (1996). Persistent changes in corticotrophin-releasing factor neuronal systems induced by maternal deprivation. *Endocrinology, 137,* 1212-1218.

LeDoux, J. (1996). *The emotional brain: The mysterious underpinnings of emotional life.* New York: Simon and Schuster.

LeDoux, J. E., Wilson, D.H., and Gazzaniga, M. (1977). A divided mind. *Annals of Neurology, 2,* 417-421.

Lemieux, A.M. and Coe, C.I. (1995). Abuse-related posttraumatic stress disorder: Evidence for chronic neuroendocrine activation in women. *Psychosomatic Medicine, 57,* 105-115.

Levine, P. (2001). *Working with the body to resolve trauma.* Paper presented at Psychological Trauma Conference sponsored by Boston University School of Medicine, Boston, MA, March.

Levine, P. and Fredrick, A. (1997). *Waking the tiger: Healing trauma.* Berkeley, CA: North Atlantic Books.

Lewis, D.O. (1998). *Guilty by reason of insanity.* New York: Ballantine.

Lewis, M.H., Gluck, J.P., Beauchamp, A.J., Keresztury, M.F., and Mailman, R.M. (1990). Long-term effects of early social isolation in Macaca Mulatta: Changes in dopamine receptor function following apomorphine challenge. *Brain Research, 513,* 67-73.

Liotti, G. (1999). Disorganization of attachment as a model of understanding dissociative psychopathology. In J. Soloman and C. George (Eds.), *Attachment disorganization* (pp. 291-317). New York: Guilford Press.

Liu, D., Diorio, J., Tannenbaum, B., Daldji, C., Francis, D., Freedmen, A., Sharma, S., Pearson, D., Plotsky, P.M., and Meaney, M.J. (1997). Maternal care, hippocampal glucocorticoid receptors, and hypothalamic-pituitary-adrenal response to stress. *Science, 277,* 1659-1662.

Luhrmann, T.M. (2000). *Of two minds: The growing disorder in American psychiatry.* New York: Alfred A. Knopf.

Lyon, G. (1996). Foundations of neuroanatomy and neuropsychology. In G. Lyon and J. Rumsey (Eds.), *Neuroimaging: A window to the neurological foundations of learning and behavior in children* (pp. 3-23). Baltimore, MD: Paul H. Brookes.

Mack, K. (1996). Nature, nurture, brains, and behavior. *The World and I,* July, 194-201.

MacLean, P.D. (1990). *The triune brain in evolution.* New York: Plenum Press.

Madanes, C. (1990). *Sex, love, and violence: Strategies for transformation.* New York: Norton.

Main, M. and Hesse, E. (1990). Parents' unresolved traumatic experiences are related to infant disorganized attachment status: Is frightened and/or frightening parent behavior the linking mechanism? In M. Greenberg, D. Cicchetti, and E. Cummings (Eds.), *Attachment in the preschool years* (pp. 161-182). Chicago: University of Chicago Press.

Main, M. and Solomon, J. (1990). Procedures for identifying infants as disorganized/disoriented during the Ainsworth Strange Situation. In M.T. Greenberg, D. Cicchetti, and E.M. Cummings (Eds.), *Attachment in the preschool years: theory, research, and intervention* (pp. 121-160). Chicago: University of Chicago Press.

Mason, J.W., Wang, S., Yehuda, R., Lubin, H., Johnson, D., Bremner, J.D., Charney, D., and Southwick, S.M. (2002). Marked lability in urinary cortisol levels in subgroups of combat veterans with posttraumatic stress disorder during an intensive exposure treatment program. *Psychosomatic Medicine, 64,* 238-246.

McCarton, C.M., Brooks-Gunn, J., Wallace, I.F., Bauer, C.R., Dennett, F.C., Bern, J.C., Bennett, F.C., Bernbaum, J.C., Broyles, R.S., Casey, P.H., et al. (1997). Results at age 8 years of early intervention for low-birth-weight premature infants: The infant health and development program. *Journal of the American Medical Association, 277,* 126-132.

McEwen, B.S. (2001). Commentary on PTSD discussion. *Hippocampus, 11,* 82-84.

McEwen, B.S. (2002). *Stress and hippocampal structural plasticity.* A paper presented at the 18th annual International Conference of the International Society for Traumatic Stress Studies. Special satellite meeting: Biological concepts related to the etiology, pathophysiology, and treatment of PTSD. Baltimore, MD.

McEwen, B.S. and Magarinos, A.M. (1997). Stress effects on morphology and function of the hippocampus. In R. Yehuda and A. McFarlane (Eds.), *Psychobiology of posttraumatic stress disorder* (pp. 271-285). New York: New York Academy of Sciences.

McGee, J. P. and DeBernardo, C. (1999). The classroom avenger. *Forensic Examiner,* May/June, 16-18.

McGoldrick, M. and Gerson, R. (1985). *Genograms in family assessment.* New York: Norton.

McLosky, L. and Walker, L. (2000). Posttraumatic stress in children exposed to family violence and single-event trauma. *Journal of the American Academy of Child and Adolescent Psychiatry, 39,* 108-115.

Meaney, M.J. (2002). *Maternal care and the development of individual differences in vulnerability for anxiety and trauma related disorders.* A paper presented at the 18th annual International Conference of the International Society for Traumatic Stress Studies. Special satellite meeting: Biological concepts related to the etiology, pathophysiology, and treatment of PTSD. Baltimore, MD.

Mills, D., Coffey-Corina, S., and Neville, H. (1994). Variability in cerebral organization during primary language acquisition. In G. Dawson and K. Fisher (Eds.), *Human behavior and the developing brain* (pp. 427-455). New York: Guilford Press.

Mlot, C. (1998). Probing the biology of emotion. *Science, 280,* 1005-1007.

Money, J. (1992). *The Kaspar Hauser syndrome of psychosocial dwarfism: Deficient statural, intellectual and social growth induced by child abuse.* Buffalo, NY: Prometheus.

Moyers, B. (1993). *Healing and the mind.* New York: Doubleday.

Nachmias, M., Gunnar, M., Mangelsdorf, S., Parritz, R.H., and Buss, K. (1996). Behavioral inhibition and stress reactivity: The moderating role of attachment security. *Child Development, 67,* 508-522.

National Clearinghouse on Child Abuse and Neglect Information. (1999). *In harm's way: Domestic violence and child maltreatment.* Washington, DC: Author. Retrieved April 13, 2001, from <http://www.calib.com/nccanch/pubs/otherpubs/ harmsway.cfm>.

National Council of Juvenile and Family Court Judges (1999). *Effective intervention in domestic violence and child maltreatment cases: Guidelines for policy and practice.* Reno, NV: Author.

National Institute of Mental Health. (2000). *A good beginning: Sending America's children to school with the social and emotional competence they need to succeed.* Bethesda, MD: Author.

Nemeroff, C.B., Heim, C., Newport, J., and Miller, A. (2002). *The role of early trauma in the pathophysiology of depression.* A paper presented at the 18th annual International Conference of the International Society for Traumatic Stress Studies. Special satellite meeting: Biological concepts related to the etiology, pathophysiology, and treatment of PTSD. Baltimore, MD.

Nijenhuis, E., Ehling, T., and Krikke, A. (2002). *Hippocampal volume in florid and recovered DID, DDNOS, and healthy controls: Three MRI studies.* Research paper presented at the 19th International Fall Conference of the International Society for the Study of Dissociation. Baltimore, MD.

Nilsson, M., Perfilieva, E., Johansson, U., Orwar, O., and Eriksson, P.S. (1999). Enriched environment increases neurogenesis in the adult rat dentate gyrus and improves spatial memory. *Journal of Neurobiology, 39,* 569-578.

Ochberg, F.M. (1996). The counting method for ameliorating traumatic memories. *Journal of Traumatic Stress, 4,* 873-880.

Ogden, P. and Minton, K. (2001). *Bio-mechanical resources: Interventions and psychological implications.* Paper presented at Psychological Trauma Conference sponsored by Boston University School of Medicine, Boston, MA, March.

Ornitz, E. (1996). Developmental aspects of neurophysiology. In M. Lewis (Ed.), *Child and adolescent psychiatry: A comprehensive textbook* (pp. 39-49). Baltimore, MD: Williams and Wilkins.

Papolos, D. and Papolos, J. (1999). *The bipolar child: The definitive and reassuring guide to childhood's most misunderstood disorder.* New York: Broadway Books.

Parkin, A. (1998). The alien hand. In R. Carter (Ed.), *Mapping the mind* (p. 52). Los Angeles: University of California Press.

Perry, B.D. (1994). Neurobiological sequelae of childhood trauma: PTSD in children. In M. Murgurg (Ed.), *Catecholamine function in post-traumatic stress disorder: Emerging concepts* (pp. 233-255). Washington, DC: American Psychiatric Press.

Perry, B.D. (1997). Incubated in terror: Neurodevelopmental factors in the "cycle of violence." In J. Osofsky (Ed.), *Children in a violent society* (pp. 124-149). New York: Guilford Press.

Perry, B.D. (2000a). *Violence and childhood: How persisting fear can alter the developing child's brain.* Retrieved March 29, 2000, from <http://www.bcm.tmc.edu/civitas> (currently <http://www.childtrauma.org>).

Perry, B.D. (2000b). *Neurodevelopment and dissociation: Trauma and adaptive responses to fear.* A plenary presented at the Seventeenth International Fall Conference of the International Society for the Study of Dissociation, San Antonio, TX, November.

Pert, C.B. (1997). *Molecules of emotion: The science behind mind-body medicine.* New York: Simon and Schuster.

Peterson, G. (1996). Diagnostic taxonomy: Past to future. In J.L. Silberg (Ed.), *The dissociative child* (pp. 3-26). Lutherville, MD: Sidran Press.

Post, R.M., Weiss, B., Smith, M., He Li, and McCann, U. (1997). Kindling versus quenching: Implications for the evolution and treatment of posttraumatic stress disorder. In R. Yehuda and A. McFarlane (Eds.), *Psychobiology of posttraumatic stress disorder* (pp. 285-296). New York: New York Academy of Sciences.

Prevent Child Abuse America. (2001). *Total annual cost of child abuse and neglect in the United States.* Retrieved March 20, 2001, from <http://www.preventchildabuse.org>.

Putnam, F.W. (1996). *Longitudinal psychobiology of sexually abused girls.* Paper presented at the New York Academy of Sciences Conference on the Psychobiology of Posttraumatic Stress. New York, NY, September.

Putnam, F. (1997). *Dissociation in children and adolescents: A developmental perspective.* New York: Guilford Press.

Putnam, F. (1998). *Why is it so difficult for the epidemic of child abuse to be taken seriously?* David L. Chadwick endowed lecture presented at the San Diego Conference on Responding to Child Maltreatment, San Diego, CA, January.

Putnam, F.W., Helmers, K., and Trickett, P.K. (1993). Development, reliability and validity of a child dissociation scale. *Child Abuse and Neglect, 17,* 731-741.

Putnam, F. and Trickett, P. (1997). Psychobiological effects of sexual abuse: A longitudinal study. In R. Yehuda and A. McFarlane (Eds.), *Psychobiology of posttraumatic stress disorder* (pp. 150-160). New York: New York Academy of Sciences.

Pynoos, R.S. and Nader, K. (1988). Psychological first aid and treatment approach to children exposed to community violence. *Journal of Traumatic Stress, 1,* 445-473.

Pynoos, R.S., Steinberg, A.M., and Goenjian, A. (1996). Traumatic stress in childhood and adolescence: Recent development and current controversies. In B.A. van der Kolk, A.C. McFarlane, and L. Weisaeth (Eds.), *Traumatic stress: The effects of overwhelming experience on mind, body, and society* (pp. 331-359). New York: Guilford Press.

Pynoos, R.T., Steinberg, A.M., Ornitz, E.M., and Nemeroff, C.B. (1997). Issues in the developmental neurobiology of traumatic stress. In R. Yehuda and A. McFarlane (Eds.), *Psychobiology of posttraumatic stress disorder* (pp. 176-194). New York: New York Academy of Sciences.

Raine, A., Meloy, J.R., Bihrle, S., Stoddard, J., Lacasse, L., and Buchsbaum, M.S. (1998). Reduced prefrontal and increased subcortical brain functioning assessed using positron emission tomography in predatory and affective murderers. *Behavioral Sciences and the Law, 16,* 319-332.

Ramey, C. and Ramey, S. (1994). Which children benefit the most from early intervention? *Pediatrics, 6,* 1064-1066

Ratey, J. (1999). *The user's guide to the brain: Bringing neuroscience into clinical practice.* Summer seminars for mental health professionals. Sponsored by Harvard Medical School. Brewster, MA, July.

Ratey, J. (2001). *A user's guide to the brain.* New York: Pantheon Books.

Ratey, J., Middeldorp-Crispijn, C., and Leveroni, C. (1995). Influence of attention problems on the development of personality. In J. Ratey (Ed.), *Neuropsychiatry of personality disorders* (pp. 79-119). Cambridge MA: Blackwell Science.

Rauch, S.L., van der Kolk, B., Fisler, R.E., Alpert, N.M., Orr, S.P., Savage, C.R., Fischman, A.M., Jenike, M.A., and Pitman, M.D. (1996). A symptom provocation study of posttraumatic stress disorder using positron emission tomography and script-driven imagery. *Archives of General Psychiatry, 53,* 380-387.

Ross, C. (1997). *Dissociative identity disorder: Diagnosis, clinical features, and treatment of multiple personality* (Second edition). New York: John Wiley and Sons.

Ross, C. and Pam, A. (1995). *Pseudoscience in biological psychiatry: Blaming the body.* New York: John Wiley and Sons.

Rossi, E.L. (1993). *The psychobiology of mind-body healing: New concepts of therapeutic hypnosis.* New York: Norton.

Rutter, M. and Rutter, M. (1993). *Developing minds: Challenge and continuity across the life span.* New York: Basic Books.

Sameroff, A.J. (1998). Environmental risk factors in infancy. *Pediatrics, 102,* 1287-1292.

Sameroff, A.J., Seifer, R., Baldwin, A., Baldwin, C. (1993). Stability of intelligence from preschool to adolescence: The influence of social and family risk factors. *Child Development, 64,* 80-97.

Sameroff, A.J., Seifer, R., Barocas, R., Zax, M., and Greenspan, S. (1987). Intelligence quotient scores of 4-year-old children: Social-environmental risk factors. *Pediatrics, 79,* 343-350.

Sapolsky, R.M. (1996). Why stress is bad for your brain. *Science, 273*, 749-750.

Sapolsky, R.M. (1998). *Why zebras don't get ulcers.* New York: W.H. Freeman.

Schiffer, F. (1998). *Of two minds: The revolutionary science of dual-brain psychology.* New York: Free Press.

Schiffer, F., Teicher, M., and Papanicolaou, A. (1995). Evoked potential evidence for right brain activity during the recall of traumatic memories. *The Journal of Neuropsychiatry and Clinical Neurosciences, 7*, 169-175.

Schiraldi, G. (2000). *The post-traumatic stress disorder sourcebook: A guide to healing, recovery, and growth.* Los Angeles: Lowell House.

Schmahmann, J.D. (1997). *The cerebellum and cognition.* New York: Academic Press.

Schneider, M.L., Clarke, A.S., Kraemer, G.W., Roughton, E.C., Lubach, G.R., Rimm-Kaufman, S., Schmidt, D., and Ebert, M. (1998). Prenatal stress alters biogenic amine levels in primates. *Developmental Pathology, 10*, 427-440.

Schore, A.N. (1994). *Affect regulation and the origin of the self: The neurobiology of emotional development.* New Jersey: Erlbaum.

Schore, A.N. (1996). The experience-dependent maturation of a regulatory system in the orbital prefrontal cortex and the origin of developmental psychopathology. *Development and Psychopathology, 8*, 59-87.

Schore, A.N. (2001). The effects of early relational trauma on right brain development, affect regulation, and infant mental health [Electronic version, pp. 1-80]. *Infant Mental Health Journal, 22*, 201-269. Retrieved October, 28, 2001, from <http://www.trauma-pages.com/shore-2001b.htm>.

Scott, J. (1979). Critical periods in organizational processes. In F. Falkner and J. Tanner (Eds.), *Human growth, Vol. 3, Neurobiology and nutrition* (pp. 223-241). New York: Plenum Press.

Sgoifo, A., Koolhass, J., De Boer, S., Musso, E., Stilli, D., Buwalda, B., and Meerlo, P. (1999). Social stress, autonomic neural activation, and cardiac activity in rats. *Neuroscience and Biobehavioral Reviews, 23*, 915-923.

Shalev, A.Y. (1996). Stress versus traumatic stress: Acute homeostatic reactions to chronic psychopathology. In B. van der Kolk, A. McFarlane, and L. Weisaeth (Eds.), *Traumatic Stress* (pp. 77-102). New York: Guilford Press.

Shapiro, F. (1995). *Eye movement desensitization and reprocessing: Basic principles, protocols, and procedures.* New York: Guilford Press.

Shepard, G.M. (1994). *Neurobiology* (Third edition). New York: Oxford University Press.

Shields, A. and Cicchetti, D. (2001). Parental maltreatment and emotion dysregulation as risk factors for bullying and victimization in middle childhood. *Journal of Clinical Child Psychology, 30*, 349-363.

Shin, L.M., McNally, R.J., Kosslyn, S.M., Thompson, S.L., Rauch, S., Alpert, L., Metzger, L.J., Lusko, N.B., Orr, S.P., and Pitman, R.K. (1999). Regional cerebral blood flow during script-driven imagery in childhood sexual abuse-related PTSD: A PET investigation. *American Journal of Psychiatry, 156*, 575-584.

Shure, M.B. (1995). *Raising a thinking child.* New York: Henry Holt.

Siegel, D.J. (1999). *The developing mind: Toward a neurobiology of interpersonal experience.* New York: Guilford Press.

Silberg, J.L. (Ed.). (1996a). *The dissociative child: Diagnosis, treatment, and management*. Baltimore, MD: Sidran Press.

Silberg, J.L. (1996b). The five-domain crisis mode: Therapeutic tasks and techniques for dissociative children. In J.L. Silberg (Ed.), *The dissociative child: Diagnosis, treatment, and management* (pp. 113-134). Lutherville, MD: Sidran Press.

Silberg, J.L. (1998). *Constructing consciousness in dissociative children: A family affair.* A workshop presented at the Fifteenth International Fall Conference of the International Society for the Study of Dissociation. Seattle, WA, November.

Silberg, J.L. (2000). *Developmental approach to the treatment of dissociative children.* A workshop presented at the Seventeenth International Fall Conference of the International Society for the Study of Dissociation. San Antonio, TX, November.

Sirevaag, A.M. and Greenough, W.T. (1987). Differential rearing effects on rat visual cortex synapses. III. Neuronal and glial nuclei, boutons, dendrites, and capillaries. *Brain Research, 424,* 320-332.

Smith, M.A., Makin, S., Kvernansky, R., and Post, R.M. (1995). Stress and glucocorticoids affect the expression of brain-derived neurotrophic factor and neurotrophin-e mRNA in the hippocampus. *Journal of Neuroscience, 15,* 1768-1777.

Southwick, S.M., Morgan, C.A., Bremner, D.J., Grillon, C.G., Krystal, J. H., Nagy, L.M., and Charney, D.S. (1997). Noradrenergic alterations in posttraumatic stress disorder. In R. Yehuda and A. McFarlane (Eds.), *Psychobiology of posttraumatic stress disorder* (pp. 125-142). New York: New York Academy of Sciences.

Sperry, R.W. (1968). Hemisphere disconnection and unity in conscious awareness. *American Psychologist, 23,* 723-733.

Spitz, R. (1945). Hospitalism: An inquiry into the genesis of psychiatric conditions in early childhood. *The Psychoanalytical Study of the Child, 1,* 53-74.

Spivak, G. and Shure, M.B. (1974). *Social adjustment of young children: A cognitive approach to solving real-life problems.* San Francisco: Jossey-Bass.

Squire, L.R. and Kandel, E.R. (1999). *Memory: From mind to molecules.* New York: Scientific American Library.

Stein, M.B., Koveroala, C., Hanna, C., Torchia, M.G., and McClarty, B. (1997). Hippocampal volume in women victimized by childhood sexual abuse. *Psychological Medicine, 27,* 951-959.

Sullivan, H.S. (1953). *The interpersonal theory of psychiatry.* New York: Norton.

Swerdlow, J. (1995). The quiet miracles of the brain. *National Geographic, 187,* June, 2-41.

Sylwester, R. (1995). *A celebration of neurons: An educator's guide to the human brain.* Virginia: Association for Supervision and Curriculum Development.

Taussig, H., Clyman, R., and Landsverk, J. (2001). A 6-year prospective study of behavioral health outcomes in adolescence. *Pediatrics, 108,* E10.

Teicher, M. (2000). Wounds that time won't heal: The neurobiology of child abuse. *Cerebrum: The Dana Forum on Brain Sciences, 2,* 50-68.

Teicher, M.H., Glod, C.A., Surrey, J., and Swett, C. (1993). Early childhood abuse and limbic system ratings in adult psychiatric outpatients. *Journal of Neuropsychiatry and Clinical Neuroscience, 5,* 301-306.

Teicher, M.H., Ito, Y., Glod, C.A., Anderson, S.L., Dumont, N., and Ackerman, E. (1997). Preliminary evidence for abnormal cortical development in physically and sexually abused children using EEG coherence and MRI. In R. Yehuda and A. McFarlane (Eds.), *Psychobiology of posttraumatic stress disorder* (pp. 160-176). New York: New York Academy of Sciences.

Terr, L. (1981). Forbidden games. *Journal of the American Academy of Child Psychiatry, 20,* 741-760.

Terr, L. (1990). *Too scared to cry.* New York: Basic Books.

Terr, L. (1994). *Unchained memories.* New York: Basic Books.

Thatcher, R. (1994). Cyclic cortical reorganization. In G. Dawson and K. Fischer (Eds.), *Human behavior and the developing brain* (pp. 232-266). New York: Guilford Press.

Thompson, P.M., Gledd, J.N., Woods, R.P., MacDonald, D., Evans, A.C., and Toga, A.W. (2000). Growth patterns in the developing brain detected by using continuum mechanical tensor maps. *Nature, 404,* 190-192.

Thormaehlen, D.J. and Bass-Feld, E.R. (1994). Children: The secondary victims of domestic violence. *Maryland Medical Journal, 43,* 355-359.

Tinker, R.H., and Wilson, S.A. (1999). *Through the eyes of a child: EMDR with children.* New York: Norton.

U.S. Department of Health and Human Services, Administration for Children and Families. (1999). *Progress report to the president on adoption.* Washington, DC: U.S. Government Printing Office. Retrieved May 3, 2001, from <http://adoptmonth.calib.com/pdf/report.pdf>.

U.S. Department of Health and Human Services, Administration for Children and Families, National Center on Child Abuse and Neglect. (1996). *Child maltreatment 1994: Reports from the states to the National Center on Child Abuse and Neglect.* Washington, DC: U.S. Government Printing Office.

U.S. Department of Health and Human Services, Administration on Children, Youth and Families. (2000). *Child maltreatment 1998: Reports from the states to the national child abuse and neglect data system.* Washington, DC: U.S. Government Printing Office. Retrieved May 30, 2001, from <http://acf.dhhs.gov/programs/cb/publications/cm98/>.

U.S. Department of Housing and Urban Development. (1999). *Homelessness programs and the people they serve: Findings of the national survey of homeless assistance providers and clients.* Washington, DC: U.S. Public Health Service. Surgeon general's report on mental health. Retrieved April 17, 2001, from <http://www.urban.org/housing/homeless/homeless.html>.

U.S. Public Health Service. (2000). *Report of the surgeon general's conference on children's mental health: A national action agenda.* Washington, DC: Author. Retrieved May 15, 2001, from <http://www.surgeongeneral.gov/cmh/childreport.htm>.

Vaidya, C.J., Austin, G., Kirkorian, G., Ridlehuber, H.W., Desmond, J.E., and Glover-Gabrieli, J.D. (1998). Selective effects of methylphenidate in attention deficit hyperactivity disorder: A functional magnetic resonance study. *Procedures of the National Academy of Sciences, 95,* 14494-14499.

van der Kolk, B. (1987). *Psychological trauma*. Washington, DC: American Psychiatric Press.

van der Kolk, B. (1994). The body keeps the score: Memory and the evolving psychobiology of posttraumatic stress. *Harvard Review of Psychiatry, 1,* 253-265.

van der Kolk, B. (1996a). The body keeps the score: Approaches to the psychobiology of PTSD. In B. van der Kolk, A. McFarlane, and L. Weisaeth (Eds.), *Traumatic stress* (pp. 214-241). New York: Guilford Press.

van der Kolk, B. (1996b). Trauma and memory. In B. van der Kolk, A.C. McFarlane, and L. Weisaeth (Eds.), *Traumatic stress* (pp. 279-303). New York: Guilford Press.

van der Kolk, B. (1997). *Trauma, memory, and self-regulation: Clinical applications of current research* (Mimeographed handout). Harvard Medical School Summer Seminars, Nantucket, MA, September.

van der Kolk, B. (2000). Trauma, neuroscience and the etiology of hysteria. *The Journal of the American Academy of Psychoanalysis, 28,* 237-262.

van der Kolk, B. (2001). EMDR, consciousness and the body. Paper presented at the Boston University School of Medicine Psychological Trauma Conference, Boston, MA, March.

van der Kolk, B., Burbridge, J., and Suzuki, J. (1997). The psychobiology of traumatic memory: Clinical implications of neuroimaging studies. In R. Yehuda and A. McFarlane (Eds.), *Psychobiology of post-traumatic stress disorder* (pp. 99-114). New York: New York Academy of Sciences.

van der Kolk, B. and Fisler, R. (1994). Childhood abuse and neglect and loss of self-regulation. *Bulletin of the Menninger Clinic, 58,* 145-168.

van der Kolk, B.A., McFarlane, A.C., and Weisaeth, L. (1996). *Traumatic stress: The overwhelming experience on mind, body, and society.* New York: Guilford Press.

van Ijzendoorn, M.H., Schuengel, C., and Bakermans-Kranenburg, M.J. (1999). Disorganized attachment in early childhood: Meta-analysis of precursors, concomitants, and sequelae. *Development and Psychopathology, 11,* 225-249.

Vythilingam, M., Heim, C., Newport, J., Miller, A.H., Anderson, E., Bronen, R., Brummer, M., Staib, L., Vermetten, E., and Charney, D.S. (2002). Childhood trauma associated with smaller hippocampal volume in women with major depression. *American Journal of Psychiatry, 159,* 2072-2080.

Wachtel, E.F. (1994). *Treating troubled children and their families.* New York: Guilford Press.

Walker, E., Gelfand, A., Felfand, M., Koss, M., and Katon, W. (1995). Medical and psychiatric symptoms in female gastroenterology clinic patients with histories of sexual victimization. *General Hospital Psychiatry, 17,* 85-92.

Wang, S., Bartolome, J., and Schanberg, S. (1996). Neonatal deprivation of maternal touch may suppress ornithine decarboxylase via downregulation of the proto-oncogenes c-myc and max. *Journal of Neuroscience, 16,* 836-842.

Waters, F.W. (1996). Parents as partners in the treatment of dissociative children. In J. L. Silberg (Ed.), *The dissociative child* (pp. 273-296). Lutherville, MD: Sidran Press.

Waters, F.W. (2000). *Bio-psycho-social approach to stabilizing the dissociative child.* Workshop presented at the Seventeenth International Fall Conference of the International Society for the Study of Dissociation. San Antonio, TX, November.

Waters, F.W. and Silberg, J.L. (1996). Therapeutic phases in the treatment of dissociative children. In J. L. Silberg (Ed.), *The dissociative child: Diagnosis, treatment, and management* (pp. 135-165). Lutherville, MD: Sidran Press.

Watzlawick, P. (1964). *An anthology of human communication.* Palo Alto, CA: Science and Behavior Books.

Webb, N.B. (1999). Play therapy crisis intervention with children. In N.B. Webb (Ed.), *Play therapy with children in crisis* (Second edition) (pp. 29-49). New York: Guilford Press.

Weinstock, M. (1997). Does prenatal stress impair coping and regulation of hypothalamic-pituitary-adrenal axis? *Neuroscience and Biobehavioral Reviews, 21,* 1-10.

Weinstock, M., Fride, E., and Hertzberg, R. (1988). Prenatal stress effects on functional development of offspring. *Progressive Brain Research, 73,* 319-331.

Werry, J. (1996). Brain and behavior. In M. Lewis (Ed.), *Child and adolescent psychiatry: A comprehensive textbook* (pp. 86-96). Baltimore: Williams and Wilkins.

White House Conference on Mental Health. (1997). Early childhood development and learning: What new research tells us about our youngest children, Washington, DC, April.

White House Conference on Mental Health. (1999). Remarks by the President, the First Lady, the Vice President, Mrs. Gore, and others. Howard University, Washington, DC, June.

Wieland, S. (1998). *Techniques and issues in abuse-focused therapy with children and adolescents: Addressing the internal trauma.* Thousand Oaks, CA: Sage Publications.

Williams, L.M. (1994). Recall of childhood trauma: A prospective study of women's memories of child sexual abuse. *Journal of Consulting and Clinical Psychology, 62,* 1167-1176.

Yehuda, R. (1997). Sensitization of the hypothalamic-pituitary-adrenal axis in posttraumatic stress disorder. In R. Yehuda and A. McFarlane (Eds.), *Psychobiology of posttraumatic stress disorder* (pp. 57-76). New York: New York Academy of Sciences.

Yoshikawa, H. (1995). Long-term effects of early childhood programs on social outcomes and delinquency. *Future of Children, 5,* 51-75.

Young, N. and Gardner, S. (1998). *Responding to alcohol and other drug problems in child welfare: Weaving together practice and policy.* Washington, DC: Child Welfare League of America.

Index

Page numbers followed by the letter "b" indicate boxed material; those followed by the letter "f" indicate figures.

Academic achievement, and interpersonal violence, 106-107

Accommodation, mental concept, 61, 123

Act to Leave No Child Behind, early interventions, 223-224

Adjunct therapy, trauma treatment, 134, 175-179, 179b-181b, 181-182

Adolescence, brain growth, 24

Adoption, foster care, 184

Adoption and Safe Families Act (ASFA), 185

Adrenalcorticotrophic (ACTH) hormone
complex PTSD, 102
stress response, 86, 87f

Adverse childhood experience (ACE) study
medical risk factor, 110, 220
reception of, 220-221

Affect-phobic, 150, 198-199

Aggression (fight), stress response, 81

Ainsworth, Mary, "strange situation," 188

Alexander and the Terrible, Horrible, No Good, Very Bad Day, 148

"Alien hand," 31

Ambivalence
stage 4 maturation, 52
trauma treatment, 151

Ambivalent attachment, 188, 189b

American Professional Society on the Abuse of Children, 227

American Psychiatric Association, PTSD diagnosis, 74

Amnesia, childhood trauma, 117-119

Amygdala
complex PTDS, 101-102
functions of, 25, 27f
maturation stage 1, 43
stress response, 83, 84, 86, 87f
stress response impairment, 88
unconscious memory system, 91-92

Andreasen, Nancy, genetic determinism, 212-213

Anger
interpersonal violence, 78
maturation stage 2, 48

Anosognosia, 33

Anterior cingulate
complex PTSD, 102, 105
function of, 94

Anterior commissure, brain organization, 27f

Antisocial behavior, attachment disorder, 49

Anxiety
complex PTDS, 100-101
trauma response, 78

Appeasement (submission), stress response, 81

Arousal
complex PTSD, 114, 116b
trauma treatment, 147

Arousal system, newborn, 43-44

Assertiveness training, trauma treatment, 175

Assessment, PTSD treatment, 140-141

Assimilation, mental concept, 61, 123

Association area, brain development, 22

Attachment
and brain development, 7
and brain structure, 19
biology of, 7-8, 12
categories of, 188, 189b, 190

Attachment disorder
Billy, 183, 188, 190-192, 198
critique of, 207-208
foster mother guidelines, 199b-201b

Attachment relationship
description of, 39
and empathy, 49
stress regulation, 54

Attachment theory
early research, 221
formulation of, 39

Attention deficit/hyperactivity disorder (ADHD)
Billy, 197
DSM-IV characterization, 125

Auditory hallucinations, simplified explanation, 145

Autobiographical memory, 90, 92, 106

Autonomic nervous system (ANS)
complex PTSD, 105
stress response, 83, 84, 85f, 87f

Autoregulation, stage 4 maturation, 54

Avoidance
Brittany, 80
Jessica, 113
Larry, 80
PTSD symptoms, 75-76
trauma treatment, 154

Avoidance attachment, attachment style, 188, 189b

Basil ganglia, stress response, 84

Battered child syndrome, 123

Battered women
childhood domestic violence, 99
trauma studies, 74

Begley, Sharon, 206, 208

Behavior problems
cause of, 4, 6
and implicit memories, 119

Behavioral reenactment, 77, 93

Belief system, child maltreatment, 130-131

Benson, Herbert, on relaxation response, 147

Betrayal trauma, 117

Billy, case study, 183-184, 186-188, 190-199, 201-202, 227

"Biological habit," 116b

Biological psychiatry, brain development, 1, 2, 4, 5f, 6

Bipolar Child, The, 129b

Bodily response, stress response, 82, 83

Body memories, trauma, 77-78, 93

Body therapy, trauma treatment, 178, 179, 181-182

Bonding, brain development, 110

Borderline disorder
in children, 128b-130b
and hemispheric integration, 109

Boundary setting, trauma treatment, 152b-153b

Bowlby, John, attachment theory, 7, 39, 221

Boys, and domestic violence, 99

Bradley
case study, 13-14, 43, 45, 46
stage 1 development, 45, 46
stage 2 development, 48, 49-50
stage 3 development, 51
stage 4 development, 55
stage 5 development, 57-60
stage 6 development, 64-66

Brain
continuous development of, 3
emotional-cognitive synchronicity, 8
functional areas, 17-19, 18f
growth of, 19, 20-22
and motion, 177-179
size of, 17

Brain chemistry
pharmacological treatment, 138

Brain chemistry *(continued)*
  trauma response, 81, 86-87, 87f, 88b, 89
Brain-deprived neurotrophic factor, (BDNF), cortisol reaction, 105
Brain development
  and abuse impact, 10, 87
  attachment theory, 8
  childhood trauma studies, 7
  and complex PTSD, 14, 101-112
  and emotional expression, 8-9, 10, 51-52
  emotional milestones, 68-71
  factors that inhibit, 4
  growth spurts, 13, 22, 23-24, 62-63, 64
  maturation stage 1, 43-45
  maturation stage 2, 46
  maturation stage 3, 50-51
  maturation stage 4, 51-54
  maturation stage 5, 55-57
  maturation stage 6, 60-64
  neural genes, 6
  and simple PTST, 14, 88b, 88-95
Brain organization
  collaboration, 34-37
  hemispheres, 28-34
  overview, 13
  triune brain, 25-28, 26f, 27f
Brain stem
  brain organization, 25, 26f
  maturation stage 1, 43
  stress response, 84, 87f
Branch Davidian crisis, trauma response, 89
Brave New Brain: Conquering Mental Illness in the Era of the Genome, 212-213
Breggin, Peter, 213
Bremner, J. Douglas
  on "disease of memory," 92
  on genetic causation, 3
  hippocampus research, 104, 106
  on memory deficits, 123
Breuer, Josef, 73

Briere, John, 227
Brittany
  developmental skills, 175
  safety/stabilization stage, 145-146
  simple PTSD case study, 79-80, 93, 137
  simple PTSD treatment, 133, 134
  symptom reduction/memory work, 149-150, 154, 165-166
Broca's area, 18f, 29
Bruer, John T., 207, 208-209, 210, 211
Bullying, maltreated children, 127
Bungee cord effect, abused children, 126
Burlingham, Dorothy, 221

Caregiver
  child development, 64
  foster mother guidelines, 199b-201b
  maturation stage 2, 46-49
Carolina Abecedarian Project, 225
Carson, Benjamin, hemispherectomy, 20
Carter, Rita, long-term memory, 103
Case studies
  Billy, 183-184, 186-188, 190-199, 201-202, 227
  Bradley, 13-14, 40, 45, 46, 48, 49-50, 51, 55, 57-60, 64-67, 203
  Brittany, 79, 80, 93, 133, 134, 137, 145-146, 149-150, 154, 165-166, 175
  Eliot, 28
  Jessica, 112-113, 133-134, 137, 141, 142, 145, 146-147, 150, 154, 166-168, 173, 175, 203
  memory systems, 90
  William, 129b
Catecholamines, trauma response, 89
Cause and effect, stage 3 maturation, 50
Cerebellar vermis
  and ADHD, 125

Cerebellar vermis *(continued)*
  and complex PTSD, 14, 98, 105,
    107
  movement stimulation, 178
Cerebellum
  brain organization, 25, 26f
  functional area, 18f
Cerebral palsy, purposeful movement,
    50-51
Child abuse. *See also* Child
    maltreatment
  behavior problems, 4
  impact of, 99-100, 104-105
Child development, psychobiological
    model of, 6, 39-68, 205
Child Dissociative Checklist, 140
Child maltreatment
  belief system formation, 130-131
  brain impairment, 15
  costs of, 214, 215f-217f, 217-221
  emotional regulation problems,
    113-114
  and identity formation, 120-123
  innovative programs, 224-228
  and interpersonal relationships,
    126-128
  mental health services, 186
  policy directions, 224-227
  and psychiatric disorders, 97, 98
  scope of, 14, 98-100
Child Sexual Behavior Inventory, 140
Child welfare system
  child maltreatment costs, 215b
  description of, 183, 184-186
Childhood PTSD, as risk factor, 218
Children
  complex PTSD behavior, 97
  brain growth, 24
  mental illness, 204
  and PTSD, 74-75, 76b, 76-79
  studies of traumatized, 95
  and traumatic memories, 93
Children's Defense Fund
  on childhood mental illness,
    204-205
  on early interventions, 223

Chowchilla kidnapping, traumatic play,
    77-78
Chronic health care, child maltreatment
    costs, 215b
Chronic pain, child maltreatment,
    219-220
Chronic traumatic stress
  impact of, 97-101
  seven core symptoms, 101
Chu, James, 100, 155
Cingulate cortex, maturation stage 2, 46
Cingulum, brain colaboration, 34
Clinton, Hillary, 206, 211
Cognition development
  and childhood experience, 8-9
  stage 4 maturation, 51, 52
  stage 5 maturation, 54, 55
  stage 6 maturation, 61
Cognitive impairment
  abused/neglected children, 123-124
  in foster children, 185-186
Cognitive restructuring, memory
    transformation, 159, 160-161
Cognitive-behavior therapy, PTSD
    treatment, 139b, 139
Collaboration, stage 4 maturation, 53
Comfort, trauma treatment, 148-150
Commissurotomy, split-brain studies,
    29
Communication
  Bradley, 51
  emotional milestones, 69
  stage 3 maturation, 50
Compartmentalization, identity
    formation, 121-122
Complementary (codependent)
    relationships, maltreated
    children, 127
Complex PTSD
  and ADHD, 125, 128b
  barriers to treatment, 133
  Billy's case study, 187-199, 227
  and brain impairment, 14, 101-112
  characterization of, 14, 100-101
  in children, 97-98
  core symptoms, 14, 101

Complex PTSD *(continued)*
  developmental skills, 14-15, 140, 168-175
  memory work stage, 14-15, 140, 156-168, 157f
  safety/stabilization stage, 14, 140, 141-147, 142b-143b
  symptom reduction stage, 14-15, 140, 147-151, 152b-153b, 153-156
  treatment goals, 133-139, 135b-136b
  treatment options overview, 138b-139b
Compulsive repetitiveness, traumatic play, 77
Concrete state, and brain growth, 24
Conscious experience, stress response, 82, 84
Conscious memory system, 90-92
Consciousness, developmental process, 122
Constitutional factors, brain development, 10-11
Contracts, trauma treatment, 142
Control, and maltreated children, 126
Corpus callosum
  and ADHD, 125
  and brain organization, 27f
  collaboration, 34
  and complex PTSD, 98, 108
  split-brain studies, 29-31
Cortex
  brain organization, 26f, 26-28
  stress response, 84, 85f, 85
Corticotropin-releasing factor (CRF)
  complex PTSD, 102, 105-106
  stress response, 86, 87f
Corticotropin-releasing factor (CRF) antagonists, 138
Cortisol
  complex PTSD, 102, 105-107, 111
  stress response, 86, 87f
  touch therapy, 176
Counting, memory transformation, 159, 163, 164

Covey, Steven, 169
Crack cocaine, and child welfare system, 184
Crawling, motor development, 50
Criminal activity, child maltreatment costs, 216b
"Critical period," developmental theory, 205, 206
Csikszentmihalyi, Mihaly, on flow, 35
"Cultural dissociation," 209-210
Curtis, Patrick, 184

Dalenberg, Constance, on survivor's cognitive errors, 160
Damasio, Antonio
  on brain function, 40
  and "Eliot," 28
  on emotional incongruity, 33-34
Declarative memory, 90, 92
"Defense operations," PTSD, 100
Dendrites
  and brain growth, 19, 22-23
  growth of, 11
Denial, PTSD defense mechanism, 100-101
Denver Developmental Screening Test, foster children, 185
Depression
  impact of maternal, 10, 204
  left hemisphere activity, 108
Desensitization
  EMDR, 180b
  memory work, 159-165
  trauma treatment, 154
Developmental skills
  Billy, 192, 196-198
  Brittany, 175
  Jessica, 173, 175
  trauma therapy, 14-15, 140, 168-175
  treatment goals, 133-134
Diagnostic and Statistical Manual for Mental Disorders (DSM-III), PTSD diagnosis, 74

Diagnostic and Statistical Manual for Mental Disorders (DSM-IV)
  ADHD, 125
  PTSD categories, 75-76
Disorganized attachment, 189b, 190
Disqualifications, definition of, 120
Dissociation
  and complex PTSD, 115b-116b, 116-117
  PTSD defense mechanism, 100-101
  stress response, 84
  and trauma studies, 73
  trauma treatment, 154-156
Dissociative amnesia, and trauma, 93, 95
Dissociative disorder not otherwise specified (DDNOS), Jessica, 113
Dissociative disorders, and complex PTSD, 106
Dissociative identity disorder (DID)
  in children, 122-123
  hippocampus volume, 104-105, 135
Dodd, Christopher, 223-224
Domestic violence, childhood maltreatment, 99
Dopamine
  and ADHD children, 125-126
  complex PTSD, 102
  stage 4 maturation, 53-54
Douglas, William O., right hemisphere stroke, 33-34
Dreams, PTSD symptoms, 76
Drug therapy, PTSD treatment, 138
Dwarfism, "Kaspar Hauser syndrome," 109

Early Childhood Development and Learning: What New Research Tells Us About Our Youngest Children conference, 206-207
Early Head Start, creation of, 206

Early intervention
  child maltreatment principle, 224, 225
  innovative programs, 225
Edelman, Marian Wright, 223
Education, PTSD treatment, 144-145
Educational assistance, PTSD treatment, 139b
Effective Intervention in Domestic Violence and Child Maltreatment Cases: Guidelines for Policy and Practice, 225
Einstein, Albert, on imagery, 57
Eliot, Lise, brain plasticity, 11
Eliot, neocortex impairment, 28
Elmira Prenatal/Early Infancy Project (PEIP), early interventions, 222-223
Emory University School of Medicine, sexual abuse study, 105
Emotion, stress response, 82-87, 85f
Emotional abuse
  childhood maltreatment category, 98, 99
  childhood trauma studies, 7
Emotional awareness, trauma treatment, 150-151
Emotional brain, 25, 26f
Emotional development
  and childhood experience, 8-9, 10
  emotional milestones, 68-71
  stage 4 maturation, 51-52
  stage 6 maturation, 61
  and trauma, 78-79
Emotional expression, and brain development, 8
Emotional intelligence
  child maltreatment principle, 224, 226
  innovative programs, 226-227
Emotional milestones, early childhood, 68-71
Emotional reciprocity, maturation stage 2, 48

Emotional regulation
  Billy, 188
  brain hemispheres, 32b, 32-33
  and childhood trauma, 7
  and complex PTSD, 113-114
  as dyadic interaction, 41
  trauma treatment, 147-148
Emotional self-regulation
  and caregiver interaction, 44
  during childhood, 8
  maturation stage 2, 48
Emotions
  brain lateralization, 109
  integration of, 151
  in stage 2 maturation, 47-48
  in stage 5 maturation, 56
  unconscious memory system, 91
Empathy
  and attachment relationship, 49
  maturation stage 6, 63
Endorphins, stress response, 86
Enriched environments, brain
      development, 11
Environmental stress, sociological
      factors, 213
Epinephrine, complex PTSD, 102
Ethical principles, universal, 174
Evaluation, stress response, 82
Exercise, adjunct therapy, 134, 177
Experience
  and brain development, 10-11
  and brain function, 3
  as "brain remodeling," 23
  cognitive organization of, 61
  neurobiologic view of, 2, 3, 4, 5f, 6
  trauma therapy, 14-15
Explicit memory, 90
Eye-movement desensitization and
      reprocessing (EMDR)
  for children, 179b-181b
  memory transformation, 159,
      164-165

Falling in love
  emotional milestones, 69
  stage 2 development, 46-49

Family
  PTSD treatment, 139b
  PTSD treatment goals, 136b
  Violence and Sexual Assault
      Institute, 227
Family foster care, 184
Fear
  maturation stage 2, 48
  processing of, 82-83
  stage 5 maturation, 57
Felitti, Vincent, ACE experience study,
      110, 220
Fetal alcohol syndrome (FAS), 4, 21
Fetal development, nervous system,
      20-21
Field, Tiffany, TRI, 176
Fight, stress response, 81, 82
First Feelings, 68
Flashbacks
  PTSD, 75
  simplified explanation, 144
  trauma treatment, 155
  traumatic memory, 93
Flight, stress response, 81, 82
Flow, brain organization, 35-37, 36f
*Flow: The Psychology of Optimal
      Experience*, 35
Focus, newborns, 43, 44-45
Foege, William, on ACE study,
      220-221
Formal operations stage, and brain
      growth, 24
Foster care
  children in, 183, 184-186
  and children with PTSD, 75
  exists from, 184
  types of, 184
Foster mother, care guidelines,
      199b-201b
Fragmentary memory
  and hippocampus, 106
  and trauma, 118
Frank Porter Child Development
      Center, Carolina Abecedarian
      Project, 225
Fraser, Sylvia, 112

Freeze response
   complex PTSD, 103
   stress response, 81-82
Freud, Anna, 221
Freud, Sigmund
   on common unhappiness, 74
   on hysteria, 73
   psychoanalytic theory, 2
Freyd, Jennifer, betrayal trauma, 117
Frontal cortex, maturation stage 2, 48
Frontal lobe
   cognitive development, 9-10
   functional area, 18f

Gamma-aminobutyric acid (GABA),
   stress response, 86
Garbarino, James, war zones survivors,
   95
Gender, PTSD, 75
Gene transcription, brain development,
   6
Genes, neurobiologic view of, 2, 3-4,
   5f, 6
Genetic determinism
   backlash view, 209
   and child maltreatment, 211-212
Genogram, memory transformation
   tool, 161
Genome Project, and mental illness, 3
Gesell Institute of Human
   Development, on action, 55
*Ghosts in the Nursery: Tracing the
   Roots of Violence,* 210
Gladwell, Malcolm, 209
Glucose metabolism, during childhood,
   22
Goleman, Daniel, on "two minds," 28
*Good Beginning: Sending America's
   Children to School with the
   Social and Emotional
   Competence They Need to
   Succeed, A,* 226
Gore, Tipper, 205, 211
Gray matter, brain, 17

Greenspan, Nancy T., *First Feelings,*
   68
Greenspan, Stanley
   child development, 13, 39, 44
   "circles of communication," 49
   on cognitive development, 61
   First Feelings, 68
   on play, 64
   on purposeful movement, 50-51
Guided imagery, 163

*Handbook for Treatment of Attachment
   and Trauma Problems in
   Children,* 199
Hanh, Thich Nhat, on feelings, 151
Harris, Eric, 131
Harris, Judith Rich, 207, 208, 209, 210,
   211
Head Start, creation of, 221-222, 226
Healing imagery, memory
   transformation, 159, 161-163
Healing touch, adjunct therapy, 134,
   176
Healthy Families America (HFA),
   home visits, 226-227
Heightened arousal
   Brittany, 80
   Jessica, 113
   Larry, 80
   PTSD symptoms, 75-76, 78
Hemispherectomy, 20
Hemispheres, brain development, 23-24
Herman, Judith
   on attachment relationship, 117
   on "cultural dissociation," 209-210
   on identity formation, 120-121
   on revictimization risk, 127-128
   trauma studies, 73, 100
   on trauma therapy phases, 139-140
Hippocampus
   and complex PTSD, 14, 98, 102,
      104, 106, 111
   and conscious memory system, 91
   functions of, 25, 27f, 103-104

Hippocampus *(continued)*
  maturation stage 2, 46
  nerve regeneration, 134-135
  stress response impairment, 89
  and traumatic memory, 93-94
Hofer, Myron
  attachment neurobiology, 13
  attachment theory, 7, 39
Home visits, HFA, 226-227
"Home-remedy therapy," 198
Hopelessness, child maltreatment, 130
Hormones
  complex PTSD, 102
  stress response, 83
  trauma response, 88b, 89
Hospitalizations, child maltreatment
    costs, 215b
Human genes, nervous system, 6
Huntington's chorea, genetic causation,
    4
Huttenlocher, Peter, dendritic density,
    19
Hyman, Steven, White House
    Conference II, 211, 212
Hyperactivity
  Billy, 188
  and child maltreatment, 124-125
Hyperarousal, complex PTSD, 113, 114
"Hyperlexia," 65
Hypothalamic-pituitary-adrenal (HPA)
    axis
  complex PTSD, 105, 106
  stress response impairment, 89
Hypothalamus, 83, 85f, 86, 87f
  functions of, 25
Hysteria, psychoanalytic history, 73
Hysterical Disorders of Warfare, 74

I Am Your Child Foundation, 206
Identity formation
  and childhood trauma, 7
  child maltreatment, 120-123

Imagination
  Bradley, 64-65
  maturation stage 5, 57
Imaging studies, traumatic dysfunction,
    94
Imitation, maturation stage 4, 52
Immobility (freezing), stress response,
    81-82
Immune system function, and complex
    PTSD, 14, 98, 110
Implicit memory, 90, 119
Infant Health and Development
    Program, 225
Infants
  attuned interactions, 8
  developmental stages, 41
  emotional milestones, 68-71
  impact of maternal depression, 10,
    204, 218
International Society for the Study of
    Dissociation, 227
International Society for Traumatic
    Stress Studies, 227
Interpersonal experience
  brain development, 11-13
  PTSD treatment, 136b, 138
Interpersonal relationships
  Bradley, 42, 43, 48
  and brain science, 2
  child maltreatment, 126-128
  and childhood trauma, 7
  maturation stage 2, 46-47
  and psychobiological model, 6
Interpersonal stressors
  emotional response to, 78
  and trauma, 74, 98
Interventions
  Bradley, 57-60
  RAND study, 222-223
  value of, 68
Interweaving, child development, 56
*Investing in Our Children: What We
    Know and Don't Know About
    the Costs and Benefits of
    Early Childhood
    Interventions,* 222

It Takes a Village, 206
It's Nobody's Fault: New Hope and
    Help for Difficult Children,
    211-212

James, Beverly
    emotion/weather metaphor, 151
    foster mother guidelines, 199b-201b
    hurricane survivors, 95
    on intimacy fears, 126
    on self-destructive behavior, 114
    on self-soothing, 147
    trauma bonding, 190
James S. McDonnell Foundation, 207
Janet, Pierre, 73
Jessica
    complex PTSD case study, 112-113,
        137, 203
    complex PTSD treatment, 133, 134
    developmental skills, 173, 175
    safety/stabilization stage, 141, 142,
        145, 146-147
    symptom reduction/memory work,
        150, 154, 166-168
Johnson, Jeffrey G., on parental
        behavior, 219
Judicial system, child maltreatment
        costs, 215b
Jung, Carl, psychoanalytical technique,
        36
Juvenile delinquency, child
        maltreatment costs, 216b

Kagan, Jerome, 40, 208
Kardiner, Abram, 74
Karr-Morse, Robin, 210
Kaspar Hauser syndrome, 109
Kendler, Kenneth, twin study, 219
Kessler, Ronald, on childhood PTSD,
        218
Kindling, complex PTDS, 101
Kinship foster care, 184
Klebold, Dylan, 131

Koplewicz, Harold, White House
        Conference II, 211-212
Kraepelin, Emil, biological psychiatry,
        2, 4
Kuhl, Patricia, on critical periods, 206

Language areas, brain, 18i, 22, 29
Language development
    Billy, 188
    Bradley, 41-43
    stage 5 maturation, 54, 55, 56
    stage 6 maturation, 61, 62
Larry, complex PTSD case study, 80-
        81, 101
Lateralization, complex PTSD, 98, 108-
        109
Law enforcement, child maltreatment
        costs, 215b
"Laying on of hands," 176
LeDoux, Joseph, on psychotherapy,
        137
Left hemisphere
    brain development, 62
    brain function, 32b, 32-33, 109
    brain organization, 13, 28-29
    and complex PTSD, 14, 98, 107-109
    coordination technique, 163
    removal of, 20
Lewis, Dorothy, death row study, 118,
        128
Limbic system
    brain organization, 25-26, 26f, 27f,
        27-28
    and complex PTSD, 14, 98, 102,
        107
    maturation stage 2, 46
    stress response, 83, 84, 85i
Locus coeruleus, stress response, 84
Logical thinking, stage 3 maturation, 50
Luhrmann, T. M., 1-2

Madanes, Cloé, therapeutic goals, 174
Magnetic resonance imaging (MRI),
        abused children studies, 108

Main, Mary, disorganized attachment, 190
Malevolent transformation, 149
Malignant belief systems, behavior problems, 4
Mammalian brain, 25
Manage care, symptom relief, 2
Mapping the Mind, 103
Masking experiments, emotional reactions, 82
Maternal attention, childhood development, 12
Maternal depression, impact of, 10, 204, 218
Maternal deprivation, sequelae of, 9
Maternal stress, brain development, 21-22
Maturation process, child development, 39
    stage 1, 43-47
    stage 2, 46-50
    stage 3, 50-51
    stage 4, 51-55
    stage 5, 55-60
    stage 6, 60-67
McEwen, Bruce
    on hormones, 220
    on neurogenesis, 134-135
Medial cortex, 94, 106
Medical neglect, childhood maltreatment category, 98
Memory
    autobiographical memory, 90, 92
    brain organization, 25-26, 26f
    and complex PTSD, 75, 106
    and dissociation, 117-119
    hippocampus's role, 103-104
    state-dependent recall, 95
    and stress response, 14
Memory systems, case studies, 90-91
Memory work
    trauma therapy, 14-15, 140, 156-168, 157f
    treatment goals, 133-134
Men, and domestic violence, 99

Mental health services
    child maltreatment costs, 215b, 216b, 218
    child maltreatment principle, 224, 227
    and foster care, 185-186
    innovative programs, 227-228
Mental illness
    as brain fragmentation, 109
    and childhood maltreatment, 97
    children with, 204
    and trauma history, 9, 10
Mental images, maturation stage 5, 55, 57, 60
Mental schema, stage 6 maturation, 61
Merzenich, Michael, 206
Metacognition, and complex PTSD, 108
Metacognitive development, stage 6 maturation, 63
Miller, George, 223-224
Mirroring, maturation stage 2, 48
Money, John, "Kaspar Hauser syndrome," 109-110
Motor areas, brain development, 22, 50-51
Motor development, stage 6 maturation, 62
Motor planning and sequencing, stage 3 maturation, 50
Motor skills, Bradley, 42
Movement, adjunct therapy, 134, 176-177, 178
Multiple Personality Disorder (MPD), 122
Multistate Foster Care State Archive, foster case recidivism, 196
Music, adjunct therapy, 176-177
Mutual engagement, Bradley, 58-59
My Father's House: A Memoir of Healing, 112
Myelinization
    complex PTSD, 107
    nervous system, 22
Myth of the First Three Years, The, 207, 209, 219

Naloxone, 138
Neglect
  ADHD children, 125
  childhood maltreatment category,
    98, 99
  childhood trauma studies, 7
  and complex PTSD, 108
Neocortex, brain organization, 27, 28
Nervous system
  fetal development, 20-21
  genes in, 6
  maturation stage 1, 43- 45
  myelinization, 22
Netherlands, child abuse study, 104-
    105
Neurobiologists, functional imagery
    technology, 3
"Neurobiology of interpersonal
    experience," 3
Neuroendocrine system, and complex
    PTSD, 14, 98, 109, 110
Neurological deficits
  and psychiatric disorders, 98
  and trauma, 101
Neurons, development of, 20-21
Neuropeptides
  complex PTSD, 102
  trauma response, 88b
Neurotransmitters, 88b, 102
Newborns
  challenges of, 43
  maturation stage 2, 47-48
Newsweek, "Your Child's Brain,"
    206, 208
Norepinephrine
  complex PTSD, 102
  maturation stage 4, 53-54
  stress response, 84
  trauma response, 88b
  Numbing, complex PTSD, 113, 114
*Nurture Assumption: Why Children
    Turn Out the Way They Do,
    The,* 207, 209

Object constancy, stage 4 maturation,
    52-53

Object permanence, stage 4 maturation,
    52-53
Occipital lobe, functional area, 18f
Ochberg, Frank, counting, 164
*Of Two Minds: The Growing Disorder
    in American Psychiatry,* 1-2,
    29, 34
Oppositional behavior,
    maltreated children, 126
    maturation stage 6, 62-63
Oppositional defiant disorder (ODD),
    and complex PTSD, 128b
"Optimistic processes," 87
Orbitofrontal cortex
    and complex PTSD, 106
    maturation stage 2, 46, 47f
    maturation stage 4, 53
    traumatic dysfunction, 94
Outward Bound, adjunct therapy, 176
Overarousal, brain organization, 43-44,
    45

Papolos, Demitri, 129b
Papolos, Janice, 129b
Parasympathetic nervous system
    and complex PTSD, 102-103, 106
    stress response, 83, 84
Parental behavior, child development,
    219
Parental education, Bradley, 59
Parents
    betrayal trauma, 117
    child development, 66
    and infant brain growth, 8
    post-trauma action, 95b
Parietal lobe, functional area, 18f
Parkin, Alan, "alien hand," 31
Pattern recognition, nervous system
    organization, 44-45
Peer relationships
    Bradley, 59-60
    and genetic determinism, 208
    social skill training, 173
Permissiveness, behavior problems, 4

Perry, Bruce
  on belief systems, 130
  on Branch Davidian children, 89
  cognitive impairment findings, 123
  on dissociation, 115b, 116b
  on EMDR, 165
  on naloxone, 138
  on reactivity, 111
  on sensitization, 109, 111
  traumatologist, 7, 205
Perry Preschool program, early
      interventions, 222, 223
Pert, Candace, peptide flow, 37
Pet scans, maturation stage 2, 46
Pharmacological therapies, PTSD
      treatment, 139b
Phenylketonuria (PKU), genetic
      causation, 4
Physical abuse
  childhood maltreatment category, 98
  childhood trauma studies, 7
  complex PTSD, 102, 104, 108
Physical growth, and child abuse, 109,
      110
Piaget, Jean
  basic mental activities, 61, 123
  development stages, 24
Pincas, Jonathan, death row study, 118,
      128
Pinker, Steven, on attachment disorder,
      208
Pituitary gland, stress response, 86, 87f
Plasticity, brain development, 11, 19-
      20, 221
Play
  and basic mental processes, 124
  Billy, 188
  maturation stage 5, 55-56
  and traumatic reenactment, 77
"Play Baby" intervention, 149-150
Play therapy, memory work, 158-159
Play Therapy with Children in Crisis,
      158
Positron-emission tomography (PET),
      brain organization, 34-35

Post-traumatic stress disorder (PTSD)
  barriers to treatment, 133
  brain development, 14
  among children, 74-75, 76b, 76-79
  and developmental skills, 14-15,
      140, 168-175
  "disease of memory," 92
  DSM criteria, 74, 75-76
  memory work, 14-15, 140, 156-168,
      157f
  prevalence of, 75
  safety/stabilization stage, 14, 140,
      141-147, 142b-143b
  symptom reduction, 14-15, 140,
      147-151, 152b-153b, 153-156
  symptoms of, 75-76
  treatment goals, 133-139, 135b-
      136b
  treatment options overview, 138b-
      139b
  types of, 79-81
Predictability, secure attachment, 190
Prefrontal cortex
  brain development, 23
  and complex PTSD, 102, 105, 111
  and infant attachment, 8
  stage 2 maturation, 46, 47f
  stage 4 maturation, 53, 54
  stage 6 maturation, 63-64
  stress response, 84, 85-86
  stress response impairment, 89
  traumatic dysfunction, 94
Prenatal insults, impact of, 21
Prepuberty, and brain growth, 24-25,
      64
Prevent Child Abuse America study, on
      child maltreatment costs, 214,
      215f-217f, 217-218, 219-220
Problem behaviors
  and complex PTSD, 97
  neurobiological view of, 4
Problem solving
  teaching, 171b-172b
  and trauma, 168-169
  trauma treatment, 169-170
Problem-solving steps, 170-171

Procedural memory, 90
Productivity loss, child maltreatment
     costs, 216b
Pruning
     brain development, 23
     maturation stage 5, 56
Psychoanalysis, emergence of, 73
Psychoanalysts, current debate, 1, 2
Psychobiological movement
     backlash against, 207-211
     development of, 205-207
Psychobiology of Mind-Body Healing,
     The, 163
Psychodynamic therapy, PTSD
     treatment, 138b, 139
Psychoeducational approach, PTSD
     treatment, 138b
Psychological abuse
     and brain lateralization, 108
     left hemisphere deficits, 107
Psychologists, current debate, 1
Psychophysiolgical reenactment, 77-78
Putnam, Frank
     on ADHD children, 125
     on cognitive impairment, 218-219
     on psychobiology, 210-211
     traumatologist, 7, 205

Quantity, stage 6 maturation, 61

Rage
     complex PTDS, 100-101
     interpersonal violence, 78
RAND study, early interventions, 222-
     223
Rape victims, trauma studies, 74
Rasmussen's encephalitis, 20
Ratey, John
     on child psychiatry, 12-13
     on childhood stress, 6
     on motion, 177-179
     neuron firing research, 45
Rebuilding Shattered Lives, 100

Reclaiming Our Children: A Healing
     Plan for a Nation in Crisis,
     213
Reconnection, adult trauma therapy,
     139-140
Reexperience
     Brittany, 80
     Jessica, 113
     Larry, 80
     PTSD symptoms, 75-77
Reflected appraisals, identity
     formation, 120
Reiner, Rob, I Am Your Child
     Foundation, 206-207
Relaxation response, 147
Religious beliefs, therapeutic goals,
     174
Remedial interventions, PTSD
     treatment, 139b
Remembrance/mourning, adult trauma
     therapy, 139-140
"Remodeling," brain development, 23-
     24
Repetition, Bradley, 42
Reptilian brain, 25, 26f
Residential (group) foster care, 184
Responsiveness, secure attachment, 190
Reunification, foster care exist, 184-
     185
Revictimization, maltreated children,
     127
Richmond, Julius, 221-222
Right hemisphere
     brain function, 32b, 32, 33, 109
     brain organization, 13, 28-29
     and complex PTSD, 14
     coordination technique, 163
Ritalin, ADHD, 197
Rituals, trauma treatment, 176
Rochester Longitudinal Study,
     cognitive risk factors, 123
Romanian orphans, developmental
     disabilities, 9-10
Ross, Colin, on survivor's cognitive
     errors, 160

Rossi, Ernest
  flow modalities, 36
  symptom scaling, 163-164
Rutter, Marjorie, on cognitive risk
      factors, 123
Rutter, Michael, on cognitive risk
      factors, 123

Sadness, maturation stage 2, 48
Safe Start, zero tolerance, 224
Safety, adult trauma therapy, 139-140
Safety/stabilization stage
  Billy, 192, 193-194
  Brittany, 145-146
  Jessica, 141, 142, 145, 146-147
  trauma therapy, 14, 140, 141-147,
      142b-143b
  treatment goals, 133-134
Sameroff, Arnold, Rochester
      Longitudinal Study, 123
Sapolsky, Robert, 86-87
Satcher, David, 204, 212
Schiffer, Fredrick, cerebral
      hemispheres, 28-29, 34
Schore, Allan
  on abusive caregiver, 191-192
  attachment neurobiology, 13
  attachment theory, 7, 8, 39
  axon generation, 44
  brain development, 40, 46-47, 125,
      191
  on complex PTSD arousal, 103
  on neurotransmitters, 53-54
  stress regulation, 54
  traumatologist, 205
Secure attachment, 188, 189b, 190
Selective serotonin reuptake inhibitors
      (SSRI), and brain activity, 14,
      138
Self, and trauma, 168
Self-anesthesia, PTSD defense
      mechanism, 100-101
Self-assertion
  stage 3 maturation, 50

Self-assertion *(continued)*
  stage 4 maturation, 51, 52
  stage 6 maturation, 62
Self-assurance, stage 6 maturation, 63
Self-awareness
  stage 6 maturation, 63
  and trauma, 168-169
  trauma treatment, 172-173
Self-destructive behavior
  complex PTSD, 113, 114
  trauma treatment, 141-142
Self-hypnosis, and dissociation, 115b
Self-organization, emotional
      milestones, 69-70
Self-reflection, stage 6 maturation, 63
Self-regulation, emotional milestones,
      68
Sensitization, description of, 109
Sensory area, brain development, 22
Sensory information, stress response,
      82-83
Sensory modalities, nervous system
      regulation, 44
Sensory-motor stage, and brain growth,
      24
Serotonin, complex PTSD, 102
*7 Habits of Highly Effective People,
      The*, 169
Sex abuse
  amnesia study, 118
  childhood behavior, 97
  childhood maltreatment category,
      98, 99
  childhood trauma studies, 7
  and complex PTSD, 102, 104, 108
  immune system disfunction, 110
  Larry, 80-81, 101
  and PTSD, 75
  twin study, 219
Shame
  Larry, 80, 81
  trauma response, 78
Shapiro, Francine, 164-165
Shatz, Carla, on critical periods, 206
"Shell shock," 73

Siegel, Daniel
  attachment theory, 7
  "neurobiology of interpersonal
    experience," 3
Silberg, Joy
  on ambivalence, 153-154
  on making sense, 144
  on traumatic reminders, 126, 154
Simple PTSD
  barriers to treatment, 133
  case study, 79-80
  developmental skills, 14-15, 140,
    168-175
  memory work, 14-15, 140, 156-168,
    157f
  parental response, 95, 95b
  safety/stabilization stage, 14, 140,
    141-147, 142b-143b
  symptom reduction, 14-15, 140,
    147-151, 152b-153b, 153-156
  and stress impairment, 88b, 88-95
  treatment goals, 133-139, 135b-
    136b
  treatment options overview, 138b-
    139b
Simpson, Matthew, Rasmussen's
    encephalitis, 20
Sleep disturbances, Billy, 188
Social skills, and trauma, 168-169
Social skills training
  PTSD treatment, 138b
  and trauma treatment, 173
Social workers, current debate, 1
Somatic symptoms, and trauma
    memory, 176
Soumi, Stephen, attachment theory, 7
Space, maturation stage 6, 61
Special education, child maltreatment
    costs, 216b
Speech therapy, Bradley, 57-58
Sperry, Roger, split-brain studies, 29-
    30
Spitz, Rene, maternal deprivation
    sequelae, 9
"Split-brain" studies, brain
    organization, 29-32

Splitting, PTSD defense mechanism,
    100-101
Starting Early Starting Smart (SESS),
    227
Startle response, trauma victim, 78
State-dependent learning, traumatic
    recall, 95
Stein, Murray, hippocampus research,
    104
Strange situation, attachment disorder,
    188
Stress
  and attachment regulation, 54
  attuned interactions, 8
  and brain development, 4, 9, 10
  and maternal attachment, 12
  during pregnancy, 21-22
Stress response
  and complex PTSD, 14, 98
  description of, 14, 81-87, 85f, 87f
  impairment of, 88-89
Stress response system, complex
    PTDS, 101-103
Studies on Hysteria, 73
Sullivan, Harry Stack
  on malevolent transformation, 149
  on reflected appraisals, 120
Supplementary motor area (SMA),
    "alien hand," 31
Symmetrical communication,
    reciprocal relationships, 127
Symptom reduction/memory work
    stage
  Billy, 192, 194-196
  Brittany, 149-150, 154, 165-166
  Jessica, 150, 154, 166-168
  trauma therapy, 14-15, 140, 147-
    151, 152b-153b, 153-156
  treatment goals, 133-134
Symptom scaling, 163-164
Synapses, dendritic density, 19

Tallal, Paula, 206
Travis, Carol, 209

Techniques and Issues in Abuse-Focused Therapy with Children and Adolescents: Addressing the Internal Trauma, 160
Teicher, Martin
    on ADHD children, 125
    brain hemisphere studies, 107-109
    on bullying behavior, 210
    cognitive impairment findings, 123
    on cerebellar vermis, 178
    on child maltreatment, 203
    traumatologist, 7, 205
    on vermis cerebellum, 107
Telling the story, memory work, 157-159
Temporal lobe
    functional area, 18f
    emotion development, 9-10
Terr, Lenore
    on dissociation, 115b
    on emotional scars, 119
    on metaphor, 158
    on PTSD defense mechanisms, 100-101
    PTSD types, 79, 100
    on shame, 78
    on traumatic play, 77
"Terrible twos," 54
Thalamus
    limbic system, 27f
    maturation stage 1, 43
    stress response, 82, 83, 85f
Therapeutic foster care, 184
Therapeutic goals
    eight accepted, 174
    trauma treatment, 133-139, 135b-136b
"Third way"
    empirical foundation of, 2-3
    genetic-environmental interaction, 4, 5f
Thought disorders, Billy, 188
Through the Eyes of a Child: EMDR with Children, 164, 179b-181b

Time, maturation stage 6, 61
Timeouts, trauma treatment, 142b-143b
Tinker, Robert, EMDR, 179b
Titration, memory work, 158
Toddlers
    brain development, 51-52
    disconnected behavior, 60-61
Touch
    brain development, 110
    trauma treatment, 176
Touch Research Institute (TRI), 176
Trauma
    changes in body chemistry, 88b
    description of, 74
    impairment scope, 134
    and neurological deficits, 101
    right hemisphere storage, 34
    and rigid thinking, 123
Trauma bonding, 190
Trauma history, risk factor, 9
Trauma studies, history of, 73-75
Trauma Symptom Checklist for Children, 140, 227
Trauma therapy
    and childhood abuse, 15
    three phases of, 14-15
    value of, 128
Traumatic amnesia, studies of, 118
Traumatic memory
    biology of, 93-95
    nature of, 92-93, 94
Traumatic play
    definition of, 77
    trauma memory, 98
Treatment goals, PTSD, 133-134,135b-136b
Triune brain, brain organization, 13, 25-28, 26f
"Two minds," 28
Type I PTSD, 79, 100
Type II PTSD, 79, 100

Unconscious memory system, 90-92
Underarousal, brain organization, 43, 45
Users Guide to the Brain, A, 12-13

Value systems, trauma treatment, 174-175
van der Kolk, Bessel
  ACE experience study, 110
  body therapy, 178
  on dissociation, 115b
  on domestic abuse, 99
  on EMDR, 165
  on hippocampus damage, 106
  on interpersonal violence impact, 106-107
  on rigid thinking, 124
  on self-protection, 175-176
  traumatologist, 7, 205
Van Derbur, Marilyn, 121, 122
Violence, and trauma, 74

Waking the Tiger: Healing Trauma, 179
Walker, Ed, 220
War, trauma studies, 73-74
"War on Poverty," 221-222
War, Stress, and Neurotic Illness: The Traumatic Neurosis of War, 74
Waters, Fran, dessert metaphor, 153
Watzlawick, Paul, on disqualifications, 120
Webb, Nancy Boyd, on play therapy, 158, 159
"Weed and Seed" program, early interventions, 223
Weinstock, Martha, maternal stress, 21

Wernicke's area
  functional area, 18f, 22
  split-brain studies, 29
What's Going On in There? How the Brain and Mind Develop in the First Five Years of Life, 11
White House Conference I, 206-207
White House Conference II, 211-212
White matter, brain, 17
Why Zebras Don't Get Ulcers, 86-87
Wieland, Sandra, on techniques, 160-161, 162, 163
Wiley, Meredith, 210
William, bipolar case study, 129b
Williams, Linda Meyer, on amnesia study, 118
Williams, Wendy, 208
Wilson, Sandra, EMDR, 179b
Withdrawal (flight), stress response, 81, 82

Yealland, Lewis, 74
"Your Child's Brain," 206

Zero tolerance
  child maltreatment principle, 224
  innovative programs, 224-225
Zigler, Edward, 221-222

WE ARE NOT ALONE: A TEENAGE GIRL'S PERSONAL ACCOUNT OF INCEST FROM DISCLOSURE THROUGH PROSECUTION AND TREATMENT by Jade Christine Angelica. (2002). "A valuable resource for teens who have been sexually abused and their parents. With compassion and eloquent prose, Angelica walks people through the criminal justice system—from disclosure to final outcome." *Kathleen Kendall-Tackett, PhD, Research Associate, Family Research Laboratory, University of New Hampshire, Durham*

WE ARE NOT ALONE: A TEENAGE BOY'S PERSONAL ACCOUNT OF CHILD SEXUAL ABUSE FROM DISCLOSURE THROUGH PROSECUTION AND TREATMENT by Jade Christine Angelica. (2002). "Inspires us to work harder to meet kids' needs, answer their questions, calm their fears, and protect them from their abusers and the system, which is often not designed to respond to them in a language they understand." *Kevin L. Ryle, JD, Assistant District Attorney, Middlesex, Massachusetts*

GROWING FREE: A MANUAL FOR SURVIVORS OF DOMESTIC VIOLENCE by Wendy Susan Deaton and Michael Hertica. (2001). "This is a necessary book for anyone who is scared and starting to think about what it would take to 'grow free.' . . . Very helpful for friends and relatives of a person in a domestic violence situation. I recommend it highly." *Colleen Friend, LCSW, Field Work Consultant, UCLA Department of Social Welfare, School of Public Policy & Social Research*

A THERAPIST'S GUIDE TO GROWING FREE: A MANUAL FOR SURVIVOR'S OF DOMESTIC VIOLENCE by Wendy Susan Deaton and Michael Hertica. (2001). "An excellent synopsis of the theories and research behind the manual." *Beatrice Crofts Yorker, RN, JD, Professor of Nursing, Georgia State University, Decatur*

PATTERNS OF CHILD ABUSE: HOW DYSFUNCTIONAL TRANSACTIONS ARE REPLICATED IN INDIVIDUALS, FAMILIES, AND THE CHILD WELFARE SYSTEM by Michael Karson. (2001). "No one interested in what may well be the major public health epidemic of our time in terms of its long-term consequences for our society can afford to pass up the opportunity to read this enlightening work." *Howard Wolowitz, PhD, Professor Emeritus, Psychology Department, University of Michigan, Ann Arbor*

IDENTIFYING CHILD MOLESTERS: PREVENTING CHILD SEXUAL ABUSE BY RECOGNIZING THE PATTERNS OF THE OFFENDERS by Carla van Dam. (2000). "The definitive work on the subject. . . . Provides parents and others with the tools to recognize when and how to intervene." *Roger W. Wolfe, MA, Co-Director, N. W. Treatment Associates, Seattle, Washington*

POLITICAL VIOLENCE AND THE PALESTINIAN FAMILY: IMPLICATIONS FOR MENTAL HEALTH AND WELL-BEING by Vivian Khamis. (2000). "A valuable book . . . a pioneering work that fills a glaring gap in the study of Palestinian society." *Elia Zureik, Professor of Sociology, Queens University, Kingston, Ontario, Canada*

STOPPING THE VIOLENCE: A GROUP MODEL TO CHANGE MEN'S ABUSIVE ATTITUDES AND BEHAVIORS by David J. Decker. (1999). "A concise and thorough manual to assist clinicians in learning the causes and dynamics of domestic violence." *Joanne Kittel, MSW, LICSW, Yachats, Oregon*

STOPPING THE VIOLENCE: A GROUP MODEL TO CHANGE MEN'S ABUSIVE ATTITUDES AND BEHAVIORS, THE CLIENT WORKBOOK by David J. Decker. (1999).

BREAKING THE SILENCE: GROUP THERAPY FOR CHILDHOOD SEXUAL ABUSE, A PRACTITIONER'S MANUAL by Judith A. Margolin. (1999). "This book is an extremely valuable and well-written resource for all therapists working with adult survivors of child sexual abuse." *Esther Deblinger, PhD, Associate Professor of Clinical Psychiatry, University of Medicine and Dentistry of New Jersey School of Osteopathic Medicine*

"I NEVER TOLD ANYONE THIS BEFORE": MANAGING THE INITIAL DISCLOSURE OF SEXUAL ABUSE RE-COLLECTIONS by Janice A. Gasker. (1999). "Discusses the elements needed to create a safe, therapeutic environment and offers the practitioner a number of useful strategies for responding appropriately to client disclosure." *Roberta G. Sands, PhD, Associate Professor, University of Pennsylvania School of Social Work*

FROM SURVIVING TO THRIVING: A THERAPIST'S GUIDE TO STAGE II RECOVERY FOR SURVIVORS OF CHILDHOOD ABUSE by Mary Bratton. (1999). "A must read for all, including survivors. Bratton takes a lifelong debilitating disorder and unravels its intricacies in concise, succinct, and understandable language." *Phillip A. Whitner, PhD, Sr. Staff Counselor, University Counseling Center, The University of Toledo, Ohio*

SIBLING ABUSE TRAUMA: ASSESSMENT AND INTERVENTION STRATEGIES FOR CHILDREN, FAMILIES, AND ADULTS by John V. Caffaro and Allison Conn-Caffaro. (1998). "One area that has almost consistently been ignored in the research and writing on child maltreatment is the area of sibling abuse. This book is a welcome and required addition to the developing literature on abuse." *Judith L. Alpert, PhD, Professor of Applied Psychology, New York University*

BEARING WITNESS: VIOLENCE AND COLLECTIVE RESPONSIBILITY by Sandra L. Bloom and Michael Reichert. (1998). "A totally convincing argument. . . . Demands careful study by all elected representatives, the clergy, the mental health and medical professions, representatives of the media, and all those unwittingly involved in this repressive perpetuation and catastrophic global problem." *Harold I. Eist, MD, Past President, American Psychiatric Association*

TREATING CHILDREN WITH SEXUALLY ABUSIVE BEHAVIOR PROBLEMS: GUIDELINES FOR CHILD AND PARENT INTERVENTION by Jan Ellen Burton, Lucinda A. Rasmussen, Julie Bradshaw, Barbara J. Christopherson, and Steven C. Huke. (1998). "An extremely readable book that is well-documented and a mine of valuable 'hands on' information. . . . This is a book that all those who work with sexually abusive children or want to work with them must read." *Sharon K. Araji, PhD, Professor of Sociology, University of Alaska, Anchorage*

THE LEARNING ABOUT MYSELF (LAMS) PROGRAM FOR AT-RISK PARENTS: LEARNING FROM THE PAST—CHANGING THE FUTURE by Verna Rickard. (1998). "This program should be a part of the resource materials of every mental health professional trusted with the responsibility of working with 'at-risk' parents." *Terry King, PhD, Clinical Psychologist, Federal Bureau of Prisons, Catlettsburg, Kentucky*

THE LEARNING ABOUT MYSELF (LAMS) PROGRAM FOR AT-RISK PARENTS: HANDBOOK FOR GROUP PARTICIPANTS by Verna Rickard. (1998). "Not only is the LAMS program designed to be educational and build skills for future use, it is also fun!" *Martha Morrison Dore, PhD, Associate Professor of Social Work, Columbia University, New York*

BRIDGING WORLDS: UNDERSTANDING AND FACILITATING ADOLESCENT RECOVERY FROM THE TRAUMA OF ABUSE by Joycee Kennedy and Carol McCarthy. (1998). "An extraordinary survey of the history of child neglect and abuse in America. . . . A wonderful teaching tool at the university level, but should be required reading in high schools as well." *Florabel Kinsler, PhD, BCD, LCSW, Licensed Clinical Social Worker, Los Angeles, California*

CEDAR HOUSE: A MODEL CHILD ABUSE TREATMENT PROGRAM by Bobbi Kendig with Clara Lowry. (1998). "Kendig and Lowry truly . . . realize the saying that we are our brothers' keepers. Their spirit permeates this volume, and that spirit of caring is what always makes the difference for people in painful situations." *Hershel K. Swinger, PhD, Clinical Director, Children's Institute International, Los Angeles, California*

SEXUAL, PHYSICAL, AND EMOTIONAL ABUSE IN OUT-OF-HOME CARE: PREVENTION SKILLS FOR AT-RISK CHILDREN by Toni Cavanagh Johnson and Associates. (1997). "Professionals who make dispositional decisions or who are related to out-of-home care for children could benefit from reading and following the curriculum of this book with children in placements." *Issues in Child Abuse Accusations*